OTHER TITLES OF INTEREST FROM ST. LUCIE PRESS

New Schools for a New Century: A Leader's Guide to High School Reform

Total Quality in Higher Education

Creating Quality in the Classroom

Teams in Education: Creating an Integrated Approach

Learning by Doing: School Restructuring

Continuous Improvement in Education Video Series:

    Adopting the New Education Paradigm

    Out of Theory into Practice

    Using Quality to Improve Administrative and Student Outcomes

The Baldrige Award for Education: How to Measure and Document Quality Improvement

Mastering the Diversity Challenge: Easy On-the-Job Applications for Measurable Results

The Skills of Encouragement

Improving Service Quality: Achieving High Performance in the Public and Private Sectors

For more information about these titles call, fax or write:

St. Lucie Press
100 E. Linton Blvd., Suite 403B
Delray Beach, FL 33483
TEL (407) 274-9906 • FAX (407) 274-9927

S$_L^t$

Designing High-Performance Schools

A Practical Guide to Organizational Reengineering

Francis M. Duffy, Ph.D., RODC

S^t_L

St. Lucie Press
Delray Beach, Florida

Phone: (407) 274-9906
Fax: (407) 274-9927

SᴸᵗL

Published by
St. Lucie Press
100 E. Linton Blvd., Suite 403B
Delray Beach, FL 33483

This book is dedicated to the memory of my father, Francis, whose ability to dream the "big dream" was passed on to me; to my mother, Romayne, who gave me strength of character; my wife, Marcia, the woman with whom I was always meant to be; and to my children, Lauren and Paul—two loving and decent young adults who have brought joy into my life.

TABLE OF CONTENTS

SECTION 1: THE FOUNDATION FOR REDESIGNING SCHOOLS

1 Characteristics of High-Performance Organizations 3
The Characteristics 3
Environment 5
Management 6
High-Performance School Organizations 8
Conclusion 13
References 14

2 The Mandate to Change 17
A Brief History of the Current Educational Reform Movement 17
Examples of Restructuring Initiatives 27
Goals 2000: Educate America Act 31
Conclusion 32
References 33

3 The Redesign Model 35
Introduction 35
The Redesign Phases 37
  Phase I: Preparing 37
  Phase II: Redesigning for High Performance 44
  Phase III: Achieving Permanence and Diffusion 54
  Phase IV: Continuous Improvement of Schooling 56
Conclusion 58
References 58

SECTION 2: HOW TO REDESIGN A SCHOOL DISTRICT

4 Phase I: Preparing 63
Introduction 63
Step 1.1: Build Support for the Redesign Project 63
Step 1.2: Identify a Starting Point 74

Step 1.3: Establish a Contract   76
Step 1.4: Form a Steering Committee   78
Step 1.5: Engage the Steering Committee in Open Systems Planning
   Activities   79
Step 1.6: Engage the Steering Committee in Redefining the Mission
   and Vision of the School District   86
Step 1.7: Establish a Change Management Structure and Process   95
Conclusion   99
References   100

5 **Phase II: Redesigning for High Performance/
   Diagnosing the Technical System** 103
Step 2.1a: Diagnose the Work System   103
Conclusion   120
References   121

6 **Phase II: Redesigning for High Performance/
   Diagnosing the Social System** 123
Step 2.1b: Diagnose the Social System   123
Conclusion   133
References   133

7 **Phase II: Redesigning for High Performance/
   Developing and Implementing Redesign Proposals** 135
Step 2.2: Develop Redesign Proposals   135
Step 2.3: Develop Implementation Plans   149
Step 2.4: Implement Selected Proposals   157
Conclusion   157
References   158

8 **Phase II: Redesigning for High Performance/
   Evaluating the Redesign Project** 159
Step 2.5: Evaluate the Process and Outcomes of the
   Redesign Effort   159
Evaluation   159
Reasons for Conducting Evaluation Research   161
Measurement   162
Research Design   164
General Guidelines for Conducting Evaluation Research   165
Specific Steps in the Evaluation Process   166
The Politics of Evaluation   168
Conclusion   169
References   170

9 Phase III: Achieving Permanence and Diffusion and Phase IV: Continuous Improvement of Schooling 173

Phase III: Achieving Permanence and Diffusion   173
   A Model for Achieving Permanence   174
   Psychological and Emotional Considerations   178
   Step 3.1: Conduct Double-Loop Learning Seminars   179
   Step 3.2: Renew Commitment to the Changes Made   181
   Step 3.3: Allocate Rewards for Desired Behaviors   181
   Step 3.4: Diffuse Changes to Entire District   182
   Step 3.5: Detect and Correct Deviations from Desired
     Outcomes   184
Phase IV: Continuous Improvement of Schooling   185
   Step 4.1: Supervise System Boundaries   185
   Step 4.2: Seek Opportunities for Continuous Improvement   186
Conclusion   186
References   187

SECTION 3: IDEAS TO SUPPORT A REDESIGN PROJECT

10 Introduction to Change Theory 191

Overview   191
Managing Complex Change   192
Models of Change   194
Change Strategies   201
Managing the Transition from the Present to the Future   203
Conclusion   205
References   206

11 Interpersonal and Group Dynamics for Change Agents 207

A Basic Philosophy for Interpersonal Communication
   During Change   207
The Emotional Aspects of Change   208
Resistance to Change   210
Conflict   215
Meeting Management   218
Group Problem Solving and Decision Making   224
Conclusion   235
References   235

12 Supervising Knowledge Work 237

Introduction   237
The Orthodox Paradigms of Instructional Supervision   238
Supervising Knowledge Work   240

Knowledge Work   240
Knowledge Work Supervision: Concepts and Principles   243
The Structure of the Paradigm   243
Conclusion   247
References   249

13 Working with a Consultant 253
Overview   253
The Context for Organization Development Consultants   254
Characteristics of Effective OD Consultants   255
Preparing to Hire a Consultant   257
Appraising a Consultant's Expertise and Credibility   258
The Contracting Process   261
Preparing for "Sticker Shock": Consultants' Fees and Expenses   263
Conclusion   266
References   267

Index 269

PREFACE

Suppose you are a school administrator or a school board member who sees the need for your school district to increase its level of organizational performance and that you are specifically interested in redesigning your district. In the language of change management specialists, you recognize the need to make changes in the operation of your district. Alternatively, you may be a consultant who has been asked to assist with a school restructuring project. As a school administrator, school board member, or consultant about to begin a school restructuring project, what should you do first?

The purpose of this book is to present a step-by-step model your district can use to redesign its anatomy (structures), physiology (flow of information and webs of relationships), and psychology (beliefs and values).

As informed school administrators, school board members, or consultants, many of you may be overwhelmed by the vast literature on school improvement that explains *why* schools need to be restructured and *what* the outcomes of restructuring ought to look like (e.g., block scheduling, year-round schooling, outcome-based education, and schools of choice). However, there is almost nothing in the literature about *how* to redesign your district to move it toward higher levels of performance. The model in this book describes how to redesign an entire school district's work system, social system, and its relationships with elements of its environment.

The redesign model described in this book is a process that helps a school district avoid the "failure of success." *The model is intended to help your school district become a high-performance learning organization that applies its collective knowledge to create educational services that have true value for all students and parents.*

This book is designed to help you develop proposals for redesigning your school district that are tailored to its environment, its work system, and its social system instead of state or national recommendations or the newest school redesign fad.

The redesign model looks complex because it is. It must be complex, because your organization is complex! The model offers a systematic way to examine critical variables that affect the performance of your district. The model also assumes that your district is a system and gives you techniques to improve all pieces of the system instead of just individual pieces of it (e.g., adopting a new curriculum or lengthening the school year). The model looks like it takes time to implement because it does take time! There are no quick fixes to school improvement. If you indulge in the quick fix, you are headed for failure.

It is important to know that you may not see improvements in the district's performance level until after the redesign project is completed. However, if applied continuously, consistently, and with patience, the redesign model presented in this book will almost certainly move your district toward higher levels of organizational performance. The literature on redesigning business organizations using similar models confirms this conclusion. Also, it is important to know that you will not perfectly achieve your new vision because that vision, in the rubric of chaos theory, is a moving target. You will, however, move toward the vision, and because the redesign process is repeated for the life of the district (through Phase IV of the model), you will move continuously toward that vision. It is your school district's lifelong journey of continuous renewal that will raise the district's level of organizational performance. Nothing less will do the job!

I hope you will find the book to be informative, descriptive, and, most importantly, useful. If I can answer any questions about the model or provide clarification about any of the ideas, please do not hesitate to contact me.

Francis M. Duffy, Ph.D., RODC
The F.M. Duffy Group
7404 Bucks Haven Lane
Highland, Maryland 20777
301-854-9800
E-mail: FMDUFFY@GALLUA.GALLAUDET.EDU

THE FOUNDATION
FOR
REDESIGNING SCHOOLS

CHAPTER 1

CHARACTERISTICS OF HIGH-PERFORMANCE ORGANIZATIONS

THE CHARACTERISTICS

The term *high-performance organization* is often found in today's business literature. The seminal thinking of Peter Vaill[1] contributed significantly to the early development of this concept. But what exactly does it mean? What does a high-performance organization look like? This chapter answers these questions.

Organizations are often thought of as systems. A system is a web of interlocked roles, work procedures, structures, and people existing in a state of interdependence. Organizations are established to manufacture a product or provide a service. Organizations that consistently deliver products or services to customers within predetermined constraints of cost, quality, timeliness, safety, and customer requirements are considered to be high-performing organizations.

There are three sets of variables that can be used to evaluate an organization to determine if it is a high-performing system: organizational-level variables, social system variables, and measurement variables.

Organizational-Level Variables—For an organization to be considered a high-performing system, the following conditions must exist at the level of the whole organization:

- The organization consistently (not 100%, however) achieves its goals for delivering its products or services while simultaneously achieving goals related to quality of work life within the organization.

- When faced with pressure to change from the external environment, the organization is flexible enough to modify its operations and social system with minimal impact on the system.

- Organizational culture, the grand vision, and organizational structures are in alignment (i.e., each supports the other as the organization strives to achieve its production/service and quality of work life goals).

- Workers have a high level of internal commitment to the success of the organization, and this commitment becomes the "energy" that drives the organization toward its goals.

Social System Variables—To be a high-performing system, the following people variables must be evident:

- People have the skills, resources, and technology to do their jobs at high levels of performance (i.e., they are *able* to do their jobs).

- People have the motivation to want to do their jobs. This motivation comes from within individuals and is not manifested because of extrinsic rewards or punishments (i.e., they must be *willing* to work).

- Through appropriate delegation, granting of autonomy, elimination of performance obstacles, and providing access to job-related information, workers have the *opportunity* to do their jobs well.

Measurement Variables—Finally, high performance can be measured by applying the following tests:

- Determine the ratio of resources consumed to the value of the product or service delivered. The perceived value must be higher than the perceived costs. In high-performing organizations, the perceived value of a product or service is significantly higher than the perceived cost of the product or service.

- Assess the timeliness with which products or services are delivered and determine the quality of those outputs. High-performing organizations deliver high-quality products and services to customers without undue delays.

- Assess whether or not the product or service meets customer requirements. High-performing organizations deliver a product or service that customers perceive as desirable and that appropriately responds to their expectations.

- Measure workers' levels of internal commitment to the goals of the organization. High-performing organizations rely on the internal commitment of workers as a primary means to achieve goals and objectives. These organizations tend not to use extensive control measures (e.g., sign-in sheets and turning in lesson plans on Fridays) to influence human behavior.

To examine other characteristics of high-performance organizations, let's start by looking at the business literature. This body of knowledge provides us with the most comprehensive descriptions of high-performance organizations. The literature describes a number of factors associated with high performance. One of the more classic publications on this topic is *In Search of Excellence* by Thomas Peters and Robert Waterman.[2] There also have been studies conducted to determine why companies succeed or fail.[3] Additionally, newer books, such as *A Passion for Excellence,*[4] *Thriving on Chaos,*[5] and *Productive Workplaces,*[6] identify management ideas for creating high performance that are derived from observations of and research on a variety of organizational types: American corporations, small businesses, and high-tech companies. Some of the major ideas from the literature are summarized in this chapter. These ideas are organized using four categories: environment, management, structure, and human resources.

ENVIRONMENT

Research provides us with three characteristics of high-performance organizations that describe an organization's relationship with its environment. These characteristics are *close to the customer*, making a *proactive response*, and having a *clear business focus*. Let's examine each one.

Close to the Customer—"Customer driven" is the force that motivates companies to become more focused on the needs of their customers. The literature is clear: successful organizations are customer driven—they thrive on sales and service overkill. Managers in these successful organizations "patrol" the boundary between the organization and its environment by staying in close communication with the customers. If management begins to take customers for granted and loses touch with customer needs, the organization finds itself in difficulty.

Proactive Response—Companies get into difficulties when their products or services become obsolete or non-competitive. Organizations need new technologies, products, services, and administrative structures to keep up with changes in their environments. Thus, high-performance organizations develop procedures for identifying opportunities for change and improvement. Major shifts in product lines or services require agility and daring. High-performance organizations take chances and do not expect everything to follow a formal strategic plan.

Clear Business Focus—High-performance organizations are very focused on what they do best. They clearly define their strengths and focus the bulk of their work on exercising these strengths. Having a clear business focus helps high-performance organizations reduce the complexity of information that is pouring in from their environments. Additionally, this clear focus also helps these successful companies conduct research and development in fields that will support their areas of strength.

MANAGEMENT

The characteristics of the management of high-performance organizations are leadership vision, bias toward action, and minimal rationality.

Leadership Vision—Successful organizations require a special kind of leadership—a kind of leadership that is visionary. The leaders of high-performance organizations provide a vision of what the organization can accomplish. They establish a sense of purpose and meaning that employees relate to and support.

Successful organizations often run on causes. The leader's vision builds commitment and excitement for the cause. Leaders of successful companies create the belief that both efficiency and innovation are possible. Jack Welch, CEO of General Electric, looks for visionaries when selecting division managers. Welch's idea of a good manager is

...somebody who can develop a vision of what he or she wants their business, their unit, their activity to do and be. Somebody who is able to articulate to the entire unit what the business is, and gain through a sharing of discussion—listening and talking—an acceptance of the vision. And [someone who] can relentlessly drive implementation of that vision to a successful conclusion.[7]

Visionary leaders are involved in central company issues and communicate face to face with many employees. They lead by example, they "walk their talk," and they are authentic. They push the dominant value of the organization with a single-minded focus. Employees in high-performance organizations do not receive mixed signals or suffer doubts about what the organizational leadership is trying to accomplish.

Bias Toward Action—High-performance companies are oriented toward action and implementation. They don't talk problems to death or delay action waiting for one more analysis to be completed. For example, PepsiCo's decision philosophy is "Ready, Fire, Aim."[8] Action-oriented managers stay in frequent touch with their employees. For example, managers at Hewlett-Packard practice "management by wandering around."

Action-oriented companies are goal directed, but they also tolerate failure. They tolerate failure because trial-and-error experimentation is a great learning tool. Managers are encouraged to take risks. For example, the CEO of a computer peripherals company said, "We tell our people to make at least ten mistakes a day. If you are not making ten mistakes a day, you're not trying hard enough."[9]

Minimal Rationality—Research on high-performance organizations indicates that they do not rely heavily on objective, quantitative decision rules.[10] Rational methods of decision making are often not fast enough, accurate enough, or able to accommodate ambiguity. At Hugh Russell in Canada, a crisis situation forced the company to move away from a highly rational decision-making process (which was called a "hard box") to a more intuitive model (called a "soft bubble"). Instead of the top managers analyzing the data and providing a solution, the managers set up many task forces to address the urgent issues. The passion, warmth, and trust arising from these groups lacked analytical rationality but saved the company.[11]

Applying the minimal rationality principle to decision making, managers of high-performance organizations also communicate through symbols that appeal to emotions instead of relying on hard facts. High-performance organizations "minimize rationality in the sense that overlapping, unplanned, and emotional processes become the source of wisdom and communication."[12]

HIGH-PERFORMANCE SCHOOL ORGANIZATIONS

The education elite do not like to think of schooling as a business. Certainly, it is not a profit-making venture. However, schooling is a non-profit enterprise in the public sector of the economy, and it has business-like goals (e.g., controlling costs, breaking even financially, delivering high-quality products and services, and maintaining excellent school–community relations). As a business, schooling can aspire to, achieve, and maintain characteristics found in high-performance organizations in other sectors of our economy.

In describing high-performing school organizations, the intention here is not to offer specific prescriptions about what the results of your restructuring effort should be. Instead, these examples are offered as ideas to stimulate your thinking about what the outcomes of your redesign effort could be.

Leadership in High-Performance Schools

Let's begin by reviewing what the literature says about leadership in high-performance organizations, especially school districts. Speicher[13] describes components of leadership in high-performance school organizations. These leaders:

- **Organize for outcomes**—These school leaders establish student learning as their organizations' bottom line. The instructional delivery system is underpinned by well-defined objectives, strategies, and outcomes.

- **Share leadership and decision making**—The people who are affected by particular decisions are involved in making those decisions. Site-based management is the primary method for achieving this level of involvement.

- **Effect staff and career development**—These leaders know that their people need to learn and grow to continue doing their jobs well. They seek and provide opportunities for this learning to occur.

- **Assess student progress and accountability**—If student learning is the school district's bottom line, then people need to know how well students are learning. Further, knowing these results helps create and maintain accountability for improving the results.

- **Apply the components of restructuring**—When restructuring is defined as a renewal process, it energizes a school organization. This increased energy helps propel the organization toward higher levels of performance.

- **Encourage school partnerships**—It is posited that school districts cannot work in isolation within their environments. They need to identify key stakeholders in their environments (e.g., business leaders, religious groups, and news media) and then develop working relationships with them.

- **Provide special programs for students who need them**—Some children have documented special needs. Often, the response to these needs comes from within the context of the instructional delivery system. Designing effective options for responding to these special needs is important.

- **Collaborate with community agencies**—High-performance schools collaborate with community agencies in serving the needs of their communities.

- **Commit to funding**—Adequate funding for the operation of schools is critical to the success of those schools.

Research on effective schools has been conducted for some time now. The basis for identifying an effective school is somewhat narrow, largely based on student outcomes on standardized tests in basic-skill areas (primarily reading and mathematics).[14] The data on effective schools usually are derived from studying inner-city elementary schools. When suburban and secondary schools are included, the implications drawn from the data are not clear. Further, the findings are often correlational, raising questions about whether the characteristics of effective principals create effective schools or if the characteristics of effective schools create effective principals.[15]

In 1990, the U.S. Department of Education identified and recognized 221 effective elementary schools. The behaviors of principals in these schools also are summarized in the literature. Doud[16] and Smith[17] identified these characteristics. A composite list of their descriptions contains the following leader characteristics:

- Knowledge of effective instructional practices
- Understanding of child growth and development
- Support of teachers
- Well-designed and coordinated instructional program
- Effective use of academic time
- Frequent assessment of student achievement
- Supervision of instruction
- Constructive feedback to teachers
- Ability to communicate orally and in writing
- Ability to use computer technology for administrative work (e.g., using computer spreadsheets)
- Understanding of political processes
- Knowledge of effective school practices
- Understanding of leadership theories and principles
- A vision of the future

Arnn and Mangieri[18] summarize the characteristics of effective secondary school principals:

- Clear academic goals
- High expectations for students
- Order and discipline
- Rewards and incentives for students
- Regular and frequent monitoring of student progress
- Opportunities for meaningful student responsibility and participation
- Teacher efficacy
- Rewards and incentives for teachers
- Concentration on academic learning time
- Positive school climate
- Administrative leadership

- Well-articulated curriculum
- Evaluation of instructional improvement
- Community support and involvement

Pajak[19] identifies the "vital ingredients for supervisory excellence." His research suggests these are:

- Ensuring open and clear communication
- Providing meaningful opportunities for staff development
- Improving the instructional program
- Managing the change process
- Motivating people by organizing around a common vision
- Observing and conferencing with teachers
- Coordinating and integrating curriculum
- Providing service to teachers
- Managing personal development of teachers
- Establishing and maintaining community relations
- Conducting research and program evaluation

Characteristics of Effective School Organizations

In the previous section, we looked at the characteristics of leaders in effective schools. Now, let's examine the characteristics of effective school organizations.

There are few commonly agreed-on indicators to determine whether a school is effective. In fact, the indicators are fuzzy, but we will examine some of them anyway.

Although there is little agreement on the specific indicators of school effectiveness, there seems to be a general principle that applies to achieving effectiveness:

A powerful and long-term commitment is required to bring about substantial, widespread, and enduring gains in the performance of students. Attention must be paid to the school as an institution and, in the final analysis, to the larger context of the school district and the environment in which schools operate. The effectiveness of the school as a whole helps determine what happens in each classroom.[20]

Most of the research on effective schools focuses on elementary schools. One of the most widely known studies was conducted in the 1980s by Ronald Edmonds and his colleagues. Edmonds reports that an elementary school is effective when lower-class (i.e., economic class) students score as high as middle-class students on basic-skills tests. Using this belief as a selection criterion, Edmonds identified effective schools as those in which there is strong leadership; an orderly, humane climate; frequent monitoring of students' progress; high expectations and requirements for all students; and focus on teaching important skills to all students.[21]

Purkey and Smith[22] and Wilson and Corcoran[23] summarized the attributes of effective schools. They found that effective schools have:

- Clear academic goals
- High expectations for students
- Order and discipline
- Frequent monitoring of student progress
- Meaningful student responsibility
- Teacher efficacy and morale
- Academic learning time
- Positive school climate
- Administrative leadership
- Community support and involvement

For every characteristic listed above there are behavioral indicators. These indicators can be used to document the existence or non-existence of these characteristics in the school organization and could be easily converted into a diagnostic tool to be used in an organizational redesign process like the one described in this book.

Other research on effective school organizations was conducted by Borger et al.,[24] Educational Research Service,[25] Ellett and Walberg,[26] Kelley,[27] and Miller.[28] A summary of the features of effective schools found in this research follows. Effective schools have:

- Teachers who believe their students can learn and hold them to high-performance standards
- Teachers and administrators who believe they can influence students
- Students who believe their accomplishments are the result of hard work

- Strong leadership from principals without being authoritarian
- School environments or climates that promote and encourage learning

CONCLUSION

The literature in business and education provides us with characteristics of high-performance organizations. However, it is one thing to know what the literature says about effective organizations and quite another to become an effective organization. The process of becoming a high-performance organization is complex and challenging. "School performance is unlikely to be significantly improved by any measure or set of measures that fails to recognize that schools are institutions [complex organizations composed of interrelated parts—systems] governed by well-established rules and norms of behavior, and adapted for stability."[29]

Another problem with reviewing research findings on high-performing organizations is that it is tempting to assume that you should model your school after the ones identified in the research. This kind of temptation is rooted in our society's continuing love affair with the "quick fix." Many of us want quick solutions to our difficult problems, and having a "model" to copy from seems to be a quick way to solve the performance problems of our organizations. However, we know that it is wrong and ineffective to do this because "...each school district (and each school within a district) has unique organizational characteristics that either constrain or enhance the effectiveness..." of a redesign effort.[30] This conclusion was also supported by Ted Sizer in an interview with John O'Neil, senior editor for *Educational Leadership*. As Sizer said,[31]

> ...we start from the assumption that good schools are unique...There's nothing that you just "put into place," nothing to implement...we strongly believe that you have to look at reform school-by-school-by-school (p. 4).

Donald Gainey[32] also supports the view that schools must follow their own paths when being redesigned:

> In our present-day pluralistic society, it is remarkable to think that any one remedy could address the diverse and changing

needs of all the people. They are all different. They come with a variety of characteristics and behaviors that change....So, why should we believe that education, which is a human enterprise, could have found the secret to meeting the educational needs of all people by developing the "one best system"? (p. 34).

The model described in this book does not offer a "one-size-fits-all" model to achieve the prescribed restructuring outcomes. Instead, it offers practical, step-by-step guidance on how to redesign a school organization so that it moves toward a higher level of organizational performance, knowing that different schools will create different results. In a very real way, the redesign model described herein is a map and compass to help you find your school district's path toward higher levels of performance.

REFERENCES

1. Vaill, P. (1989). *Managing as a performing art: New ideas for a world of chaotic change.* San Francisco, Calif.: Jossey-Bass Publishers.
2. Peters, T.J. and R.H. Waterman (1982). *In search of excellence.* New York: Harper & Row, 1982.
3. Maidique, M.A. and R.H. Hayes (1984). "The art of high technology management," *Sloan Management Review.* 25, pp. 17–31; Hedberg, B.L.T., P.C. Nystrom, and W.H. Starbuck (1976). "Camping on seesaws: Prescriptions for a self-designing organization," *Administration Science Quarterly.* 21, pp. 41–65; Banaszewski, J. (September 1981). "Thirteen ways to get a company in trouble," *Inc.* pp. 97–100.
4. Peters, T.J. and N. Austin (1985). *A passion for excellence: The leadership difference.* New York: Random House.
5. Peters, T.J. (1987). *Thriving on chaos.* New York: Knopf.
6. Weisbord, M.R. (1991). *Productive workplaces: Organizing for dignity, meaning, and community.* San Francisco, Calif.: Jossey-Bass Publishers.
7. Mitchell, R. and J.H. Dobrzynski (December 14, 1987). "Jack Welch: How good a manager?" *Business Week.* pp. 92–103.
8. Dunkin, A. (February 10, 1986). "Pepsi's marketing strategy: Why nobody does it better," *Business Week.* pp. 92–103.
9. Peters, T.J. (December 1984). "An excellent question," *Inc.* pp. 155–162.
10. Hedberg (see reference 3).
11. Hurst, D.K. (May–June 1984). "Of boxes, bubbles, and effective management," *Harvard Business Review.* pp. 78–88.
12. Daft, R.L. (1989). *Organization theory and design,* 3rd edition. St. Paul, Minn.: West Publishing, pp. 555–556.

13. Speicher, D. (1989). "Leadership in high-performance organizations," *School Administrator.* 46, p. 6.
14. Lunenburg, F.C. and A.C. Ornstein (1991). *Educational administration: Concepts and practices.* Belmont, Calif.: Wadsworth Publishing.
15. Ibid., p. 341.
16. Doud, J.L. (1989). *The K–8 principal in 1988.* Alexandria, Va.: National Association of Elementary School Principals.
17. Smith, D.C. (1990). *Principals for 21st century schools.* Alexandria, Va.: National Association of Elementary School Principals.
18. Arnn, J.W. and J.N. Mangierie (1988). "Effective leadership for effective schools: A survey of principal attitudes," *NASSP Bulletin.* 72, p. 3.
19. Pajak, E. (September 1990). "Dimensions of supervision." *Educational Leadership.* 48, 1, pp. 78–81.
20. Lunenburg and Ornstein (see endnote 14), p. 435.
21. Edmonds, R.R. (1982). "Programs of school improvement: An overview," *Educational Leadership.* 40, pp. 4–11.
22. Purkey, S.C. and M.S. Smith (1983). "School reform: The district policy implications of the effective schools literature," *Elementary School Journal.* 85, pp. 353–388; Purkey, S.C. and M.S. Smith (1983). "Effective schools: A review," *Elementary School Journal.* 83, pp. 427–452.
23. Wilson, B.L. and T.B. Corcoran (1983). *Successful secondary schools.* New York: Falmer Press, pp. 59–65.
24. Borger, J., C. Lo, S. Oh, and H. Wallberg (1985). "Effective schools: A quantitative synthesis of constructs," *Journal of Classroom Interaction.* 20, 2, pp. 12–17.
25. Educational Research Service, Inc. (1983). *Effective schools: A summary of research.* Arlington, Va.: ERS, Inc.
26. Ellett, C.D. and H.J. Walberg (1979). "Principals' competency, environment, and outcomes," In H.J. Walberg (Ed.). *Educational environments and effects: Evaluation, policy and productivity.* Berkeley, Calif.: McCutchan.
27. Kelley, E.A. (1980). *Improving school climate: Leadership techniques for principals.* Reston, Va.: National Association of Secondary School Principals.
28. Miller, S.K. (February 1983). "Thinking about school climate: Past and present." Paper presented at the meeting of the National Association of Secondary School Principals, Dallas, Texas.
29. Chubb, J.E. (1988). "Why the current wave of school reform will fail," *Public Interest.* 90, p. 29.
30. Duffy, F.M. (1990). "Soil conditions, cornerstones, and other thoughts: A treatise for school superintendents," *Wingspan.* 5, 2, pp. 3–7.
31. Sizer, T. in O'Neil, J. (February 1995). "On lasting school reform: A conversation with Ted Sizer," *Educational Leadership.* 52, 5, pp. 4–9.
32. Gainey, D.D. (1993). *Education for the new century: Views from the principal's office.* Reston, Va.: National Association for Secondary School Principals.

CHAPTER 2

THE MANDATE
TO CHANGE

A BRIEF HISTORY OF THE CURRENT
EDUCATIONAL REFORM MOVEMENT

The history of American education is a history of reform movements; for example, the reformers during the period 1900–1950 were known as *administrative progressives*. These reformers had common training, interests, and values. They were the first generation of professional leaders who would serve lifelong careers as city superintendents, education professors, state education officers, or foundation officials. They had a fundamental and common faith in the science of education.

The administrative progressives supported changes they thought would produce efficiency, equity (as *they* defined it), accountability, and expertise. They called their program of reform "reorganization." The reorganization movement, which is the opposite of what we mean today by restructuring, was remarkably successful. Many of the reforms made by this movement persist today. A summary of some of the accomplishments of this movement shows how successful the administrative progressives were in institutionalizing their changes:

- The control of urban school districts was centralized in small, elite boards and decision making was delegated to experts (i.e., to school superintendents).

- Small, rural districts were consolidated and one-room schools were abolished.

- "Largeness" was celebrated, as opposed to "smallness."

- Curricula were designed to match assumed differences of ability and economic destiny of students, as opposed to giving all students a solid grounding in academic subjects.

- Hierarchies of curriculum experts and supervisors were created to tell teachers what and how to teach, as opposed to giving them greater autonomy in the classroom.

- Efforts were made to replace the vagaries of local lay politics with the authority (or science) of educational practice.

In the 1950s, and even more intensely in the 1960s, critics attacked the reforms of the administrative progressives. A new politics of education emerged, with many groups demanding a role in the decision-making process. These new politics were significantly empowered by the Brown versus the Board of Education desegregation case and the civil rights movement. The message resulting from these two events was not lost on groups such as Hispanics, feminists, or parents of handicapped children. These new, socially motivated politics undermined the status quo and modified old structures of power and school programs.

Changes made in schools during the 1960s included:

- Mandated racial desegregation (primarily through busing)

- An attack on institutional sexism (e.g., by improving hiring practices)

- New bilingual education programs

- An introduction of ethnic curricula (e.g., black studies curricula)

- New, focused attention on the needs of students with disabilities

- The equalization of school finance

- State and federal government mandates for greater parental involvement through school–community councils

- African-Americans demanding greater community control of schools in urban ghettos

- Expansion of course electives in school curricula, which resulted in greater student choice

- Creation of alternative schools, as well as schools within schools and schools without walls

- Attacks on IQ testing and academic tracking
- Teacher demands for greater power over their professional lives, especially through such means as unionization and the establishment of teacher centers

In sum, reformers of the 1960s demanded dispersion and decentralization of educational decision making, as well as an increased role for federal and state governments.

However, as the changes of this period were incorporated into the school system, no new coherent model of school governance emerged; in fact, the same old model from previous eras prevailed. The educational system responded by merely grafting these newly mandated changes onto the old structure of the system. The result was larger, more complex, and fragmented bureaucracies to deal with the mandated changes.

The primary result of the reform movement of the 1960s was not decentralization as it existed in the 1800s, nor was it modest centralization like the administrative progressives sought. Instead it was, as John Meyer[1] calls it, "fragmented centralization." As noted by Meyer, fragmented centralization meant that *everybody and nobody* was in charge of public education, and the result was that educational leaders—the insiders—lost their sense of control over schooling.

After nearly two decades of turmoil in education, 1980 saw the emergence of a new reform movement—the "Back to Basics" movement. The popular diagnosis of the 1980s was that the existing crisis in education was the result of the educational ferment during the 1960s and 1970s. This ferment, it was believed, disrupted learning, thereby resulting in a decline in educational achievement which, in turn, endangered the nation's competitiveness.

The early 1980s saw a spate of reports, books, and articles on the condition of the American education system. For example, in April 1983, *A Nation at Risk: The Imperative for Educational Reform*[2] was released by the National Commission on Excellence in Education. This report criticized the performance of American schools by suggesting several major causes of their poor performance: the curriculum was too diluted with elective courses, academic standards were too low, students spent less time studying and used their in-school time inefficiently, and few highly qualified students were entering the teaching profession, thereby suggesting the need to overhaul teacher preparation programs.

In September 1983, the Carnegie Foundation for the Advancement of Teaching released a report called *High School: A Report on Secondary*

Education in America.[3] The report, which was a bit more optimistic about our nation's schools than many of the other reports of that era, proposed a 12-point "Agenda for Action" to remedy some of the problems facing the schools. Examples of these recommendations are to:

- Develop a core curriculum focused on literacy and language with additional requirements in art, health, work, and community service

- Expand guidance services to help students with career planning beyond high school

- Encourage diverse teaching techniques with flexibility in scheduling and an emphasis on student participation

- Establish school–business partnerships

In addition to these four specific recommendations, there were several suggestions for improvement related to teachers' level of preparation, salaries, workloads, and incentives for professional development.

John Goodlad wrote a report on reform, *A Place Called School: Prospects for the Future,*[4] published in 1983. This report resulted from Goodlad's eight-year study of public schools entitled "A Study of Schooling." The bulk of the report describes and analyzes what he thinks schools and schooling are all about. He proposes an agenda for school improvement. Several of Goodlad's recommendations are to:

- Increase local school site control
- Provide teachers with more planning time
- Develop a core curriculum
- Design ungraded classes that maximize the interaction between older and younger children
- Use peer teaching and cooperative learning
- Develop teams of teachers, with leadership being provided from within the teams
- Create a fourth phase of schooling for students 16 to 20 years of age, organized around experimental education and community agencies and focused on independent work, study, and volunteer service as a transition to adult life

In 1984, *Horace's Compromise: The Dilemma of the American High School*[5] was published. This was the first major publication resulting from *A*

Study of High Schools, co-sponsored by the National Association of Secondary School Principals and the Commission on Educational Issues of the National Association of Independent Schools. *Horace's Compromise,* written by Ted Sizer, is based on direct observations of public and private high schools in the United States and abroad. The title alludes to a fictional high school teacher whose characteristics are a composite of many of the teachers observed in the study. Through the eyes of this fictional character, Sizer describes the practical problems of education and the compromises that are often forced by the system. Among his many ideas for improving high schools, Sizer suggests:

- High schools should be devoted to the development of mind and character.

- The high school curriculum should be simplified by reducing it to four main areas: inquiry and expression, mathematics and science, literature and the arts, and philosophy and history.

- New student evaluation systems should be developed that are based on multiple indices of student performance, instead of course credits.

- Teachers should be given more time to respond to students' work through a personalized form of coaching that would require reductions in student–teacher ratios.

- Bureaucratic structures should be altered to give local school staffs an opportunity to develop high expectations for students that are built upon trust rather than formal regulations.

Two other significant reports of the mid-1980s were *Tomorrow's Teachers,*[6] published in 1986 by The Holmes Group, and *A Nation Prepared: Teachers for the 21st Century,*[7] also published in 1986 by the Carnegie Task Force on Teaching as a Profession. Both of these reports focus on reforming teacher preparation programs, and both suggest that initial teacher preparation should occur at the graduate level of education. Both also stress the need for teachers to have command of their subject matter, primarily by majoring in the field that they wish to teach during their undergraduate years. The Holmes Group report suggests that professional preparation courses should be improved by teaching specific subjects that are based on recent research. The Carnegie report also suggested the establishment of a national standards board to develop and administer licensing examinations.

Additionally, The Holmes Group report recommends a career ladder with three levels: instructor, professional teacher, and career professional. The Carnegie report proposes to restructure the teaching force into four categories: licensed teachers, certified teachers, advanced certificate holders, and lead teachers.

These and other reform-minded books and reports immediately preceded the current interest in restructuring schools, an interest that emerged around 1986.

Today, many critics believe that effective educational reform must result in the restructuring of schools. Advocates of restructuring often call for such changes as an increase in the decentralization of authority, more autonomy for teachers with opportunities for collegial decision making, getting students to think and to demonstrate their competence, more parental involvement, and smaller schools.

Restructuring has become a buzzword of the 1990s. However, becoming a buzzword does not mean that restructuring is actually happening. For example, John Goodlad,[8] as quoted in *Education Week* in 1988, said: "We are rapidly moving toward the use of the word 'restructuring' whenever we talk about school reform at all....This is becoming another catchword when the truth of the matter is that hardly any schools are restructured." In the same *Education Week* article, Michael Kirst[9] was quoted as saying that "Restructuring is a word that means everything and nothing simultaneously....It is in the eye of the beholder."

Mary Anne Raywid[10] has written about restructuring in such a way as to shed some light on the meaning of the term. She describes three distinct kinds of school reform efforts: pseudo-reform, incremental reform, and reform by restructuring.

Pseudo-reform provides changes that are really quite superficial. These include building repairs, expanding exceptions to school policies, lengthening the school day, and increasing minimum achievement scores for school athletes.

Sheer rhetoric, or "symbolic politics," Raywid says, is the most common kind of pseudo-reform. Purkey, Rutter, and Newman[11] confirmed the widespread existence of symbolic politics in a study of high school reforms. Their study surveyed high school principals and asked them if school improvement projects were occurring in their schools. Then, they surveyed teachers in the same schools about the nature of these projects. More than half of the teachers in more than half of the schools that reported the existence of school improvement projects were unaware of their existence! In other words, there was a lot of "sheer rhetoric" about the changes.

Raywid suggests that another frequent example of pseudo-reform is the establishment of a task force, for example, a school improvement task force. She notes that sometimes the convening of the task force *is* the reform. Some cynics of the task force structure claim that the effectiveness of the task force can be restricted to symbolic reforms right from the beginning, depending on how the task force is constituted. Regarding this observation, Raywid says, "To include on a task force all interest groups with a stake in the issues virtually insures the continuation of the status quo" (p. 140).

Incremental reform is more ambitious than pseudo-reform. It aims to improve educational practice. Most reform proposals are of this type. They typically focus on new arrangements or on the implementation of a new practice.

One of the difficulties associated with incremental reform is that schools are notoriously difficult to change. One major reason for this difficulty is the interconnectedness among various parts of the school organization. Several reformers (e.g., H. Dean Evans and Ted Sizer) have noted that in order to change almost anything of significance in schools, a great deal must be changed simultaneously. This condition is reflected in the title of an article by H. Dean Evans[12] in the *Phi Delta Kappan*: "We must begin educational reform every place at once." Like a successfully completed jigsaw puzzle, every piece is connected to everything else. You cannot change one piece without altering those pieces that are connected to it. Incremental reforms tend to focus on one piece of the organization without considering required changes in other connected pieces.

Restructuring focuses on the fundamental arrangements of the school organization that either support or constrain effective educational practice. According to Raywid, because of the interconnectedness of various components of the school organization, any change in the school organization, no matter how minor it may initially appear, will require major changes. Thus, when reasonable and desirable changes appear too complex or too unworkable, it might be time to examine the underlying organizational structures that make them too complex or unworkable. This is what restructuring is all about.

Many critics are convinced that schools are put together in the wrong way and that it is now time to reconsider such fundamental structures as:

- How we group children for instruction
- How we divide and package material for instruction
- How we evaluate student learning

These critics point out that even after a dozen years of serious educational reform efforts to improve the quality of schools, educators still hear exactly the same horror stories that drew the educational community to the excellence movement in the first place (e.g., falling test scores, rising dropout rates, and the continuing discovery of yet another set of schools deteriorating rapidly).

For these and other reasons, in 1986 the excellence movement took a noticeable turn away from "reform" and toward "restructuring." Raywid points out that proponents of restructuring propose one or both of two significant changes:

- A fundamental and pervasive alteration in the way we organize and institutionalize education

- Alterations in the way in which public schools are governed and held accountable

However, supporters of restructuring hardly agree on what aspects of the school organization should be changed. In spite of this lack of agreement about specific changes, two broad restructuring strategies have emerged:

- Site-based management
- Schools of choice

Both of these strategies, although obviously different in their goals, have common features. Both represent some kind of decentralization of decision making, seek to broaden the current base of educational decision making, and talk of changed accountability structures. The goals of each strategy are briefly described below.

Site-Based Management

Site-based management seeks to improve schools by altering the ways in which schools are governed. There are two key moves to accomplish this goal. First, decision-making power for budget, staff, and instruction is shifted from a central office to the individual schools; second, decision making in an individual school is shared among administrators, teachers, parents, and the community. The underlying logic is that each school decides for itself which kinds of changes and improvements it will undertake.

The practice of site-based management is relatively new and, therefore, there is not a lot of evidence to support its effectiveness. However, there is evidence to suggest some major difficulties in instituting this kind of restructuring. The evidence includes observations that:

- Central office staff are highly resistant to shifting authority to individual schools.

- Shared decision making in individual schools is often set up as a process of giving teachers a *voice* in an advisory body, but not giving them a *vote* in a decision-making body

- At its worst, a site-based management group becomes just another committee that is neither identified nor elected by the faculty but appointed by the building principal.

- Research indicates little correlation between site-based management and increased student achievement.

Schools of Choice

The schools-of-choice strategy is based on the premise that parents ought to be able to choose the school their child attends. This strategy is advocated by reformers such as Mary Ann Raywid, who says, "The record of the last two decades makes choice a more promising strategy" (p. 142). The relative success of the choice strategy seems to lie in school officials freeing and supporting teachers to design and implement distinctive programs from among which families can choose. Teachers are invited (not assigned) to become program designers and innovators by working together with other teachers with similar interests.

More than 20 states have adopted some form of parental choice, according to the U.S. Department of Education. These plans range from those allowing students to transfer to any public school they desire to initiatives permitting students to take some classes at local colleges. President George Bush cited choice among public and private schools as a cornerstone of school improvement. Policy analysts John Chubb and Terry Moe[13] of the Brookings Institution gave the movement a lift with their book *Politics, Markets, and America's Schools*. The book, based on longitudinal data, calls for restructuring education by allowing parents to choose among both public and private schools.

Some critics of choice, for example, Al Shanker,[14] president of the American Federation of Teachers, argue that choice does not necessarily translate into students flocking to better schools, because parents might rank such factors as convenience above academic quality. According to Shanker, "The assumption that the choices people would make would be based on academic quality is wrong" (p. 354). Another critic of choice, Diane Berreth,[15] deputy director of the Association for Supervision and Curriculum Development, cites concerns that choice might stratify schools along racial or socio-economic lines. She also says that choice "is being significantly oversold" given available research evidence. Moreover, Berreth claims that educators may neglect more promising initiatives such as school-based management if hard-sell campaigns for choice go unchecked. She believes that good schools are good because of the commitment, the talent, and the knowledge of the educators who work in them and the engagement and motivation of the parents and students. Those conditions exist in schools with choice and in schools without choice.

In addition to the suggestions for school-based management and schools of choice, the National Governors Association (NGA) has developed a framework for school restructuring similar to that expressed by other experts. The NGA says that restructuring should focus on the following:

1. Curriculum and instruction should be modified to support higher-order thinking skills by all students. Also, the use of instructional time must be more flexible, learning activities must be made more challenging and engaging, and student grouping practices should promote student interaction and cooperative learning.

2. Authority and decision making should be decentralized so that the most educationally important decisions are made at the school site. Teachers, administrators, and parents should set the basic direction of the school and determine strategies and organizational and instructional arrangements needed to achieve them.

3. New staff roles must be developed so that teachers may work together more readily to improve instruction. Experienced and skilled teachers should provide support to beginning teachers, plan and develop new curricula, or design and implement staff development. An increased use of paraprofessionals should be considered. In addition, principals need to provide the vision to help shape new school structures, lead talented teachers, and take

risks in an environment that rewards performance rather than compliance.

4. Accountability systems must be designed to clearly link rewards and incentives to student performance at the building level. Schools must have more discretion and authority to achieve results and then be held accountable for results. States must develop measures to assess valued outcomes of performance of individual schools and link rewards and sanctions to results.

EXAMPLES OF RESTRUCTURING INITIATIVES

At this point, you might be interested in some real-world examples of responses to the mandate for improved schools. There are many examples of proposed and actual restructuring efforts, some of which are described below.

The Coalition of Essential Schools—This coalition was developed by Theodore Sizer. The characteristics of this coalition are as follows:

- Particular schools voluntarily agree to embrace the coalition's principles and to work with other schools of the coalition.

- The coalition consists mostly of high schools and middle schools.

- Its efforts are directed toward restructuring the high school experience (e.g., shifting from a focus on the teacher-as-worker to that of the student-as-worker).

- There is a shift from test scores as a measurement of student achievement to the use of portfolio assessments and public exhibitions as ways to assess student learning outcomes.

- The coalition brings teachers and others together to discuss ways to encourage students to be workers and ways to organize and administer student exhibitions of their learning.

National Network for Educational Renewal—This network was established by John Goodlad. Its characteristics are as follows:

- It has 14 school–university partnerships.

- The focus of each partnership is on restructuring K–12 schooling and restructuring teacher and school administrator preparation programs.

- It has an ingredient of self-interest (i.e., the universities have an interest in gaining and sharing knowledge, while the schools have an interest in pragmatic suggestions for change), and this self-interest establishes a productive tension between the theory and practice that is used to guide restructuring efforts.

- Teachers, university faculty, administrators, and community leaders join together to examine their activities at their schools and to create alternative solutions to problems.

Chicago's Corporate/Community School—In 1988, 16 businesses (including Sears, Baxter International, and United Airlines) donated $2 million to start a model school to prove that the public education system could work. They decided to establish and run an elementary school with a pre-school through 5th grade program. Using a lottery, 200 minority students from Chicago's poverty-stricken Lawndale section were selected to attend the school. The principal, Elaine Mosley, was given authority similar to her counterparts in the business world. She had the authority to give raises to good teachers and to fire bad ones. Her performance was also under careful scrutiny—if the students' math and reading scores did not increase, she would be fired at the end of her three-year contract. Teachers were highly involved in the decision-making processes of the school. Ms. Mosley, who was the principal of a suburban Chicago elementary school prior to this assignment, was quoted as saying, "All this is possible and doable in every school. It only requires focus and believing that every child deserves the highest quality education possible."

Chiron Middle School in Minneapolis, Minnesota—This school is not really a school at all, if one conceives of a school in a traditional way. Opened in the fall of 1988, Chiron students spend 12-week sessions rotating among several "learning centers" that are strategically located in areas throughout the community—areas whose resources are suitable for experiential learning. For example, in 1989, one center met at the agricultural campus of the University of Minnesota, another was located in a former parochial school in the middle of the performing arts neighborhood in Minneapolis, and a third shared space with college evening classes in a former store in the center of the business district. The specific ideas that resulted in the development of the school were found in proposals submitted in response to a district competition to create a better school.

Other Examples—Examples of pilot demonstration schools throughout the United States that are involved in various kinds of restructuring efforts include:

- Schools for the 21st Century in the state of Washington
- Carnegie Schools in Massachusetts
- Public schools of Dade County, Florida
- Public schools of Jefferson County, Kentucky
- The National Education Association's "Mastery in Learning" project
- The "Teachers-as-Leaders" project of the American Federation of Teachers
- The Relearn Network
- Demonstration schools at the University of Georgia at Athens
- The League of Professional Schools at the University of Georgia at Athens
- Public schools of Santa Fe, New Mexico

In 1992, the New American Schools Development Corporation (NASDC), which was formed by American business leaders to support the development and dissemination of innovative school programs, selected and funded 11 proposals for innovation in school designs. Several of the 11 design teams that won awards are listed below:

1. The proposal for the Bensenville New American School project in Bensenville, Illinois (near Chicago) describes how students will spend considerable time connecting their class lessons with work at community-based sites (e.g., local businesses and government offices). The design conceives of the entire community as the campus for the students. The design team also proposed that schools be open year-round from 6 a.m. to 10 p.m.

2. The Los Angeles Learning Centers project suggests a "moving diamond" matrix within which each child will be connected with an older student, a teacher, a parent or parents, and a community volunteer. Students and adults will help by providing tutoring, referring students to relevant services, and just interacting with the children.

3. The proposal for the Odyssey Project in Gaston County, North Carolina suggests that students should be grouped loosely into

five levels of schooling: alpha (ages 0–3), beta (3–6), gamma (7–10), delta (11–14), and odyssey (15–18). Students move from one level to the next only after they accomplish the required performance outcomes. The schools will operate year-round, with a regular ten-week term followed by a three-week mini-term.

4. The Roots and Wings project directed by Robert Slavin of the Johns Hopkins University uses an approach named "never-streaming." With this approach, an array of special services, including tutoring and family support, make it possible for students to remain in regular classrooms rather than being pulled out for special education. Schools are non-graded and use strategies such as cooperative learning and cross-age tutoring.

5. The Community Learning Centers of Minnesota project intends to act on a new state law that allows teachers to establish a "charter school." According to the law, teachers have the freedom to organize schools differently as long as students meet agreed-upon outcomes.

6. The remaining grant winners are:
   - ATLAS Communities, One Davol Square, Providence, Rhode Island
   - Audrey Cohen College, New York, New York
   - The Co-Nect School, Cambridge, Massachusetts
   - Expeditionary Learning, Cambridge, Massachusetts
   - The Modern Red Schoolhouse, Indianapolis, Indiana
   - The National Alliance for Restructuring Education, Washington, D.C.

Many of the above proposals share common features. For example:

- Many of the teams attempt to better align learning opportunities inside and outside of the school. Some of the projects provide opportunities for students to work on community service projects, allow the schools to stay open longer to offer adult learning opportunities, and enhance the connection between schools and employers.

- A few of the proposals intend to focus on providing a more personalized learning environment for students.

- Several of the projects use some form of outcome-based education that will be linked to national or world-class standards. This linkage replaces traditional expectations for students to complete a series of courses or to occupy a class seat for the requisite number of hours.

- Several design teams propose ways to improve schools' responses to children who require special services and to reduce the demand for those services.

- Another common thread among several of the proposals is finding better ways to organize the work of teachers and other adults in the schools.

For more information about each of the above projects, including mailing addresses, contact NASDC, 1000 Wilson Boulevard, Suite 2710, Arlington, Virginia 22209.

GOALS 2000: EDUCATE AMERICA ACT

The Goals 2000: Educate America Act was passed by Congress. The debate of that legislation served as an imperative for the careful assessment of options and opportunities for general and special education in America. The act provides a framework for meeting a set of national goals by doing the following:

- Promoting coherent nationwide systematic education reform
- Improving the quality of teaching and learning in the classroom
- Defining appropriate federal, state, and local roles
- Establishing valid, reliable, and fair mechanisms for building consensus on reform
- Assisting in the development of international standards of competence and developing student assessment measures
- Supporting initiatives at the federal, state, and local levels to provide equal opportunity to meet the new standards
- Providing a framework for reauthorization of all federal education directives and programs
- Stimulating development of certification standards to upgrade the teaching profession (from the Department of Education, 1993)

The act lists several specific goals for the nation and emphasizes that these goals are for *all* students—disadvantaged, disabled, gifted, and those with limited proficiency in English. The goals are summarized below:

1. **School readiness**—All students will begin school ready to study at their appropriate level. A special effort will be made to ensure that all children are given proper nutrition. Children with disabilities will receive services and programming that are developmentally appropriate.

2. **School completion**—The act sets a goal of 90% of all American students completing a kindergarten through 12th grade program of study. This includes students who are currently identified as being from minority groups and students with disabilities.

3. **Student achievement**—All students will take and successfully complete an assessment of skills determined to be appropriate and essential to students in grades 4, 8, and 12. In addition to the traditional areas of focus, the thrust of this assessment will include problem solving and reasoning skills. The assessment will be applicable to students with disabilities and students from minority groups.

4. **Mathematics and science**—The act specifically states that American students will be first in the world in mathematics and science by the year 2000. With regard to special education and other student populations, the goal will be to increase the number of mathematics and science classes these children take by at least 50%.

5. **Adult literacy and lifelong learning**—The goal is that by the year 2000, all Americans will be literate and able to compete in the global economy. This includes and is perhaps more closely directed to minorities and students with disabilities.

6. **Safe and drug-free schools**—A final goal focuses on creating a safe school environment for children.

CONCLUSION

The past 100 years has seen several significant educational reform movements. Each of these movements made its mark on the educational system. The current reform movement had its origins in the early 1980s.

The first wave of this reform movement started with the 1983 report *A Nation at Risk;* the second wave followed with the 1986 Carnegie report entitled *A Nation Prepared,* and the third, and current, wave of reform, now known as restructuring, emerged almost concurrently with the second wave in 1986.

Although there is little agreement about specific changes that should be made in the organization of schools, two broad restructuring strategies have evolved: site-based management and schools of choice. Each has its proponents and critics. There are also many field-based examples of restructuring projects. However, none of these projects seems to be systemic in method or design (i.e., the restructuring focuses only on a few pieces of the school system and not on the entire system). If these projects are not systemic, then it is likely that the improvements that are made will not persist or will be canceled out by problems in other parts of the school system.

This book describes a process model to help school practitioners, like you, conduct a systemic and systematic examination of their districts' performance, determine what needs to be improved, lay out a framework for redesigning the district to support desired changes, develop and implement action plans for change, evaluate the change effort, and work hard to make the changes permanent (which is known as institutionalization). An overview of this systemic and systematic redesign model is described in the next chapter. Then, Chapters 4 through 9 walk you through each step of the model in more detail.

REFERENCES

1. Meyer, J.W. (1980). *The impact of the centralization of educational funding and control of state and local educational governance.* Stanford, Calif.: Institute for Research on Educational Finance and Governance, Stanford University.
2. National Commission on Excellence in Education (1983). *A nation at risk: The imperative for educational reform.* The Report of the National Commission on Excellence in Education.
3. Boyer, E.L. (1983). *High school: A report on secondary education in America* (ERIC Document Reproduction Service No. ED 242 227).
4. Goodlad, J.I. (1983). *A place called school: Prospects for the future* (ERIC Document Reproduction Service No. ED 236 137).
5. Sizer, T.R. (1984). *Horace's compromise: The dilemma of the American high school.* Boston: Houghton Mifflin.
6. The Holmes Group (1986). *Tomorrow's teachers* (ERIC Document Reproduction Service No. ED 270 454).

7. Task Force on Teaching as a Profession (1986). *A nation prepared: Teachers for the 21st century* (ERIC Document Reproduction Service No. ED 268 120).

8. Goodlad, J. in L. Olsen (1988). "The restructuring puzzle," *Education Week.* November 2, p. 7.

9. Kirst, M. in L. Olsen (1988). "The restructuring puzzle," *Education Week.* November 2, p. 7.

10. Raywid, M.A. (October 1990). "The evolving effort to improve schools: Pseudo-reform, incremental reform, and restructuring," *Phi Delta Kappan.* 72, 2, pp. 139–143.

11. Purkey, S.C., R.A. Rutter, and F.M. Newman (1986–87). "U.S. high school improvement programs: A profile from the high school and beyond supplemental survey," *Metropolitan Education.* pp. 59–91.

12. Evans, H.D. (1983). "We must begin educational reform every place at once," *Phi Delta Kappan.* November, pp. 173–177.

13. Chubb, J. and T. Moe (1990). *Politics, markets and America's schools.* Washington, D.C.: Brookings Institution.

14. Shanker, A. (1990). "The end of the traditional model of schooling and a proposal for using incentives to restructure schools," *Phi Delta Kappan.* 71, 5, pp. 345–357.

15. Berreth, D. (1991). In personal correspondence with the author.

CHAPTER 3

THE REDESIGN MODEL

INTRODUCTION

A model for designing high-performance schools is depicted in Figure 3.1. The purpose of this redesign process is to help school districts become superior learning organizations that apply their accumulated knowledge to create true value educational services for students and their parents. The desired outcome of this redesign process is the reconstruction of a school district's anatomy (its formal structures), psychology (its culture, beliefs, and values), and physiology (its flow of information and web of relationships).

The redesign model has four phases and is cyclical in nature. Phase I is a set of preparation activities conducted by a district-wide Steering Committee that assesses the expectations and requirements of the district's environment, clarifies or redefines the district's mission and vision, and establishes a change management structure and process. Phase II is a process to redesign the technical and social systems of a cluster of interrelated schools that is targeted to begin the redesign process for the purpose of moving that cluster toward higher levels of organizational performance. The process is facilitated by an internal or external consultant in collaboration with a Steering Committee and a

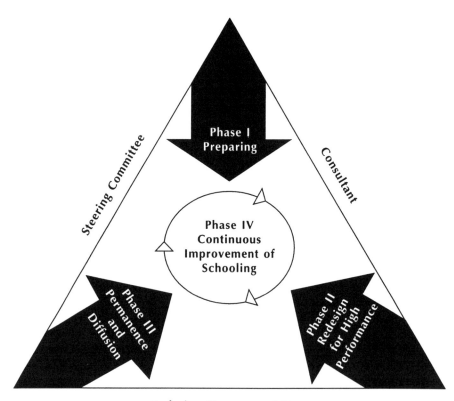

FIGURE 3.1 Model for Designing High-Performance Schools

Redesign Management Team composed of teachers and administrators. Once the redesign improvements are made, they are stabilized and then diffused to all other schools in the district until the entire organization is redesigned. This is Phase III.

After the improvements are stabilized and diffused, the Redesign Management Team then begins a process of continuous improvement that identifies and acts upon opportunities for incremental improvements in both the technical and social systems of the district and in its relationship with the environment. This is Phase IV. After a predetermined period of time, the district returns to Phase I of the model. This four-phase redesign process continues for the life of the organization. Each of the phases is described below and in more detail in subsequent chapters.

THE REDESIGN PHASES

Phase I: Preparing

Step 1.1   Build support for the redesign project

Step 1.2   Identify a starting point

Step 1.3   Establish a contract

Step 1.4   Form a Steering Committee

Step 1.5   Engage the Steering Committee in Open Systems Planning activities

Step 1.6   Engage the Steering Committee in redefining the mission and vision of the school district

Step 1.7   Establish a change management structure and process

Step 1.1: Build Support for the Redesign Project

The first step toward redesign is to build political support for the redesign project. Without political support (from within and outside of the school district), chances are the redesign effort will fail. Kotter[1] presents eight common mistakes businesses make while applying organizational reengineering processes. Several of the errors occur during Phase I of the redesign model described in this chapter. The first error Kotter describes is the failure of leadership to establish a great enough sense of urgency to motivate people to support the redesign process. A lack of urgency does not attract the support needed for the success of the redesign process. Kotter claims that well over 50% of organizational redesign efforts fail at this point; thus, Step 1.1 becomes exceedingly critical to the success of your redesign effort.

Three key activities can help build support for your redesign goals.

Recognize Needs and Opportunities—This activity is conducted by collecting information about the need to redesign the school district. This can be done informally by talking to individuals or groups or more formally by conducting needs assessments. Either way, the purpose of this activity is to collect data about the need to redesign the district.

In addition to assessing the need to make improvements, you must also identify opportunities the district can take advantage of to move toward higher levels of performance. The basic guiding question here is: What opportunities are there? (For example, there might be a "window of opportunity" to get federal or state funding or there might be a prospect of becoming a national model for other school districts to emulate.)

Hall, Rosenthal, and Wade[2] examined more than 100 companies using reengineering processes to redesign themselves. Out of this group, they completed a detailed analysis of 20 companies to identify factors contributing to the success (or failure) of the redesign process. They identified two categories of variables: breadth and depth. The variables within each category represent needs and opportunities for an organization. Each category is discussed below.

- **Breadth**—The work process to be redesigned must be sufficiently defined in terms of its cost or customer value. Narrowly focusing on a small number of process variables does not yield bottom-line results for the organization.

- **Depth**—The redesign process must penetrate to the organization's core to fundamentally change six crucial elements of the organization's infrastructure. Hall et al. call these elements "depth levers." These six levers are roles and responsibilities, measurements and incentives, organizational structures (e.g., policies, formal rules), information technology, shared values, and job skills.

The redesign process described in this chapter starts with a clean slate to plan and build a new infrastructure to support the evolving vision for the school district. It is critical to avoid the "we can't do that because..." mentality because this leads to a classic reengineering pitfall: trying to fix the status quo. Hall et al. observe that businesses that try to fix the status quo fail at reengineering, whereas businesses that do a "clean slate" redesign of the depth levers achieve dramatic success.

Assess Readiness for Change—In addition to recognizing needs and opportunities relating to your redesign project, you must also assess people's readiness to change. Readiness to change means that people recognize and accept the need to change and that they will at least support the effort. Assessing readiness to change is more of an art than a science, but it is an important part of the preparation phase. At least 25% (a "critical mass") of the key stakeholders must support the redesign project in order to proceed successfully. Kotter's[3] analysis of failed organizational redesign efforts suggests that the second error organizations make is not building a sufficiently powerful critical mass of people to support the redesign effort. He claims that "...whenever some minimum mass is not achieved early in the effort, nothing much worthwhile happens...in the most successful cases, the coalition [his name for a critical mass] is always pretty powerful—in terms of titles, information and expertise, reputations and relationships" (p. 62).

Another way of thinking about assessing readiness for change is to use a metaphor attributed to Gleicher.[4] The metaphor is $D \times V \times F > R$, where D = level of dissatisfaction with the status quo, V = a clear, powerful vision, F = discernible first steps toward the vision, and R = resistance to change. If any of first three variables are at or near zero, then the product of those three variables is at or very close to zero and thereby insufficient to overcome R. The larger the values of D, V, and F, the more likely it is that R will be surmounted.

Conduct an "All-Hands" Meeting—Dannemiller and Jacobs[5] specialize in large-scale change. An important element of their change model, which they have used successfully with large businesses like Ford Motor Company, is a structured meeting early in the redesign process which is attended by everyone in the organization, and they do mean everyone! In organizations where it is physically impossible to have everyone in the same room at the same time, a series of meetings can be held using the same structure and process until everyone in the organization has participated in one of these meetings.

There are several purposes of the all-hands meetings. First, the meetings are used to build support for the redesign project by presenting employees with available information about the purposes and desired direction of the redesign project. Second, the meetings are structured to surface, honor, and respond to valid resistance to the proposed project. Third, the meetings model the kind of employee participation that will be critical to the success of the redesign project as it unfolds and which will be central to the effective functioning of the newly designed school district.

Step 1.2: Identify a Starting Point

The redesign paradigm presented in this book assumes that a school district wants to improve instruction throughout the *entire* district by starting with a cluster of interconnected schools. Starting at this level is supported by Sirotnik.[6] He argues that school reform must begin at the building level because teachers are repositories of first-hand experience and are the primary agents of change. Further, Sirotnik suggests that individual schools should be viewed as centers of change instead of objects of change.

It is important to start small because the redesign process is too complex, in most cases, to be used simultaneously in all schools within a district. The cluster that is selected as the starting point is called the *target*. The target is neither the best nor the worst in the district. It has good schools with room for improvement. If the best or worst clusters are used, practitioners might attribute the success or failure of the redesign effort to the status of the target (e.g., "Well, the only reason they succeeded is because they have the best students in the district." or "They had no chance of succeeding. There was no leadership in those schools."). After successfully making improvements in the technical and social systems of the target cluster and after improving its relationships with its environment, the changes and organizational learning resulting from this experience are then diffused to other clusters until the entire district is redesigned for high performance.

Step 1.3: Establish a Contract

Once the target cluster is selected, a contract is negotiated with the administrator(s) and teachers. The contracting phase involves clarifying expectations, negotiating the involvement of staff, identifying and acquiring needed resources, and reaching consensus on the overall purpose of the redesign effort.

Because either an internal or external consultant is used to facilitate and support the redesign process, his or her role must be negotiated at this point. The consultant must also enter into either a formal or informal contract with the school district for services to be rendered. Tips for working with consultants are provided in Chapter 13.

Step 1.4: Form a Steering Committee

The Steering Committee provides strategic leadership for the redesign project by overseeing the redesign process for the entire school district. Thus, it is very important to have people from different parts of the district on the Steering Committee. Members of the Steering Committee must include the superintendent of schools, one principal from each level of schooling (i.e., elementary, middle, and high school levels), one teacher from each level of schooling, and one union representative (if appropriate). Additionally, some school districts may choose to include parents and students on the Steering Committee. The size of the group should not exceed ten members, because larger groups are exceedingly difficult to manage.

Soon after establishing the Steering Committee, the consultant provides the committee with team-building experiences. Developing the Steering Committee into a high-functioning team is a critical part of the process because its strategic leadership is crucial to the long-term success of the redesign effort.

Step 1.5: Engage the Steering Committee in Open Systems Planning Activities

These activities serve the purpose of helping the Steering Committee view the school district as an open system that is affected by and that affects its environment. Open Systems Planning (OSP) activities are facilitated by the outside consultant.

The environment is subdivided into three primary segments: the *contextual environment*, which includes elements outside of the organization that affect what happens inside the organization but are beyond the influence of the organization (e.g., federal and state laws, rules and regulations set by the state department of education, and private schools that compete with the district for students); the *transactional environment*, which includes elements outside the organization that affect the organization but are, in turn, affected by the organization (e.g., the community, parents, and accrediting agencies); and the *internal environment* of the organization (e.g., stakeholders such as management groups, employee groups, and individuals).

To analyze the various components of the environment, the outside consultant helps the Steering Committee go through a process of OSP.[7] The OSP process is often divided into four major tasks: (1) describe the major historical, social, and physical features of the organization; (2) identify the key internal stakeholders (e.g., managers, groups of employees, and individuals); (3) identify the key stakeholders in the transactional environment of the organization (e.g., parents and community groups); and (4) describe the contextual environment of the organization (e.g., state and federal laws, rules and regulations of the state department of education, "best practices" in the field of education, and the educational reform movement).

Step 1.6: Engage the Steering Committee in Redefining the Mission and Vision of the School District

Using the results of the OSP activities, the Steering Committee reviews the basic mission of the school district (i.e., it reassesses the basic reason for its existence or, in other words, redefines the business it is in). Then, the Steering Committee uses the mission statement as the basis for developing a vision statement (i.e., a concise, vivid, and powerful verbal picture of the district's core values and a description of "where [they] wish to head, the kind of organization [they] wish to create..."[8] The redefinition of the mission and vision of the school district should call into question every assumption underlying the process of schooling in the district. Support for this kind of deep restructuring is provided by educational leaders such as Albert Shanker.[9]

The concept of visioning was developed by Ronald Lippitt.[10] He called it "preferred future." According to Lippitt, the most serious trap organizations fall into when developing a vision is to limit involvement to a small team that plans for the whole. Kotter[11] identifies two errors in the reengineering process related to visioning. The first is that the organization lacks a well-defined, easily articulated vision. According to Kotter, if you cannot communicate your vision in five minutes or less and get a reaction that indicates both understanding and interest, your work is not done yet. The second visioning error is that the dream is undercommunicated. Kotter says that the vision must be communicated using *all* communication channels.

Step 1.7: Establish a Change Management Structure and Process

To manage the redesign process effectively, the Steering Committee designs a change management structure and process. The recommended change management structure has three parties: the Steering Committee, a Redesign Management Team (RMT), and a consultant. This structure is shown in Figure 3.2.

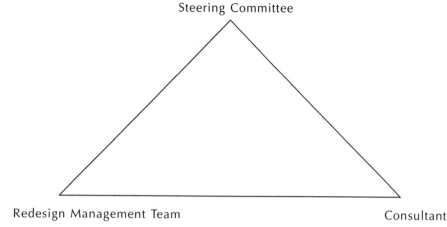

FIGURE 3.2 A Three-Party Redesign Management Structure

The Steering Committee was described earlier. The RMT provides tactical leadership for the redesign project and is formed by recruiting administrators and faculty from the target cluster who have the knowledge, ability, and willingness to participate effectively on the RMT. An additional selection criterion is that people selected for the RMT must be in full support of the redesign effort. Additionally, one member of the Steering Committee sits on the RMT. This dual membership is important to assure excellent communication between the RMT and the Steering Committee. Many school districts already have the RMT structure in the guise of school improvement teams.

Once the RMT is formed, the consultant provides team-building experiences. The RMT receives the same initial training as the Steering Committee. In addition to the basic training, the RMT members begin to learn about the process of and techniques for diagnosing the technical and social systems of their cluster.

The knowledge and experience of the consultant are also very important. The Steering Committee should choose a consultant who has (1) superior interpersonal communication skills, (2) an excellent knowledge of organizational redesign, and (3) a successful track record as an organization development consultant. Chapter 13 provides in-depth advice about how to find and work with external consultants.

Phase II: Redesigning for High Performance

Step 2.1a	Diagnose the technical system of the target cluster
Step 2.1b	Diagnose the social system
Step 2.2	Develop redesign proposals
Step 2.3	Develop implementation plans
Step 2.4	Implement selected proposals
Step 2.5	Evaluate the process and outcomes of the redesign effort

The purpose of Phase II activities is to conduct a systematic and systemic analysis of the technical and social system of the target cluster to identify specific ways to reconstruct its anatomy (structures), physiology (flow of information and relationships), and psychology (culture, values, beliefs). The desired outcome of Phase II activities is a comprehensive proposal to reconstruct the technical and social systems of the cluster of schools that begin the process and its relationship with its environment.

Step 2.1a: Diagnose the Technical System of the Target Cluster

The technical system is "the total collection of processes, procedures, instructions, techniques, tools, equipment, machines, and physical space that are used in transforming an organization's inputs into the desired output (product or service). "'X' is transformed into 'Y' by doing 'Z'."[12] In school organizations there are two primary types of work processes in the technical system: non-linear knowledge work (classroom teaching) supported by a linear instructional program (K–12).

First, analyzing and redesigning the linear instructional program of the target cluster will be discussed, and then information on how to analyze and redesign non-linear knowledge work will be presented. In both the linear and non-linear work processes, one of the primary goals of the technical system is to identify and correct variances (errors or disturbances in the work process) so that the organization can achieve its goals successfully. For the target cluster, this means that educators must constantly strive to identify and eliminate or control errors in the instructional program and in classroom teaching that may reduce the effectiveness of the teaching–learning process.

Diagnosing the Linear Work Process

In knowledge organizations, linear work processes are usually secondary to non-linear, knowledge work processes. The supportive linear instructional program of the target cluster is analyzed by an instructional audit that begins with the identification of the major inputs, outputs, and feedback mechanisms. Then, the RMT examines the linear instructional program by mapping boundaries between and among grades, teams, or departments, including the point where children come into the system, points at which children make transitions from one grade to the next, and points at which important concepts and skills are imparted. The analysis continues by identifying key errors (actual or potential) in the instructional program, assesses the impact of the errors, and evaluates how people currently control the errors.

Next, the RMT identifies and describes the major inputs to the instructional program. These inputs include technical and financial resources (human resources are assessed as part of the diagnosis of the social system). All resources imported into the cluster to operate the instructional program are assessed for appropriateness and adequacy.

Another task for the RMT is to identify the major outputs of the target cluster. A major output for a school is student learning as measured by achievement tests or other assessment techniques. Included in this list are the standards and criteria used by the target cluster to assure quality education. Once the outputs are identified, the characteristics of the customers (i.e., the students and their parents) who benefit from the outputs (the learning) are described.

Next, the RMT identifies the specific goals and performance measures for each output. The identification of goals includes both output goals (quantity, quality, cost, and time) and process goals (e.g., efficiency, procedures, gaps in the instructional program caused by vacations, holidays, and so forth). The RMT also examines the information used to set instructional goals and identifies the sources of this information. Another part of this analysis identifies customer expectations for quality, cost, service, and so forth. Finally, this part of the analysis charts teacher–student ratios, class enrollments, grade enrollments, and so on in such a way that trends can be spotted and responded to early.

The analysis also assesses the impact of other related organizational support systems on the linear work process of the target cluster, especially other support systems (e.g., management and secretarial staff). Additionally, the comprehensive analysis clarifies the demands that are made on the social system of the target cluster to operate, coordinate, and maintain the technical system. It also identifies opportunities to improve quality control within the technical system of the cluster.

Finally, the RMT assesses the feedback loop in the socio-technical system of the target cluster. The feedback loop is the channel through which various units, groups, and individuals in the cluster receive feedback on their performance so they can take corrective actions. This assessment is done by mapping the feedback loop and marking important steps in the feedback process. Additionally, the types of information provided through feedback are listed and described.

Diagnosing Non-Linear Knowledge Work in Schools

In schools, classroom teaching is the core knowledge work process. Knowledge work[13] is non-linear and non-routine.

To analyze non-routine knowledge work in the target cluster, a different analysis technique is applied. With linear work, a variance analysis technique that identifies and charts errors or potential errors on a matrix chart is used. Because knowledge work is non-routine work, this traditional method cannot be used effectively. Instead, the RMT examines the information exchange process (described below) used by the teachers, administrators, and supervisors;[14] identifies gaps and errors in the exchange process; and then redesigns the information exchange process to eliminate or control the errors. Work procedures and technological devices that support classroom teaching are also examined and corrected. Occasionally, as with grading procedures, traditional socio-technical system analysis techniques are applied to identify and chart variances in these supportive linear procedures.

In knowledge organizations, information feeds the workplace. "If school practitioners are cognitive beings whose actions are directed by their own conscious and unconscious thought processes; then the information that feeds those thoughts and choices becomes a primary resource for effective work."[15] Thus, the quality, quantity, and flow of information within a school system need to be improved if classroom teaching is to become more effective.

The conscious and unconscious thought process within the heads of knowledge workers (professionals working in schools) is called a *deliberation*.[16] Knowledge workers deliberate (or think) about many topics. Some of these information topics are critical to their effectiveness on the job. These are called *key deliberations*. Other topics are not critical. Some even distract the knowledge worker from topics he or she should be deliberating. Some deliberations result in decisions; others do not. To identify the current key information topics, the RMT lists and rank orders the critical topics teachers, administrators, and supervisors need to deliberate. This process is essentially an information exchange process.

At some point, a knowledge worker's deliberation process reaches out to solicit the input of others. Knowledge workers reach out by discussing topics with people they think can be of help. This reaching out creates an exchange of information. The places where information is exchanged are called *forums*. Forums can be structured (e.g., regularly scheduled team meetings), semi-structured (e.g., off-site training workshops), or unstructured (e.g., two colleagues conversing over coffee). The forums for the exchange of information are identified and described during the analysis.

The people included in a knowledge worker's deliberations are called *participants*. These people exchange their advice, opinions, or insights with the knowledge worker who, in turn, shares his or her information. Sometimes the knowledge worker involves the right people in his or her deliberations and sometimes not. The analysis must identify and describe the current participants in the deliberations.

When knowledge workers take action based on the exchange of information that occurs, they often follow prescribed work procedures (e.g., evaluation procedures) and use technological devices to assist them (e.g., computer systems). In schools, these procedures and devices support classroom teaching. The current procedures and devices used in the deliberation process are also identified and described during the analysis.

The information exchange process—deliberations, forums, participants, and supportive work procedures and technological devices—is the most important part of the non-linear work process in the technical system of a school. To analyze this kind of knowledge work, the RMT engages teachers and support staff in a diagnostic process that focuses on variances (errors or potential errors) that exist in the deliberations, forums, participation, and supportive work procedures and technological devices. To improve non-routine, non-linear knowledge work, teachers, administrators, and supervisors learn to participate more effectively in the information exchange process by deliberating more effectively about appropriate topics, involving appropriate participants, engaging others within appropriate forums, and using appropriate supportive work procedures and technological devices. Pasmore[17] refers to this kind of improvement process as "managing deliberations."

Step 2.1b: Diagnose the Social System

To continue the redesign process, the RMT analyzes the target cluster's social system. The social system is composed of the *participants* in the information exchange process, as well as the roles that each participant fills. The social system is a web of individual attitudes and beliefs, role definitions, skill sets, relationships among and between people, the potential for motivation and job satisfaction, and organizational culture. The desired outcome of this analysis is a comprehensive proposal describing ways to redesign the social system to create the social architecture needed for people to exchange a sufficient amount of quality information on a timely basis.[18]

Information is exchanged between and among individuals who form, disband, and reform temporary coalitions to explore common interests or concerns. The purpose of these temporary coalitions is to help teachers and administrators accomplish their work goals more effectively. The inherent nature of these temporary groups creates a web-like organization that functions much differently than an organization designed using Taylorist[19] principles of scientific management. Pava[20] refers to this web-like design as a reticular organization. Specific, in-depth guidance about networks of teams is provided by Lipnack and Stamps.[21] Additional guidance on the nature of collaborative work communities is offered by Schindler-Rainman and Lippitt.[22]

After the RMT identifies the information topics that are key to the effectiveness of classroom teaching, it identifies which people ideally should be participating in the process of exchanging information about effective teaching. Next, the RMT attempts to characterize the predominant values that each participant in the information exchange process consistently demonstrates while engaged in these deliberations. These values are easily inferred, because as people work with others long enough, they can predict which side of an issue the others will take. After working with others, people also begin to know the values that the others have (e.g., they begin to know if another person values good employee relations, good student relations, strict performance evaluations, or giving minimal merit pay increases).

After the values are listed, the RMT marks those values that are in conflict. If, for example, teachers and principals are expected to engage in an exchange of information about how to conduct effective performance appraisals and teachers say the process should be flexible while principals say it should be strict, then there is conflict between the values of these participants.

When conflict exists, the participants in an information exchange need to make trade-offs to reach consensus regarding the point of contention. During the diagnostic process, the RMT attempts to identify explicitly the trade-offs that need to be made to achieve consensus. Identifying intelligent trade-offs is important because the participants are interdependent and they are, hopefully, interested in gaining long-term benefit for the school district.

Another level of analysis described by Cotter[23] relates four sets of organizational variables to vertical and horizontal relationships in an organization. These variables are Goal setting, Adaptation, Integration, and Long-term development. The acronym for these variables is GAIL.

Goal setting includes, for example, policies and practices for financial budgeting, allocating funds, degree of autonomy, clarity of goals, and coordination among units of the organization. Adaptation focuses on assessing the appropriateness of such current organizational practices as long-term planning, feedback from customers, managerial support for innovation, and measurement procedures. Integration refers to practices and structures such as disseminating information, communicating, coordinating, cooperating, and resolving conflict. Long-term development includes variables such as staffing plans, recruitment, selection criteria, and performance evaluations.

The analysis of the GAIL variables gathers data on who interacts with whom to perform goal setting, adaptation, integration, and long-term development functions. The interactions are evaluated in terms of who is involved, how often the interactions occur, how effective they are, and how people feel while participating in the interactions.

Another part of the analysis of the social system identifies and describes the critical skill sets needed by teachers. One example of how this is done comes from the Canadian Imperial Bank of Commerce (CIBC).[24] Hubert Saint-Onge, Vice President for Learning Organizations and Leadership Development for CIBC, started identifying critical work skills by asking a simple question: "What must our people know to serve customers?" With this question as its guiding criterion, CIBC developed competency models that described the various talents needed for each category of employee. Each model contained about four dozen competencies. Next, CIBC abolished training. Instead, it made employees responsible for their own learning by asking them to use their competency models to plan their own training and education to do their *current* jobs better—not to win a promotion. Then, the supervisors were expected to track how fast their teams learned the required skills and to identify gaps in the skill sets.

A process for identifying critical work skills is performance technology (PT).[25] PT is a process that thinks of "...job performance as something that occurs within a system of goals, measurements, incentives, skills, consequences, feedback, and more."[26] PT recognizes that teachers-as-knowledge-workers are asked to think. Much of their thinking "behavior" is inside their heads; thus it is covert behavior. Further, teachers-as-knowledge-workers face a wide variety of challenges. They have to figure out what to do as they go along in their work. They must "configure" their performance somewhat differently every day.

The covert nature of knowledge work leads elitists to claim that the work of teachers cannot be described using behavioral language. PT, however, provides a very powerful way to describe critical skills needed by knowledge workers. The key to the process is to specifically define the outcomes expected of teachers' work. For example, if you want teachers to think critically, then you need to be specific and ask: "Think critically about what?" You also need to ask: "What teaching behaviors will we accept as evidence that what we're looking for in teaching exists?"

The final analysis of the social system examines the formal organizational role of each participant to assess the degree to which their roles meet specific psychological criteria that contribute to motivation and job satisfaction.[27] These criteria are:

- **Autonomy and discretion**—Psychologically attractive work provides a good mix of opportunities to be responsible and to exercise self-management in response to clear guidelines for behavior.

- **Opportunity to learn and continue learning on the job**—Psychologically attractive work provides many opportunities to learn new knowledge and skills, especially those that will improve on-the-job performance. However, these learning opportunities must offer reasonable challenges and timely feedback on the effects of one's learning.

- **Optimal variety**—Work that is psychologically attractive permits teachers, administrators, and supervisors to seek a reasonable amount of variety in their work activities. This opportunity helps to reduce boredom and fatigue while simultaneously encouraging the development of a satisfying rhythm (i.e., an alternating cycle of variety) in one's activities.

- **Opportunity to exchange help and respect**—Work that is psychologically attractive generates conditions under which colleagues can and do exchange help and respect. Building in this feature requires making mutual help and assistance an intrinsic element of job expectations. It also requires encouraging recognition of individual capability and achievement.

- **Sense of meaningful contribution**—Psychologically attractive work provides teachers, administrators, and supervisors with a sense that their contributions are important and valued.

- **Prospect of a meaningful future**—Work that is psychologically attractive promises advancement, which fosters personal growth and offers appropriately higher compensation.

Step 2.2: Develop Redesign Proposals

The results of the organizational diagnoses point to problems to solve and opportunities to take advantage of if the target cluster wants to move toward a higher level of organizational performance. Not all of these problems or opportunities can be responded to by the cluster because of financial, technical, or human constraints.

To select problems and opportunities to respond to, the RMT reviews the district's mission and vision statement again. These documents provide the RMT with redesign criteria for making decisions about which problems to address and which opportunities to capture. Additionally, the RMT considers the needs and expectations of *key stakeholders* (individuals, groups, and organizations that have a significant interest in the outcomes of schooling). These needs and expectations also serve as redesign criteria. Finally, the RMT considers the needs and expectations of the Steering Committee (which have been communicated to the RMT through the Steering Committee's representative on the RMT).

The RMT selects some redesign goals for the target cluster and develops specific proposals for achieving those goals. The proposals contain specific action plans and an assessment of the quantity and quality of resources that the target cluster needs in order to implement the proposals.

The proposals developed by the RMT are submitted to the Steering Committee for review and approval. The Steering Committee makes the final decision about which proposals go forward and which are set aside.

Because one member of the Steering Committee sits on the RMT, the proposals that are submitted should not be a surprise to the Steering Committee. Because the Steering Committee has been kept apprised of the RMT's work throughout the process, its review and approval should be relatively straightforward.

Step 2.3: Develop Implementation Plans

The RMT will have many proposals to implement and they must be implemented in a logical sequence that increases the effectiveness of the redesign process. For example, if one of the proposals calls for a change in how teachers are evaluated in the target cluster, then an antecedent change must occur in school district policies for evaluation and collateral changes must occur in the supervisory process. If antecedent and collateral changes are not made, then the desired redesign improvements will bump into significant obstacles that could threaten the success of the implementation. The importance of removing obstacles to desired redesign improvements was noted by Kotter[28] as one of eight errors made by businesses engaged in reengineering.

Step 2.4: Implement Selected Proposals

Redesign proposals are implemented according to the implementation plan. The Steering Committee provides strategic guidance for the implementation process, whereas the RMT provides tactical guidance for the implementation effort. When planning implementation, it must be understood that the process of reconstructing the cluster's anatomy, physiology, and psychology takes time. The time needed is reinforced by Kotter:[29]

> The most general lesson to be learned from the more successful cases is that the change process goes through a series of phases that, in total, usually require a considerable length of time. Skipping steps creates only the illusion of speed and never produces a satisfying result (p. 59).

One of the eight reengineering errors identified by Kotter relates to the amount of time needed to produce desired improvements. The error is for an organization to declare victory too soon. For one reengineering effort, Kotter and people from inside the organization calculated the amount of change that occurred each year for seven years. They used a scale of 1 to 10, where 1 is the lowest amount of change. Their analysis indicated the following:

Year 1 = rating of 2 (a low amount of change)

Year 2 = rating of 4

Year 3 = rating of 3

Year 4 = rating of 7

Year 5 = rating of 8

Year 6 = rating of 4

Year 7 = rating of 2

The peak year for important changes was year 5—a full three years into the reengineering effort.

Because of the amount of time needed to produce permanent change, it is important to intentionally design short-term wins into the process. Short-term wins are improvements that can be made early and often. These wins create and maintain the momentum needed to persevere to the end. Not planning these early, short-term wins, according to Kotter, is another error businesses make while participating in reengineering.

During implementation, formative evaluation techniques are used to assure that the entire redesign project, and the implementation of each proposal, stays on course. The evaluation data are fed back to the people responsible for implementing each proposal and are used to make course corrections and modifications.

Step 2.5: Evaluate the Process and Outcomes of the Redesign Effort

After all of the proposals for redesigning the target cluster are implemented, the Steering Committee, RMT, and consultant evaluate the redesign process and outcomes. The importance of evaluation was reinforced by Hall, Rosenthal, and Wade.[30] They identify four ways for organizations to fail at reengineering, one of which is to measure only the implementation plan and not evaluate the outcomes across time.

The results of the evaluations are also used during the diffusion stage of the redesign project, when the Steering Committee begins to spread the improvements to other clusters in the district. The evaluation results are used to determine if the redesign process is on course toward the vision and to make improvements in the overall redesign process.

Changes in organizations often disappear after a period of time. An old French saying captures this phenomenon: "plus ça change, plus c'est la même chose" ("the more things change, the more they stay the same"). In other words, organizations often produce a lot of changes and then revert back to their old ways, only to start changing again at a later time and then reverting, and changing, and reverting, and.... If a school district wants to achieve permanent improvements in the functioning of the target cluster, then this phenomenon cannot be allowed to occur. The improvements made as a result of the redesign process must become a permanent feature of the cluster's landscape and the knowledge workers' mindscapes.

Phase III: Achieving Permanence and Diffusion

Step 3.1	Conduct double-loop learning seminars
Step 3.2	Renew commitment to the changes made
Step 3.3	Allocate rewards for desired behaviors
Step 3.4	Diffuse changes to entire district
Step 3.5	Detect and correct deviations from desired outcomes

Kotter's[31] eighth error contributing to the failure of reengineering efforts is when an organization fails to anchor the improvements in its culture; in other words, it fails to make the changes permanent. Further, the literature is replete with examples of pilot projects that never spread throughout the entire organization. Failure to diffuse improvements results in a failed redesign effort. Thus, the purpose of this phase of the redesign model is to make improvements permanent within each re-designed cluster of schools and to spread those improvements throughout the entire school district until the entire organization is redesigned for high performance.

Step 3.1: Conduct Double-Loop Learning Seminars

To make redesign improvements permanent, the Steering Committee and RMT conduct a series of seminars where all employees within the cluster discuss not only *what* happened, but *how* it happened. "Double-loop" learning was first described by Argyris and Schön.[32] Single-loop learning, according to Argyris and Schön, is where organizations see a problem and fix it. The problem with single-loop learning is that no learning occurs about how to avoid or prevent similar problems in the future. If people in the target cluster want to see significant organizational improvement and if they want to ensure the long-term success of their knowledge organization, then they need to learn how to solve their own problems. Learning how to solve problems adds a second loop to the organizational learning process which significantly increases the overall effectiveness of the organization. The second loop also engages organizational members in a process of inquiry that questions underlying, but untested, assumptions, values, beliefs, and actions. The purpose of this kind of inquiry is to create a learning organization.

Step 3.2: Renew Commitment to the Changes Made

Gaining commitment to the improvements made in the target cluster requires sophisticated communication strategies. Achieving permanent changes also requires ongoing communication. Thus, the Steering Committee and RMT conduct quarterly all-staff meetings to: (1) ensure that people are continuing to support and learn from the changes that were made; (2) provide a forum for surfacing emerging issues, concerns, and problems; and (3) serve as a structured forum for reinforcing the school district's mission and vision statements. The Steering Committee must use every available channel of communication.

Step 3.3: Allocate Rewards for Desired Behaviors

To achieve permanent improvements in the target cluster and, later, to spread the improvements throughout the school district, the Steering Committee and RMT must also pay particular attention to the district-wide reward system. The Steering Committee and the RMT ensure that people in the target cluster are being rewarded for behaviors that support the mission, vision, and redesign improvements. This principle is important because behavior that is rewarded is repeated, and behavior that is repeated eventually becomes a permanent feature of organizational and individual behavioral repertoires.[33]

Step 3.4: Diffuse Changes to Entire District

Another problem to be managed during the redesign process is diffusion. Because the redesign process starts with an interconnected network of schools, the improvements made in this cluster need to be diffused, or spread, to all other schools in the district. Effective diffusion is critical to the success of the redesign project.

The amount of time necessary to diffuse improvements throughout an organization varies. The literature[34] suggests that the average amount of time is between 18 and 36 months. The variability in the time frame is related to the complexity of the organization and the problems it faces.

Step 3.5: Detect and Correct Deviations from Desired Outcomes

Finally, a permanent formative evaluation and feedback process is instituted. This process monitors the status of changes that were made, provides data for correcting unwanted deviations from desired outcomes, and helps identify new opportunities for additional improvements. This formative evaluation becomes the basis for continuous improvement of the school system.

Phase IV: Continuous Improvement of Schooling

Step 4.1	Supervise system boundaries
Step 4.2	Seek opportunities for continuous improvement

Step 4.1: Supervise System Boundaries

There are boundaries between subsystems in an organization. Often these boundaries represent functional differences (e.g., 5th grade teachers do not teach 6th grade subject matter, and instruction in elementary schools differs from instruction in high schools). These boundaries must be managed to reduce variances (i.e., errors in the work processes) and to ensure quality.

There are several boundaries that need to be supervised. First, there is the boundary that exists between the linear instructional program and non-linear classroom teaching. This boundary is characterized by curriculum guides, instructional policies, grading policies, and so forth. The second set of boundaries exists between grades. There is an invisible boundary between grades, and this interface needs to be examined and managed to assure timely and accurate sharing of information between grades. The third boundary exists between the social system and the technical system. There is a necessary symbiotic relationship that needs to exist between these two subsystems, and the boundary between them (represented by personnel policies and the like) needs to be managed. Finally, there is also a permeable and invisible boundary between the entire system and its environment. Since the boundary with the environment is permeable, the system affects and is affected by the environment on a frequent basis. There is a critical organizational need to manage this boundary in order to protect the social and technical systems of the target cluster from unnecessary intrusions by elements of the environment. These boundaries can be managed using a new paradigm of instructional supervision called Knowledge Work Supervision®.[35]

Knowledge Work Supervision is designed to manage the redesign process (the process is described in more detail in Chapter 12). This new supervision process is managed by a Knowledge Work Supervisor, who, in addition to managing the redesign process, supervises the boundaries between grades and between the system and its environment. Supervision of boundaries includes, for example, developing information management procedures to control the quality, quantity, and timeliness of information exchanges within the district and between the district and its environment; assuring quality communication between and among grade levels (especially between elementary and middle schools and between middle schools and high schools); assessing customer needs and expectations; and acting as a buffer to protect teachers from environmental stimuli that might hinder their efforts to teach.

Step 4.2: Seek Opportunities for Continuous Improvement

After the work process, social system, and environmental relationships of the entire school district are redesigned for high performance, the redesign process shifts its focus to the continuous improvement of schooling. Continuous improvement identifies incremental ways to improve work processes, the social system, and environmental relationships on an ongoing basis. Total quality management tools and processes[36] are useful during this phase.

After a predetermined period of continuous improvement (e.g., at the end of five years), the RMT returns to Phase I of the redesign process to seek new ways to significantly improve the district's technical and social systems and its relationship with its environment. The redesign process (preparing → redesigning for high performance → achieving permanence and diffusion → continuous improvement → preparing, and so on) continues for the life of the school district.

CONCLUSION

Current approaches to restructuring schools are inadequate because they focus primarily on prescribing the desired outcomes of restructuring (e.g., schools of choice, outcome-based education, or longer school years) without describing how to restructure a school district in a systemic and systematic manner. These prescriptive approaches to school restructuring cannot move an entire school system toward higher levels of organizational performance because they amount to nothing more than tinkering with the system. To improve the performance of an entire school system, practitioners can use the paradigm described in this chapter. It is a comprehensive, systemic, and systematic model derived from several interrelated areas: knowledge work, business process reengineering, socio-technical systems design (especially Pava[37] and Pasmore[38]), quality improvement, and organization development.

REFERENCES

1. Kotter, J.P. (March–April 1995). "Leading change: Why transformation efforts fail," *Harvard Business Review*. pp. 59–67.
2. Hall, G., J. Rosenthal, and J. Wade (November–December 1993). "How to make reengineering really work," *Harvard Business Review*. pp. 119–131.
3. Kotter (see reference 1), p. 62.
4. Gleicher, D. in Beckhard, R. and R. Harris (1987). *Organizational transitions*. Reading, Mass.: Addison-Wesley.
5. Dannemiller, K.D. and R.W. Jacobs (December 1992). "Changing the way organizations change: A revolution of common sense," *The Journal of Applied Behavioral Science*. 28, 4, pp. 480–498.
6. Sirotnik, K.A. (1987). "The school as the center of change." Paper presented at the Breckenridge Forum for the Enhancement of Teaching, Southwestern Bell Invitational Conference, San Antonio, Texas, August 18–21, 42 pages (ERIC Document Reproduction Service No. ED 292 170).

7. Jayaram, G.K. (1976). "Open systems planning," In W.G. Bennis, K.D. Benne, R. Chin, and K. Corey (Eds.). *The planning of change,* 3rd edition. New York: Holt, Rinehart, and Winston, pp. 275–283.
8. Block, P. (1991). *The empowered manager: Positive political skills at work.* San Francisco, Calif.: Jossey-Bass Publishers, p. 107.
9. Shanker, A. (January 1990). "The end of the traditional model of schooling—and a proposal for using incentives to restructure our public schools," *Phi Delta Kappan.* 71, 5, pp. 345–357.
10. Lippitt, R. (1983). "Future before you plan," In R.A. Ritro and A.G. Sargent (Eds.). *The NTL managers' handbook.* Arlington, Va.: NTL Institute.
11. Kotter (see reference 1).
12. Lytle, W.O. (1991). *Socio-technical systems analysis and design guide for linear work.* Plainfield, N.J.: Block-Petrella-Weisbord, Inc.
13. For example, Drucker, P.F. (1969). *The Age of Discontinuity: Guidelines to our changing society.* New York: Harper & Row; Drucker, P.F. (1985). *Management tasks, responsibilities, practices.* New York: Harper & Row; Drucker, P.F. (1993). "Professionals' productivity," *Across the Board.* 30, 9, p. 50; Edvinsson, L. (1994) in T.A. Stewart (October 3, 1994). "Your company's most valuable asset: Intellectual capital," *Fortune.* 30, 7, p. 71; Knights, D., F. Murray, and H. Willmott (1993). "Networking as knowledge work: A study of strategic interorganizational development in the financial services industry," *Journal of Management Studies* (Oxford, England). 30, 6, pp. 975–995; Saint-Onge, H. (1994) in T.A. Stewart (October 3, 1994). "Your company's most valuable asset: Intellectual capital," *Fortune.* 30, 7, p. 74; and Stewart, T.A. (October 3, 1994). "Your company's most valuable asset: Intellectual capital," *Fortune.* 30, 7, pp. 68–74.
14. This approach should not be confused with the Cognitive Coaching model developed by Costa, A. and R. Garmston (1985). "Supervision for intelligent teaching," *Educational Leadership.* 42, pp. 70–80. Their model focuses on the cognitive skills of individual teachers.
15. American Association of School Administrators (1994). "Seeking new connections: Learning, technology, and systemic change." Executive summary of an invitational seminar hosted by AASA and the Northern Telecom Integrated Community Networks Group, p. 4.
16. Pava, C.H.P. (1983). *Managing new office technology: An organizational strategy.* New York: The New Press.
17. Pasmore, W.A. (1992). *Sociotechnical systems design for total quality.* San Francisco, Calif.: Organizational Consultants, Inc.
18. Pava, C.H.P. (Spring 1983). "Designing managerial and professional work for high performance: A sociotechnical approach," *National Productivity Review.* pp. 126–135.
19. Taylor, F.W. (1915). *The principles of scientific management.* New York: Harper & Row.
20. Pava (see reference 16), p. 132.

21. Lipnack, J. and J. Stamps (1993). *The TeamNet factor: Bringing the power of boundary crossing into the heart of your business.* Essex Junction, Vt.: Oliver Wight Publications.

22. Schindler-Rainman, E. and R. Lippitt (1980). *Building the collaborative community: Mobilizing citizens for action.* Riverside, Calif.: University of California Extension.

23. Cotter, J.J. (1983). "Designing organizations that work: An open sociotechnical systems perspective." Paper distributed at a workshop on sociotechnical systems design. North Hollywood, Calif.: John J. Cotter & Associates, Inc.

24. Stewart, T.A. (October 3, 1994). "Your company's most valuable asset: Intellectual capital," *Fortune.* 30, 7, pp. 68–74.

25. Gordon, J. (May 1992). "Performance technology: Blueprint for the learning organization?" *Training.* pp. 27–36.

26. Ibid., p. 28.

27. Emery, F.E. and E. Thorsud (1976). *Democracy at work: The report of the Norwegian Industrial Democracy Program.* Leiden: Nijhoff.

28. Kotter (see reference 1).

29. Ibid., p. 59.

30. Hall, Rosenthal, and Wade (see reference 2).

31. Kotter (see reference 1).

32. Argyris, C. and D. Schön (1974). *Theory in practice: Increasing professional effectiveness.* San Francisco, Calif.: Jossey-Bass Publishers; Argyris, C. and D. Schön (1978). *Organizational learning.* Reading, Mass.: Addison-Wesley.

33. Thorndike, E.H. (1966). *Human learning.* Cambridge, Mass.: Massachusetts Institute of Technology Press.

34. For example, Pasmore, W.A. (1988). *Designing effective organizations: The sociotechnical systems perspective.* New York: Wiley & Sons.

35. Duffy, F.M. (1994). "Designing high performance schools through instructional supervision." Presentation at the fall conference of the Council of Professors of Instructional Supervision, Fordham University, New York; Duffy, F.M. (1995). "Supervising knowledge work," *NASSP Bulletin.* 79, 573, pp. 56–66.

36. For example, Arcaro, J.S. (1995). *Teams in education: Creating an integrated approach.* Delray Beach, Fla.: St. Lucie Press; Bonstingl, J.J. (1992). *Schools of quality.* Alexandria, Va.: Association for Supervision and Curriculum Development; Crosby, P.B. (1979). *Quality is free: The art of making quality certain.* New York: New American Library; Crosby, P.B. (1986). *Running things.* New York: McGraw-Hill; Deming, W.E. (1982). *Out of crisis.* Cambridge, Mass.: MIT Press; Taguchi, G. and D. Clausing (1990). "Robust quality," *Harvard Business Review.* 68, 1, pp. 65–72; Ishikawa, K. (1985). *What is quality control? The Japanese way.* Englewood Cliffs, N.J.: Prentice-Hall; Juran, J.M. (1989). *Juran on leadership for quality.* New York: The Free Press.

37. Pava (see reference 16).

38. Pasmore (see reference 17).

HOW TO REDESIGN
A SCHOOL DISTRICT

CHAPTER 4

PHASE I:
PREPARING

INTRODUCTION

The *preparing phase* of the redesign process is critical. Good planning increases the probability of the redesign project resulting in permanent improvements to the target cluster and, ultimately, to the entire district. Doing it poorly predictably dooms your project to the garbage bins where all failed change efforts are discarded. A failed redesign effort also hardens people's resolve to resist any future efforts to improve the district.

STEP 1.1: BUILD SUPPORT FOR THE REDESIGN PROJECT

Recognizing Need and Opportunity

Before change actually occurs, the organization must recognize the need to change. Embedded in the need to change are opportunities for significantly improving the quality of schooling you provide children in your community. Before jumping into a redesign effort, you must assess the degree to which stakeholders recognize the need to redesign the district. If you are the only one who sees the need, you might as well forget about starting a redesign project.

Administrators often focus only on "needs": What doesn't work? What hinders organizational performance? What's missing? You must clearly understand what these needs are. If the motivation to redesign the district is narrowly focused on the negative, the wrong, or the bad, then these needs become an emotional burden to overcome. An obsessive focus on needs can make the situation worse, especially if people begin to feel they are failures or incompetent.

To balance out your assessment of the need to redesign the target school(s), you should also determine what *opportunities* exist for the school(s) and focus on the value to be gained by redesigning the school. It tends to be easier for people to "buy in" to a redesign effort when they feel good about where they and the target school are going and if they know why they are being asked to make the journey. When both a statement of need and a description of opportunity exist, there is compelling motivation to improve the organization. There is a push from the past conditions (the needs) and a pull from the future (the opportunities). When being both pushed and pulled, so to speak, people often find it easier to disengage from the "old" organization and move toward the "new" one.

Opportunities can be identified by asking such questions as: What is really possible in this redesign effort? and What core values (e.g., see Patterson[1]) are served? Answers to these questions feed into a vision of the future. The vision is a purpose statement that touches people at an emotional level and gives meaning and spirit to the redesign effort. It enables the redesign project to happen and acts as its main driving force. (Suggestions for developing a vision statement are presented later in this chapter.)

Examples of questions for assessing needs and opportunities prior to beginning your redesign effort are shown in Worksheet 4.1. The answers to the questions clarify the rationale for the redesign project. The questions are used by the superintendent and his or her top staff prior to making a decision to proceed with a redesign project. The worksheet is a tool to help them think through their own positions on whether to pursue the goals of organizational redesign.

Assessing Readiness for Change

Changes occur and become relatively permanent when several important conditions exist in the organization. The presence of these condi-

1. What is creating the need for change? (Think about public pressure, results of educational research, results of local surveys, and so forth).
2. What opportunities or advantages exist for us if we redesign the school district? What is positively compelling about redesigning?
3. To what level do building administrators understand and accept these needs and opportunities?
4. To what degree do teachers understand and accept these needs and opportunities?
5. To what degree do other stakeholders understand and accept these needs and opportunities?
6. How clear are we, the top leaders, about our collective intention to plan and carry out a successful redesign project? If we are not clear about our intentions to support the project, what actions may be necessary to bring us together to strengthen our collective support for the redesign project?
7. What forms of resistance exist? What actions need to be taken to reduce the resistance and gain support?

WORKSHEET 4.1   Questions for Assessing Needs and Opportunities

tions, all at the same time, creates a "window" through which a change can pass successfully.[2] The presence of one or two of these conditions might be sufficient to start a change process, but they may not be enough to make the change permanent (making a change permanent is often referred to as *institutionalizing* the change). Beer[3] identifies several essential preconditions to change: key managers must be dissatisfied, the top manager must be committed and ready to lead, slack resources must exist and the resources must match the size and kind of change, and political support must exist.

Key Managers Must Be Dissatisfied

This is an absolutely necessary condition that must exist prior to beginning the redesign project. These key managers must include the principals of the target cluster. If the key managers do not see the need to change and the opportunities that can be realized, then there is no way that your redesign effort will succeed.

These managers must be unhappy with the status quo. Further, the principals in the target cluster must be able to identify specific problems that could become the focus of the redesign process. They must make a commitment to the redesign process. If you, or a consultant, wander around the district trying to coerce or entice principals to participate in the project, the project could fail for lack of their internal commitment to change.

The Top Manager Must Be Committed and Ready to Lead

In addition to the support and leadership of the superintendent, the top managers in the target cluster (i.e., the building principals) must be committed to the redesign project and must lead it. Without this commitment and leadership, the principals can neither model new, desired behaviors and attitudes nor adequately confront the traditional norms of the organization. When an organization is making a transition from the current state to a desired future state, traditional norms and organizational structures are weakened. It is in these moments that a top manager's effective leadership is crucial.

For these reasons, it is wise to start the redesign project with principals who are friendly to the goals, processes, and values or sociotechnical systems design. Sometimes, managers support a proposed redesign project verbally, but their behaviors make it clear that they are not committed to providing strong and visionary leadership for the redesign project. Thus, you, or a consultant, must make an early assessment of your principals' potential for commitment to and leadership of the redesign project within their schools.

Slack Resources Must Exist and Must Match the Size and Kind of Change

You must have money to spend on the redesign project, and you must have people available to help. You will need extra computers, meeting rooms, and other resources available for use by the Redesign Management Team (RMT). Some of the cost factors for a redesign project include the following.

Substitute Teachers—The redesign process requires a RMT composed of people from within the target cluster and at least one person from the Steering Committee (as described in Chapter 3). Some members of this team must be teachers. These members, ideally, should be released from their regular duties to assume responsibilities on the RMT. A less than ideal arrangement would be to give them release time during the school day and release them from one-half of their responsibilities. Either way, you will need financial resources to pay for substitute teachers.

Consultant Fees—The average daily consulting fee for the continental United States is $1,200 per day plus expenses. Because you cannot afford to have a consultant on site for 260 days (the actual number of work days in a year), you need to figure out about how many days you will need him or her.

The early steps of the process usually require a lot of the consultant's time. As the consultant trains people on the Steering Committee and the RMT, team members assume some of the consultant's responsibilities. At a minimum, you should expect to have a consultant on site four days per month during the first three months, two days per month for the next six months, and then one or two days every other month for the length of the project. (Remember that the literature on organizational redesign suggests that the average length of a redesign project is 18 to 36 months.). The specific time and cost requirements for a consultant are worked out during the contracting step of Phase I. Additional advice on contracting with a consultant is provided in Chapter 13.

In addition to the fees paid to the redesign consultant, you may also need to hire training consultants to teach people new skills and ideas (e.g., you may need to hire a special consultant to train people on outcome-based education if that is a direction in which your redesign effort takes you).

Office Space for the RMT—The RMT needs to work as a team. It would be helpful to provide the RMT with an office area where members are physically located a door or two away from each other. This physical proximity allows them to interact on an impromptu basis as well as on a more structured basis. At the least, the team leader should have a private office, which can also serve as a central location for the team's records. If the office is large enough, it might also be equipped to serve as a meeting area for the team.

Meeting Room Expenses—If you cannot provide office space to accommodate RMT meetings, one thing is for sure: do not hold meetings in classrooms. They are uncomfortable for adults and not organized to support effective meetings. Ideally, you should have a table large enough to seat all the participants. The chairs should be cushioned and comfortable. Note pads, pencils, flip charts, colored markers, and other supplies should be made available. Light refreshments should be provided. Meeting rooms should look professional and be adequate for working professionals.

If such meeting rooms are not available in your district, then you may need to budget money to rent space in a hotel or meeting facility in the area. Do not succumb to the temptation to use school classrooms. They really are not meant to be meeting rooms.

Travel Expenses for Team Members—Occasionally, organizations beginning a redesign project will send Steering Committee and RMT members to visit other organizations that are engaged in redesign projects. These visits involve travel costs. Additionally, selected members of the Steering Committee or RMT might also participate in specialized training. Attending this training results in travel expenses.

Special Equipment—RMT members need access to their own computers. Ideally, each member of the team should have his or her computer with state-of-the-art word-processing and graphics programs installed. It is also advisable to network the computers so that each RMT member has access to all redesign-related computer files through his or her personal computer.

Resources for Diffusing the Redesign Improvements—Remember, your redesign effort begins with a target cluster of schools. After the target cluster is successfully redesigned, then what it learned is diffused to other clusters in the district until the entire district is redesigned. You will need to establish additional RMTs in your district until all the schools have been redesigned.

Additionally, as you start to diffuse the redesign improvements to other schools, several schools can redesign themselves simultaneously. During each year of the redesign project, the redesign work is gradually expanded until all the schools in your district are redesigned. For example, if you have 18 schools in your district, a redesign involvement schedule might look like this: start with one school, expand to redesign three more schools, expand again to include six more schools, and finally include the last eight schools. In this kind of gradual expansion, the RMT members for the first target cluster serve as trainers and consultants to the new RMTs, the RMTs from the second round of redesign work would serve as trainers and consultants to the third round, and so forth.

Political Support Must Exist

Before beginning a comprehensive redesign of your school district (starting with the target cluster), you must assess the level of political support for this kind of effort (assessing the level of support is Step 1.1 of Phase I of the redesign model). A general rule of thumb is found in the metaphor of organizing a parade:

> To organize a parade in a town you need to assume that 25% of the people in the town will help plan and march in it, 50% will stand on the side-lines and watch it, and the remaining 25% will be against it.

This 25% rule-of-thumb is also reported in the literature (e.g., in Pasmore's[4] writings). You need at least 25% of each key stakeholder group inside the district (teachers, union leaders, and administrators) in support of a redesign effort just to get the ball rolling in the right direction. Additionally, you need the support of external key players (e.g., parent groups and the school board). Assessing where people stand on the idea of redesigning your district is a critical first step in the preparation phase of the redesign model.

To assess the level of support for your redesign effort, you can conduct a force-field analysis[5] to identify and weigh the forces for and against a proposed change. There are a number of different ways to depict your analysis; one is shown in Worksheet 4.2. This chart assumes that the "forces" are groups who are for or against the proposed change effort.

Again, you will need the support of at least 25% of the internal and external key players before you can effectively begin to move forward (this means 25% of the teachers, administrators, and staff). If you do not have that level of support, then you must take steps to secure it.

Another way to think about the concept of forces is to think about conditions that support or constrain the redesign project. Worksheet 4.3 illustrates how you can chart the supportive and constraining conditions that might impact a redesign effort.

You can employ a number of techniques to collect force-field data on the level of support for your redesign project.

Strength of Forces	Teachers	Union	Administrators
High			?
Medium	+	–	
Low			
+ = supports redesign, – = opposes redesign, ? = neutral or unknown.			

WORKSHEET 4.2 Force-Field Analysis Chart (Forces as Groups)

Conduct a Survey—Develop a survey form with questions related to attitudes toward redesigning the school district. Distribute the survey to all employees (teachers, support staff, union leaders, administrators). Use different colored paper for each group so you can identify the groups. Analyze the results to assess each group's relative level of support for the redesign effort.

The survey questions are designed in two ways. Most of the questions use a rating scale that yields results that can be manipulated mathematically (e.g., a scale of 1 to 5, where 5 equals "strongly support" and 1 equals "strongly oppose"). At the end of the survey, have one or two open-ended questions, where people can add comments that shed light on why they feel the way they do.

Conduct One-on-One Interviews—You can do these yourself or use a neutral third party to conduct them. For the majority of the interviews, however, it is advisable to use the services of a neutral third party. The third party designs an interview protocol that fits your needs

Forces Supporting Redesign	Current Situation	Forces Opposing Redesign
High community support →	Current district performance	← Teachers' fear of change
Educational literature →		← Organization's norms
Administrator pressures →		← Well-learned behavior

WORKSHEET 4.3 Force-Field Analysis Chart (Forces as Conditions)

and then conducts the interviews and records notes. The notes are analyzed later to search for patterns of opposition or support. The results
are shared in a formal report supported by written documentation that
is confidential.

Conduct Group Interviews—Use the same techniques as used in the
one-on-one interviews, but in a group setting. Sometimes these interviews are called focus groups. The size of the focus group should be no
larger than 15 people (small groups are easier to manage and they increase the likelihood that everyone will have a chance to speak). Sometimes group interviews can be recorded on audio-cassettes, especially if
the interviewer is a neutral third party who guarantees the participants
that the tapes are only for his or her personal use and will not be listened to by those in power.

Take the results of your data collection effort and chart them. It
doesn't matter what the chart looks like as long as it shows a visual
picture of the forces for and against the redesign project and the relative
strength of each force.

If the results of your data collection process indicate there are more
forces opposing your goal of redesigning the district than in support of
it, then you have three possible choices: (1) forget about it; (2) jump in
and do it anyway, regardless of the opposition; or (3) postpone starting
the redesign project and conduct activities to reduce opposing forces
while maintaining supporting forces.

If you really believe in the necessity of redesigning the district, then
it is obvious that you cannot forget about doing it. However, the second
decision generates a lot of ill will, hurt feelings, political backlash, and
ultimate failure of the effort. Thus, the most reasonable decision would
be to postpone action on the redesign project until you can build the
support you need by reducing the forces of opposition while maintaining, not increasing, the supporting forces.

According to Lewin,[5] the third alternative mentioned in the preceding paragraph can only be effective if you focus on reducing the opposing forces while maintaining, not increasing, the supporting forces. A
short personal anecdote illustrates why this principle is important:

> A few years ago I was the chairman of a university committee
> established to redesign the faculty governance system of my
> university. An informal force-field analysis indicated that one
> of the strongest supporters of the change was the president of
> the university. So, we attempted to reduce faculty resistance

to the changes by touting the president's support—that is, we were trying to increase one of the significant supporting forces. Well, to make a long story short, because the faculty didn't trust the president's motivation for the proposed changes, their resistance increased. We had to abandon our tactic quickly. Luckily, our quick switch from playing up the president's support to playing down the president's support worked and the governance system was totally redesigned.

The point of this story is not that supporting forces are unimportant—they are exceedingly important. However, if you try to play up supporting forces, this tactic can potentially backfire. Instead, Lewin suggests you focus on activities designed to reduce the opposing forces while maintaining supporting forces.

There are several ways to reduce opposing forces. Some of the techniques are discussed later in Chapter 11 under the topic of resistance to change. Another technique is to undertake educational activities whereby organization members, community members, and school board members are educated about the need to redesign your district.

Your educational activities should be designed carefully. You do not want these activities to be proselytizing sessions or lectures on the benefits of redesign. Instead, they should be designed to present rational and emotional reasons why the redesign needs to happen while also promoting group discussion.

Organizing these discussion groups in the correct way is critical to the success of the educational effort. Here are a few principles to follow:

- Conduct an "all-hands" meeting to talk about the proposed redesign effort. Invite *everybody*—teachers, secretaries, janitors, cooks, specialists, tutors, teacher aides, and so forth). Don't leave anybody out! If you can't fit all district employees into one building, then conduct several all-hands meetings (by region or by building).

  In the all-hands meeting, begin painting a verbal picture of the vision you have for the school district. Present sound rational reasons coupled with powerful emotional reasons. Use stories to make your points. In your stories, use a variety of linguistic images—auditory images (images that are linked to sounds), visual images (images that are linked to sights), kinesthetic images (images that are linked to tactile senses), and olfactory images (images that are linked to smells).[6] Provide information with a good balance between just enough detail and the "big picture." Summarize by listing several finely tuned topics that you want people to discuss before they decide whether to support the redesign effort. These topics, then, become the focus of organized discussion groups.

- Construct discussion groups using a random selection process. Use mixed groups of teachers and staff (including support staff such as teacher aides, specialists, and secretaries), faculty, union leaders, administrators, school board members, and, if you like, parents and students.

- Choose group discussion leaders who not only support the proposed redesign effort but also have the interpersonal skills to facilitate a group meeting.

- Train the group leaders by providing them with the information they need and by clarifying what you expect to happen as a result of the meetings.

- Train all the group leaders to use the same group discussion format so there is consistency across groups.

- Limit discussion topics for each meeting. Only one or two topics should be discussed in a 45-minute meeting.

- Each group needs a secretary to record the concerns people have. Prepare a response to all of the concerns that are communicated to you.

- Conduct as many meetings as you need to cover the critical topics.

Experience suggests that one of the most effective ways to change people's attitudes is through group discussion. If you try to tell a person to change his or her attitude, he or she probably won't. If you try to "re-educate" an individual to have a better attitude, your efforts probably will fail. However, if you put reasonable people together in mixed groups, under the guidance of a skilled facilitator, to discuss a variety of topics focusing on *why* the district needs to be redesigned, chances are that consensus will develop in support of the redesign project.

The educational activities described above offer a process for helping people develop commitment to the redesign process instead of forcing them to respond through control measures. When people act based on their commitment instead of in response to control measures, organizational effectiveness is increased.[7] Thus, it is imperative to begin modeling this commitment-building process early in your redesign project by involving people as much as possible. This proposition is supported by Pasmore, Frank and Rehm:[8]

> In high performance organizations we know that people are expected to be committed to the success of the organization. People move from being employees to being members; from hired hands to volunteers who can engage their heads, hearts, and hands; from simply meeting their psychological needs for security to meeting social needs through involvement; from a focus on individual jobs to a focus on teamwork; from being uninformed to being informed about relevant business information; from value-less to accepting the values of participation and teamwork; from being powerless to having at least some power to influence local decision making; from no voice in the organization to at least a limited voice; from having a single skill to having multiple skills; from a time orientation of "putting in my eight" to one of concern for the longer term success of the enterprise.... (p. 3).

STEP 1.2: IDENTIFY A STARTING POINT

Beer's list of preconditions that must exist before an organization initiates a complex, system-wide change effort was mentioned earlier. Those same conditions apply here, and they should be used to identify and select your first redesign site.

School districts are made up of many individual schools—elementary, middle or junior high, and high schools. Trying to redesign all of the schools in a district at once would be extraordinarily difficult. Fortunately, the literature on socio-technical systems design offers guidance on selecting an appropriate starting place for your redesign project.

The initial redesign site is often referred to as the *target*. The identification and selection of the target cluster of schools is a very important step in the redesign process. Further, motivation to engage in a redesign effort must come from *inside* the target cluster. It is clear that organizations completing successful change projects do not rely on authority figures to *push* them toward change—they lead the way from within.

"Self-selection" to initiate the redesign project does not mean that a principal and teachers cannot be recruited to begin the project. However, the recruitment process must give participants the opportunity to make a "free informed choice"[9] about whether or not to go first.

You, or the consultant, must resist the temptation that Miles[10] calls the "Mafia Contract." If you used this approach, you would direct the consultant, or others, to "fix" a manager or a school. Identifying a starting place in this manner would almost guarantee failure for your project.

If there are several possible "volunteer" clusters from which to choose, it is not wise to start with a cluster that is in terrible shape, because the redesign process will become bogged down in the extraordinary problems of that cluster. It is also not advisable to start with your best cluster because the remaining schools will look at the improvements and attribute the success to the fact that the cluster was "the best in the district." For those districts that are building new schools, it is also not desirable to start with these so-called "greenfield sites."

So, where do you begin? You begin with an average cluster of interconnected schools that is doing well but is in need of some improvement. This kind of cluster becomes a role model for other clusters in the district when it is time to diffuse what was learned from its redesign experience.

A critical characteristic of a school district that is useful for selecting a starting point for the redesign effort is its network of "feeder schools." There are three levels of schooling in American school districts: elementary schools, middle or junior high schools, and high schools. Elementary schools feed into middle schools; middle schools feed into high schools. This network of schools creates "clusters" of interrelated schools. Thus, if you want to improve a high school, it will have a "feeder" pathway leading down through one or more middle schools and one or more elementary schools. The site selection question, then, is: What is the target cluster? It is the high school and the entire "feeder" network, or cluster, for that high school. In most cases, this cluster of schools becomes the target to initiate the redesign process and is treated, therefore, as a single system during the redesign process. These interrelated schools are, in fact, a system, and if you want to make improvements in individual schools within that system, then you must also make collateral improvements in the other connected schools.

When starting the redesign process with a cluster of schools, you start the redesign activities with the school farthest "downstream" in the cluster (i.e., the high school) and work backwards (upstream) through the feeder pathways until the entire cluster is redesigned. This "start downstream–work upstream" approach is logical because you start by defining the outputs for the K–12 instructional program and then redesign each preceding level of schooling, moving upstream, to support the desired outputs. In a nutshell, the way the process works is like this. Redesign the high school first, then redesign the middle schools to support the improvements made in the high school, and then redesign the elementary schools to support the changes made in the middle schools and the high school. The bottom line for this approach is: Be a systems thinker!

The process of targeting a cluster to start the redesign process should include all of the building principals. In a structured meeting, explain why the redesign project is important to the district. Invite the principals to ask questions and to seek clarification. It is important to explain the criteria you have chosen to select the cluster that will start the redesign project. Finally, solicit recommendations for the target cluster from the principals. Also during this meeting, you are assessing which of the principals support the proposed project and which are not yet on board (techniques for dealing with resistance to change are described in Chapter 12).

STEP 1.3: ESTABLISH A CONTRACT

After a cluster has been identified as a likely candidate to start the redesign project, you need to identify and hire a consultant to work with you. You can work with an *internal consultant* or an *external consultant*. An internal consultant is a current employee of the school district who has the technical and interpersonal skills to facilitate the redesign project. An external consultant is an outside expert who has the technical and interpersonal skills to facilitate the project. Sometimes organizations pair an internal consultant with an external consultant so there is always someone readily available to offer advice and guidance on the redesign project. (Specific tips for working with consultants are provided in Chapter 13.)

Another consideration when working with internal consultants is release time. The internal consultant must be released from his or her regular duties in order to assume responsibility for facilitating the redesign project. It is grossly unfair and highly ineffective to assign responsibilities for the redesign project on top of regular responsibilities.

A final consideration when working with internal consultants is to make it exceedingly clear what will happen to the consultant after the redesign project is completed. Some school personnel might volunteer for the job, thinking it is a promotional opportunity. You must clearly indicate whether or not a promotion is possible. If this expectation is not clarified and the internal consultant *thinks* that a promotion is possible, when it does not happen he or she may be bitter and angry. It's a lot easier, and more ethical, to clarify expectations up front.

Another part of the contracting step is to work with the principal, teachers, and staff of the target cluster that will begin the redesign process. You must meet with them. First, meet with the principal(s) to explain, once again, what will be happening. In an all-hands meeting (and I do mean *all*-hands—secretaries, support staff, janitors—everybody), the principal explains the redesign project. You will be there as a back-up person. Remember, it's the principal's meeting, not yours.

The purpose of the all-hands meeting is to establish a psychological contract with the teachers and staff regarding the redesign project that they will be undertaking. They need to know what will be involved (even if it is a little vague at this point), who will be involved, how people will be affected (which you may not be able to answer at this early stage), and how much it will cost in terms of people's time and commitment (some people might also be interested in how much money it will cost). Even if you do not have all the answers to these and other questions, it is important to communicate with people to respond to their psychological needs. (Remember Maslow's hierarchy of human needs?[11] Physical, safety, social, ego, and self-actualization needs exist in all of us.)

When communicating about the redesign project, remember "Duffy's Laws of Human Behavior":

- **Duffy's First Law of Human Behavior**—People make decisions they think are in their best interests. Even if those decisions ultimately turn out to be wrong, when they were initially made people made them on the basis of how much they might benefit.

- **Duffy's Second Law of Human Behavior**—People seek to avoid pain and to experience pleasure. The lesson here is to describe the redesign project in positive terms that are uplifting, motivating, and emotionally powerful.

- **Duffy's Third Law of Human Behavior**—Behavior that is rewarded is repeated. Behavior that is repeated is learned. The lesson here is that when you see behavior that supports the new vision of the school district, reward it!

STEP 1.4: FORM A STEERING COMMITTEE

After you decide to proceed with the redesign project, establish a district-wide Steering Committee (SC). The purpose of the SC is to provide strategic oversight for the entire redesign effort—starting with the first cluster of schools until the entire district has been redesigned. Strategic oversight includes reviewing and approving all redesign proposals for improvements. The SC's responsibilities also include evaluating the process and outcomes of the entire redesign effort. To assure consistency when implementing redesign proposals, it is recommended that membership on the SC remain intact until the entire school district is redesigned.

Selecting members for the SC is critical. The first selection criterion is size. An effective working group should have no more than ten and no less than five people on it. Other critical selection criteria relate to who serves on the SC. If you want true improvements to be made, do not appoint people who represent groups within the school district. Mary Anne Raywid[12] makes this point when she says, "To include on a task force all interest groups with a stake in an issue virtually insures the continuation of the status quo" (p. 140). A SC composed of representatives guarantees that these people will fight for their groups' interests instead of the interests of the entire organization—it guarantees that the status quo will be maintained. Although you do not want group representatives on the SC, you do want people who are familiar with stakeholders' issues and concerns. Here is a list of people you might consider appointing to the SC:

- Superintendent (symbolically very important to have the superintendent directly involved in the redesign process)
- Three teachers—one from each level of schooling (elementary, middle, and high school)
- Three principals—one from each level of schooling
- One community member

STEP 1.5: ENGAGE THE STEERING COMMITTEE IN OPEN SYSTEMS PLANNING ACTIVITIES

The education elite do not like to think of schooling as a business, but it is! It is a non-profit business in the service sector of our economy. It has customers, suppliers, competitors, regulators, unions, and other important stakeholders (e.g., families and communities). Although schools do not have a profit motive, they still need to set and meet business-like goals and objectives. Doing an analysis of a school district's environment is just as important as doing a similar analysis for a computer software development company.

A school district's *transactional environment* is the external world of people, institutions, and trends that affect, and are affected by, the district. An environmental analysis is a methodical examination of (1) customer needs and how to meet them and (2) the needs of other important stakeholders (e.g., suppliers, competitors, regulators, unions, communities, and families). One technique for doing an environmental analysis is called *Open Systems Planning* (OSP), which was developed by Jayaram.[13] The key results of this analysis are a profound understanding of the environmental demands on your district and an understanding of how the district currently responds to those demands. The analysis process also helps you perceive the district as a whole *socio-technical system* that interacts with an external environment.

In Phase I of the redesign model, the SC does OSP for the entire school district because it needs to develop a "big picture" for the entire redesign project. The big picture then becomes a "screen," or filter, for making decisions about which redesign proposals to support and which to reject.

There are four major tasks to be completed during OSP, as follows.

1. Define the System—When defining the system of the entire school district, it is useful to use large flip charts so you can actually draw a map illustrating the boundaries. Include the following information on your map:

- Actually draw a map representing the school district as a whole system (for an example, see Worksheet 4.4).

- Then draw a similar map for the target or cluster of schools that are to begin the redesign project.

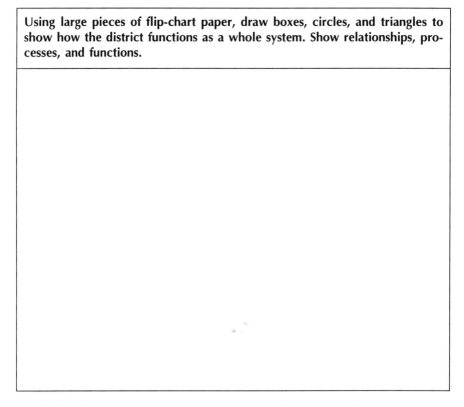

Using large pieces of flip-chart paper, draw boxes, circles, and triangles to show how the district functions as a whole system. Show relationships, processes, and functions.

WORKSHEET 4.4   Draw a Map of the School District as a Whole System

- On the maps, list the major "suppliers" to each of the schools (e.g., for a high school, list all of the feeder schools, starting with the middle schools and working backwards to the elementary schools). Other suppliers include colleges and universities that tend to provide most of your teachers and administrators, suppliers of materials and resources, and so on.

- List the major customers. For schools, the customers are parents of school-age children. Sometimes students are considered customers; at other times, they are thought of as "workers." As workers, students become "internal customers." You might consider segmenting your customer base to identify various subgroups that "purchase" your services. To assist your assessment of the customers, answer the following questions:

- ○ Who are the customers (internal and external)?
- ○ What products or services do they expect from us? (You can use a chart like the one shown in Worksheet 4.5.)
- ○ What are their requirements for the products or services?
- ○ How do we measure their satisfaction?

- Write the names of other stakeholders who influence, care about, or rely upon the performance of the school district. Then, identify those stakeholders who exert the strongest influence on the district. To help you with this step, answer the following questions:
  - ○ Who are the stakeholders?
  - ○ Where are they located?
  - ○ Why are they stakeholders?
  - ○ How do we measure their satisfaction?

  To chart information about stakeholders, you can use Worksheet 4.6.

Services and Products	Customers	Suppliers	Critics	Competitors

WORKSHEET 4.5 Service and Product Matrix

	Key Player Roles (Place a * in the appropriate cell for each key player listed)			
Key Players	Customer	Supplier	Critic	Competitor

WORKSHEET 4.6   Key Player Analysis

- Look at your map, discuss it, and identify major learning from this overall view. Develop ideas for improving the organization's response to its environment.

- Summarize the major historical, social, and physical features of the district using Worksheet 4.7.

2. Identify Strengths, Weaknesses, Opportunities, and Threats (SWOT Analysis[14]) in the Environment—Make a list of the SWOTs that exist in the district's environment. It is helpful to chart these variables using Worksheets 4.8 to 4.11. To help with this analysis, answer such questions as:

- What opportunities exist in our relationship with stakeholders?

- What opportunities exist in our relationship with our customers?

- What change efforts are currently underway in the district that might offer opportunities for the redesign project?

3. Summarize Major Learning—This is a relatively simple task. Discuss the results of the OSP analysis and then make a list of the major findings.

Major Historical Features
Major Social Features
Major Physical Features

Worksheet 4.7   Summary of the Major Historical, Social, and Physical Features of the Organization

THE PRESENT		THE FUTURE	
Strengths	Weaknesses	Opportunities	Threats

WORKSHEET 4.8   SWOT Analysis

Significant issue or trend in the external environment	How might this issue or trend affect the school district?

WORKSHEET 4.9   Issues and Trends Analysis

Probability of
Occurrence

100%				
75%				
50%				
25%				
0%				
Strength of Threat	None	Low	Moderate	Strong

WORKSHEET 4.10   Threat Analysis (Negative Effects on the School District)

Probability of
Occurrence

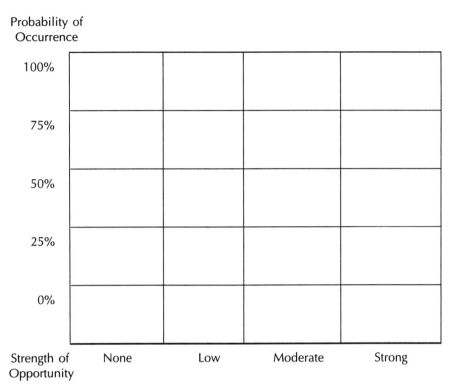

WORKSHEET 4.11   Opportunity Analysis (Positive Effect on the School District)

4. Describe Criteria for the Redesigned Organization—Using the major findings from the previous activities, begin painting a picture of how you want the entire redesigned school district to look, feel, and sound. This picture serves as a guidepost for the cluster of schools that will start the redesign process. The picture gives the target cluster a frame of reference and parameters within which to work. Finally, this picture becomes the core of the new vision statement that you will develop in the next step of the preparation phase.

In 1982, the National Association of Secondary School Principals constituted a Task Force on School Climate to "...investigate the available literature and instrumentation in this domain."[15] The product of this analysis was an interactive model of the school environment. This model[16] provides an alternative set of variables for conducting OSP. The model assesses variables in the following environments of an individual school within a district: societal environment, school district and community environment, and school or classroom (i.e., internal) environment. Within each of these environments are specific variables that can be identified and assessed for OSP.

STEP 1.6: ENGAGE THE STEERING COMMITTEE IN REDEFINING THE MISSION AND VISION OF THE SCHOOL DISTRICT

What Is a Mission Statement?

A mission statement is a simple one- or two-sentence statement about the basic reason for your organization's existence. Your mission statement needs to show people "organizationally correct" decisions in plain English. Knowing what is correct is empowering. Think about a mission statement using a sports analogy. Football teams have a simple, common, powerful mission: score touchdowns to win games. Every player knows what the team must do to win—cross the opposing team's goal line. All the players' actions on the field are focused on crossing that line. Many organizations, and very often school organizations, are confused about their "goal line." Your mission statement needs to define the goal line for your school district. By focusing your mission statement on what you really want, it becomes the goal line that relentlessly focuses people's attention, effort, and action.

What Is a Vision Statement?

The vision statement provides the context for the redesign effort. As such, it becomes the primary driving force for all decision making and action. The structure of the school district, leadership style, management practices, and strategic plans are all secondary to the vision. All of these variables take their lead from that which gives them life and definition—the vision!

"Vision is a mental journey from the known to the unknown, creating the future from a montage of current facts, hopes, dreams, dangers, and opportunities."[17] Vision is the difference between short-term tinkering (like lengthening the school day) and long-term change. Vision inspires people to change. The editors of *Fortune* magazine said, "The new paragon of an executive is a person who can *envision* a future for his organization and then *inspire* his colleagues to join him in building that future [emphasis added].[18]

Vision is central to the activities of redesigning your school district. It paints a picture of where you want the district to go and what you want it to become. A vision does not have all of the numbing details of that future, but it does paint a general picture of the future. A powerful vision spells out clearly what you want and inspires people to achieve it. It articulates a destination that everyone would like to reach.

A vision describes a crusade for the district—a quest toward ideals. These ideals, by definition, are always just out of reach. Being just out of reach creates motivational fuel that drives people toward the pursuit of a high-performing school district. Vision also gives meaning and direction to work. It captures imagination. It mobilizes emotional and physical energy. It communicates to people that their efforts will make a difference.

According to James Belasco,[19] an empowering vision meets three criteria:

- It *focuses* on the organization's strategic advantages.
- It provides *inspiration* to deliver those advantages consistently.
- It has *clarity* so it can be used as a decision-making criterion.

The first task in developing a vision is identifying the strategic advantages that your school district enjoys. Does your district exist in a wealthy suburban area that is known for financially supporting its schools? Are your school buildings all relatively new and free of damage? Do you have a curriculum that is attractive to parents? Are potential teachers beating down your doors to get a job in your district? Are you known for having an outstanding teaching staff, even though your district is in an inner-city area? Are your students' achievement scores consistently higher than those of neighboring school districts? What distinguishes your school district from all others?

If you cannot identify the strategic advantages of your district, then you must use the redesign process to develop some advantages. Transforming your district into a high-performing district will, in itself, give you the strategic advantages that you might so desperately need.

Your vision statement must also inspire people to achieve district-wide goals. Inspiration does not come from a vision of doing more of the same, just differently. You must craft the vision statement to appeal to the emotions of people. You can do this by designing your vision to inspire people to serve your district's primary customers—children and their parents—more effectively. Your faculty and staff need to see that the vision represents a means to serve some greater good.

Another element of your vision statement that can make it inspirational is to construct it so that it adds value to others. History's greatest leaders have united people with the power of their value-adding visions. Mahatma Gandhi convinced 450 million Indians to struggle for his vision of independence. Martin Luther King, Jr., convinced 20 million African-Americans to reach out for his vision of equality. John F. Kennedy motivated 210 million Americans to accept his vision of putting a man on the moon in the 1970s.

For school districts, a vision that adds value is one that aims to educate children effectively so that they can contribute to the net value of our society. It talks about helping children become lifelong learners. It addresses children's educational, physical, social, and emotional needs within the context of schooling. Your vision needs to tap into these inspirational wellsprings.

Your vision also has to be clear. Clarity is powerful. Lucidity enables your staff to use the vision as a screen to filter out which decisions and actions support the district's goals and which do not. Clarity is achieved by using a short, simple, plain-English statement of your vision. A fifteen-page vision statement does not provide clarity. A one-page vision statement written in plain, but powerful, English can provide exceptional clarity.

The school district's vision must also be compelling. To be compelling, it must be compatible with the faculty and staff's values and their personal aspirations. When the vision speaks to their values and aspirations, they can clearly see how they can contribute to its realization. The vision must activate both spirit and ownership. It must find a pathway to people's hearts, as well as to their minds. People yearn to give meaning to their work—meaning that goes beyond financial and ego needs. A compelling vision is one for which people will take a stand.

Here are examples of a mission and vision statement for a fictitious consulting company.

Sample Mission Statement

[In one sentence, restate the basic business purpose of your organization.]

The Eagle Ridge Consulting Group provides state-of-the art management training to small and mid-size businesses by producing and delivering the most marketable and effective management development training in the United States while maintaining the highest standards of quality, cost, and client satisfaction.

Sample Vision Statement
The Eagle Ridge Consulting Group

[For some practical advice on building a vision statement, see Belasco.[20]]

QUALITY FOCUS

We will commit our individual abilities and team efforts to achieve the highest quality results in all aspects of our products and services.

CUSTOMER ORIENTATION

We will seek out and satisfy our clients' needs and constantly strive to exceed their expectations. We will add value to our products and services by delivering more than we promise at no additional charge. We recognize that the quality of our training has an impact on the performance of our clients' organizations.

CONTINUOUS IMPROVEMENT

We will continuously seek ways to improve our organization. We will constantly seek ways to improve as individuals and to enhance the functioning of our teams.

PARTICIPATION AND INVOLVEMENT

We will seek input from all quarters of the organization to find the best solutions to problems we face. We will also seek input to improve the quality of work life in our organization. We will share information, resources, and ideas. We will develop the skills needed to maintain an exciting work environment where decisions are made at the most appropriate level.

PEOPLE FOCUS

We will ensure a cooperative partnership among all members of The Eagle Ridge Consulting Group. We will construct and maintain a culture marked by mutual trust, respect, a sense of dignity, and valuing diversity. We will provide opportunities for all employees to reach their maximum potential and to experience more secure and satisfying employment in a safe, healthy, and motivating work environment.

COST CONSCIOUSNESS

We will continuously improve operating efficiency and reduce costs based on the recognition that every action we take can influence external as well as internal costs. We recognize that the cost of our products and services affects our attractiveness in the marketplace.

When planning to develop or refine your vision, you must involve people in the process. Vision building is one of the best opportunities to get people working together in a synergistic way. Often the process of building the vision is as powerful as the actual written statement, and widespread participation in the vision-building process is often one of the best ways to help people develop a sense of ownership of the vision. A vision designed by the people at the top of the organization and then imposed on the organization often results in resistance and cynicism. Because you want people to own the vision—not resist it—the way in which you design your vision-building process is critical to your success.

Who Creates the Vision?

First, the superintendent drafts a framework of values and beliefs that he or she has for the school district. Then, this draft is given to the SC, which then initiates an intensive vision-building process for the entire district. To do this, the SC gathers input from all the important stakeholders. With the assistance of a consultant who is part of the redesign effort, SC members craft the vision statement by adding their own personal visions for the school district. Then, the SC incorporates acceptable elements of the stakeholders' expectations. Next, it shares the drafts of the vision statement with the stakeholders to get their reactions and suggestions for improvement. This process continues until there is consensus.

Conduct a Vision-Building Workshop for the Steering Committee

Workshop Climate

The design of your vision-building workshop is critical. The context within which the SC begins this process can have a significant effect on the outcome. When designing the workshop, consider incorporating the following elements into the workshop climate:

- Freedom to think creatively
- A work environment that is relaxing and fun

- Time built into the schedule for personal reflection
- A safe work environment that encourages and supports risk taking
- A work environment that incorporates pleasant colors, soft music, and elements of nature
- A group climate that recognizes the value of everyone's contributions so that people feel valued by the group

Workshop Format

Step 1—Prior to the workshop, collect and summarize needs assessment data that were collected from important internal and external stakeholders. The superintendent prepares the first draft of the vision statement by outlining his or her core values and beliefs regarding the future of the district.

Step 2—Distribute the summarized results and the superintendent's draft to each member of the SC and ask them to study this information to identify ways to enrich the new vision statement.

Step 3—Develop an agenda for the vision-building workshop and distribute it at least one week in advance of the meeting. Allow enough time for reflective thinking, discussion, and writing. A two- or three-day workshop format is often adequate for this first round of vision building.

Step 4—Select a meeting site that is physically attractive and comfortable. If possible, the meeting site should not be in one of the school buildings. Work with the meeting site managers to assure that the meeting room is big enough to accommodate everyone comfortably, that it has good temperature controls, and that it is aesthetically attractive. Provide light meals and refreshments.

Step 5—Line up all of your equipment and supplies. You will need an easel, a couple of large flip charts, colored markers, masking tape, note pads, and pencils. A laptop computer would be helpful for entering the results of each day's work. If the meeting facility has a computer available, you may be able to print out the results of each day's work so that everyone can have "hard copy" for the next day. Some meeting facilities may have a computer-based brainstorming network available for your use. For example, Gallaudet University, in Washington, D.C., has a computer network that is often used to collect and organize information provided by individual faculty and staff. Individuals sit at their own computer stations and enter their thoughts, feelings, perceptions, and suggestions about a particular question or problem. Then, the computer system collates all this information so that everyone has access to all the entries. Results are projected on a large screen that all can see. Individuals can then build on each other's work. This information is then used to help the administration make decisions on critical issues.

Workshop Process Tips

Tip 1—Start on time! It is wrong to delay the start of a meeting because a couple of people are late. It is not right to punish those people who made an effort to be there on time. After the meeting has started, do not stop to bring any latecomers up to speed. Let them catch up on their own after the meeting.

Tip 2—At the beginning of the meeting, set the mood. Review the purpose of the vision-building workshop. Clarify expectations. Review the agenda. Post the agenda on a large sheet of flip-chart paper. Constantly refer to the agenda to ensure that the group stays on the task.

Tip 3—Allow time for individuals to develop their personal vision statements. The first hour or so should be devoted to this task. Individuals use the results of the needs assessment data combined with their own personal feelings and thoughts to envision their preferred future for the school. The following questions can be used to guide individual thinking:

- What does this school district stand for? What purpose do we serve?
- What will it be like to work in this district if we make this vision reality?
- What will this newly redesigned school district feel like, look like, sound like?
- Why is this redesign effort so important to us?
- What, in particular, do I value about this effort?
- What can our newly redesigned school district do to add value to the children's education?
- What can we possibly hope to achieve through this effort?

Tip 4—After crafting their individual perceptions of a desired future, participants share their visions with the total group. The essential themes, elements, and components of these visions are written down on flip-chart paper. At this point, there should be no discussion, evaluation, or criticism of the individual vision statements. People's ideas are welcomed, valued, and accepted without question (except if there is a need for clarification).

Tip 5—Scan the various flip-chart sheets to identify common threads, themes, and dreams. Focus on key words, phrases, and images. Write down the common factors on a clean sheet of flip-chart paper.

Tip 6—Discuss the common factors. Aim the discussion at developing a unified statement that is reached by consensus and by blending the values and beliefs of many people. Remember that consensus is not unanimity. Consensus means that even though some people do not totally agree with a suggestion, they feel that they can live with it. Consensus-building skills are discussed in Chapter 11.

Tip 7—Using the agreed-upon themes, build the vision using components such as:

- Philosophy
- Strategic direction
- Organizational beliefs and values

Tip 8—Examine carefully the content of the vision that was reached by consensus. Determine the implications of the content. Assess the impact of the choice of words on the school district, its priorities, constraints on its operation, its functioning, and its culture. Focus your assessment on variables such as:

- **Opportunities and risks**—Identify the positives and negatives, and calculate the potential risks of implementing the vision.

- **Critical success factors**—Identify the factors that will ultimately affect the success of the vision (e.g., money, human resources, technical skills, government support, and community support).

- **Sequence of major steps toward the vision**—Develop a logical, step-by-step progression of milestones that mark the way toward the realization of the vision. Also, identify the possible impact that each step might have on another step.

Post-Workshop Action Steps

Step 1—After the conclusion of the vision-building workshop, write the draft of the vision statement that was reached by consensus. Edit the draft so that it is clear, precise, emotionally powerful, and compelling. Share a copy of this draft with all workshop participants and request feedback.

Step 2—Distribute the draft to stakeholders. Use an iterative process for testing and revising the draft (i.e., identify each group of stakeholders that must be involved in the feedback process, share the draft of the vision with the first group, incorporate their feedback into a second draft, share the second draft with the next group, incorporate their feedback, and so on). Conduct small-group meetings with each group of stakeholders. Solicit their responses and suggestions. Record the input on large sheets of flip-chart paper. Pay particular attention to people's emotional responses to the vision statement. If the responses are bland or complacent, the vision statement is missing the mark.

Step 3—Because the vision statement must be translated into a more practical and precise mission statement, goals, objectives, and priorities, you must analyze the impact that the vision statement has on the old ways of doing things in the district. This requires careful, methodical analysis. You need to identify the functions of the district and assess the impact of the vision statement on those functions. Do this for all of the functions of the district. At this point, you also must test the vision for realism and feasibility—but beware of conservatism and traditionalism because they are the demons of "more of the same" and complacency. Fine-tune the vision statement to respond to any concerns that were generated during this step of the process.

Step 4—Communicate the final vision statement throughout the school district and to external stakeholders.

Step 5—Nurture the support of internal and external stakeholders.

Step 6—Translate the vision into immediate, visible actions, even though you have not yet developed specific redesign proposals. Having a vision statement is not enough! The walls of many organizations are decorated with well-intentioned, but ignored, visions. People must use the vision to make it real. Empower your faculty and staff to use the vision—now! Each member of the SC must clearly identify the behaviors that support the vision and then *demonstrate* those behaviors. For example, if your vision statement calls for decentralized decision making, then find ways to delegate decision making—now! Live the vision consistently. Talk about it every chance you get. Incorporate it into all documents, meetings, and so forth. Become compulsive about describing and living the vision. Find ways to incorporate the vision into the culture of the organization. Look for new symbols to represent the vision. Live it! Breathe it! Become it!

Step 7—Transmit the vision statement to the members of the RMT. Charge them with the responsibility of using the vision statement as a screen for developing and selecting proposals for redesigning your school district.

STEP 1.7: ESTABLISH A CHANGE MANAGEMENT STRUCTURE AND PROCESS

The final step in the preparation phase is to design a change management process. In Chapter 3, the general design of the redesign model was displayed as a triangle. The structure of the model has three primary roles (SC, RMT, and consultant) and four phases (preparing, redesigning for high performance, achieving permanence and diffusion, and continuous improvement of schooling). This structure represents the redesign process that the SC now must formally adopt and operationalize.

Establishing a Redesign Management Team

The first action the SC takes to operationalize the redesign model is to charter a RMT. The RMT is the workhorse of the redesign project. This team is almost totally responsible for Phase II of the redesign process. It does the organizational diagnoses, develops proposals for improving the cluster, designs implementation plans, and plans for the evaluation of the process and outcomes of its piece of the redesign project. The RMT provides tactical leadership for the redesign project.

The RMT is composed of principals from the target cluster and several teachers and staff from those schools. Additionally, one member of the SC also serves on the RMT to assure communication between the RMT and the SC. Finally, the consultant acts as an advisor to the team. To have an effective working group, no more than ten people should be appointed to the RMT.

As the redesign project unfolds and more clusters are involved, new RMTs are established. RMTs that successfully complete their redesign projects provide training to new RMTs and serve as process consultants to them.

The SC drafts marching orders for the RMT. These marching orders are called a charter. A charter establishes the rules under which the RMT must function. Boundaries are set. Guidelines are outlined. Power is delegated. Action is authorized. Here is a fictitious example of a charter that can be used as a model.

Charter for a Redesign Management Team

I. Rationale—Socio-technical systems design is a widely used and effective process for moving an organization toward higher levels of performance. In uncertain times, this process provides an organization with clarity of purpose, depth of perception, and the power of a compelling vision supported by data. Given these desired resultant conditions (clarity, depth, and power), an organization not only survives but thrives.

In today's environment, schools are being pushed to restructure so that children can receive a better education, teachers can feel better about the quality of their workplace, and community members will value the education that is being provided. We, too, are beginning a process to redesign our school system and the Redesign Management Teams (RMTs) play a central role in this process.

II. Purpose of the RMT—RMTs are established to provide tactical leadership for the initiation of our district's redesign process. They are chartered by the superintendent of schools and the Steering Committee (SC) with full support of the School Board.

III. Membership on the RMT—The chairperson of each RMT will be a principal from the cluster of schools being redesigned. One member of the SC will serve on the RMT to establish and maintain a communication link between the RMT and the SC. Five teachers from the targeted cluster who have the competence and willingness to serve on the RMT will be asked to serve. Two teachers selected from other parts of the school district will also be appointed. Finally, the consultant serves as a non-voting member of the team and will facilitate team meetings as well as provide training to team members.

IV. **Responsibilities of the RMT—**
   A. Plan and conduct organizational assessments for their cluster, including:
      1. An assessment of the cluster's environment (as described earlier in this chapter)
      2. A review of the school district's new mission and vision statements (those that were developed earlier in the process by the SC)
      3. An assessment of the cluster's technical system
      4. An assessment of the cluster's social system
      5. An assessment of the cluster's relationship with its environment (using data from the Open Systems Planning process conducted earlier)

   B. Design specific proposals to move the cluster toward higher levels of organizational performance. These proposals meet the following criteria:
      1. They are linked directly and clearly to the school district's mission and vision.
      2. They are derived from the results of the organizational assessments.
      3. They include action plans with an estimate of human, technical, and financial costs of implementation.
      4. They are prioritized and sequenced in the order in which they should be implemented.
      5. They include suggestions for changing broader, district-level policies and organizational structures that might stand in the way of successful implementation.

   C. Report regularly to the SC:
      1. The SC member on the RMT will report to the SC at its regularly scheduled meetings.
      2. The chair of the RMT will present oral and written progress reports to the SC as needed.
      3. The RMT will submit a final report of its work to the SC. The report includes a full set of redesign proposals, a master implementation plan, and pro-

cedures for evaluating the process and outcomes of the redesign effort.

V. Human, Technical, and Financial Resources—To function effectively, the RMT needs the following resources:
   A. Release time during the day
   B. Staff support to prepare charts, graphs, and reports
   C. Computer hardware and software
   D. Money to copy and bind the final report

VI. Proposed Time Frame for the RMT's Work—
   A. The RMT will begin training in September.
   B. Organizational assessments will begin in October and conclude in November.
   C. First drafts of redesign proposals will be submitted to the SC in December.
   D. Final report is due in February.
   E. Implementation of the redesign proposals begins in March.

Train the RMT

The RMT cannot be expected to function without training in the core principles of socio-technical systems design. This training should be designed and delivered by the consultant. Training topics include:

- Principles of socio-technical systems design
- Meeting management skills
- Managing conflict
- Doing organizational assessments
- Effective interpersonal skills during times of change

Other training topics evolve as members of the RMT work together.

Defining the Relationships Among the Three Parties

To manage the redesign process effectively, the relationships among the three primary parties need to be defined carefully. Although the RMT's charter describes its responsibilities and establishes a reporting relationship between the RMT and the SC, it does not go far enough in defining proper working relationships between and among the three parties. Here are some criteria that can be used to develop these relationships:

- The SC makes all decisions about which redesign proposals to accept and which to reject.

- The school district's mission and vision statements must guide the SC and RMT's deliberative processes. These statements contain decision-making criteria for the SC and design criteria for the RMT.

- The RMT is an advisory group to the SC. Even though they are working on redesigning their cluster of schools, that redesign must fit with the grand vision of the school district. It is the responsibility of the SC to keep this grand vision in front of people's eyes, in their ears, and in their hearts so that all redesign decisions fit clearly with that vision.

- The consultant is a socio-technical systems design expert who provides guidance on how to carry out the redesign process. He or she also designs and delivers training to support the process. He or she does not have a vote on either the SC or the RMT. It is the responsibility of the SC and the RMT—not the consultant— to administer and lead the redesign effort.

- Although the consultant does not have a vote in the redesign process and does not manage or lead the process, it is imperative that he or she be kept informed about the process and outcomes of the redesign effort. This level of communication assures that the consultant remains a vital link in the change management structure.

CONCLUSION

This concludes Phase I: Preparing. As discussed, preparing for a redesign effort is a comprehensive phase that focuses on activities that are absolutely critical for laying the foundation for an effective redesign project. Without a solid foundation, your project will probably fail and your resources will be squandered. The dire consequences of leading your district into a redesign project that called into question every aspect of the district's operation, disrupted the status quo, affected the learning of your community's children, and ultimately failed could produce severe negative political consequences for you and your supporters.

The next chapter walks you through Phase II: Redesigning for High Performance. The redesigning phase begins with an in-depth assessment of the targeted cluster's technical and social systems. These assessments are described in detail in Chapters 5 and 6. Chapter 7 presents ideas and tips on how the RMT can develop and implement high-quality redesign proposals. Chapter 8 discusses techniques for conducting formative and summative evaluations of the process and outcomes of your redesign project. In Chapter 9, suggestions are provided to make redesign improvements in the target cluster permanent, diffuse those improvements to other clusters in the district, and initiate Phase IV of the redesign model (i.e., the continuous improvement of schooling).

REFERENCES

1. Patterson, J.L. (1993). *Leadership for tomorrow's schools.* Alexandria, Va.: Association for Supervision and Curriculum Development.
2. For example, Franklin, J.L. (1976). "Characteristics of successful and unsuccessful organization development," *Journal of Applied Behavioral Science.* 12, 4, pp. 471–492; Myerseth, O. (1977). "Intrafirm diffusion of organizational innovations: An exploratory study." Doctoral thesis, Graduate School of Business Administration, Harvard University.
3. Beer, M. (1980). *Organization change and development: A systems view.* Santa Monica, Calif.: Goodyear Publishing Company, pp. 227–230.
4. Pasmore, W. (1988). *Designing effective organizations: A sociotechnical systems approach.* New York: John Wiley & Sons.
5. Lewin, K. (1951). *Field theory in social science.* New York: Harper and Row.
6. Laborde, G.Z. (1984). *Influencing with integrity.* Palo Alto, Calif.: Syntony Publishers.
7. Walton, R.E. (1985). "From control to commitment in the workplace," *Harvard Business Review.* March–April, pp. 77–84.
8. Pasmore, W., G. Frank, and R. Rehm (1992). *Preparing people to participate in organizational change: Developing citizenship for the active organization.* Cleveland, Ohio: Pasmore & Associates.
9. Argyris, C. (1970). *Intervention theory and practice: A behavioral science view.* Reading, Mass.: Addison-Wesley.
10. Miles, R.E. (1972) in M. Beer (1980). *Organization change and development: A systems view.* Santa Monica, Calif.: Goodyear Publishing Company, p. 79.
11. Maslow, A.H. (1954). *Motivation and personality.* New York: Harper and Row.

12. Raywid, M.A. (October 1990). "The evolving effort to improve schools: Pseudo-reform, incremental reform, and restructuring," *Phi Delta Kappan.* 72, 2, pp. 139–143.
13. Jayaram, G.K. (1976). "Open systems planning," in W.G. Bennis, K. D. Benne, R. Chin, and D. Corey (1976). *The planning of change,* 3rd edition. New York: Holt, Rinehart, and Winston, pp. 275–283.
14. For example, Piercy, N. and W. Giles (1989). "Making SWOT analysis work," *Marketing Intelligence and Planning.* 7, 5, 6, pp. 5–7.
15. Howard, E.R. and J.W. Keefe (1991). *The CASE-IMS school improvement process.* Reston, Va.: National Association of Secondary School Principals, p. 1.
16. Miller, S.K. (1993). *School climate.* Reston, Va.: National Association of Secondary School Principals.
17. Hickman, C.R. and M.A. Silva (1984). *Creating excellence: Managing corporate culture, strategy, and change in the new age.* New York: New American Library, p. 151.
18. Main, J. (September 28, 1987), "Wanted: Leaders who can make a difference," *Fortune.* p. 92.
19. Belasco, J.A. (1990). *Teaching the elephant to dance: Empowering change in your organization.* New York: Crown Publishers, p. 99.
20. Belasco, J.A. (1990). *Teaching the elephant to dance: Empowering change in your organization.* New York: Crown Publishers.

CHAPTER 5

PHASE II: REDESIGNING FOR HIGH PERFORMANCE/ DIAGNOSING THE TECHNICAL SYSTEM

STEP 2.1A: DIAGNOSE THE WORK SYSTEM

In this chapter, you will learn how to diagnosis the technical (or work) system of the target cluster. The work system is "the total collection of processes, procedures, instructions, techniques, tools, equipment, machines, and physical space that are used in transforming the organization's inputs into the desired outputs. 'X' is transformed into 'Y' by doing 'Z.'"[1] In most of today's knowledge organizations, there are two types of interrelated work processes in the work system: linear and non-linear. In knowledge organizations, the non-linear work system is the primary (or core) process, whereas the linear work system plays a supportive role. Schooling is a combination of linear (the K–12 instructional program) and non-linear (classroom teaching) work processes.

Linear work is composed of activities that are repetitive and done step by step (such as an assembly line). The essential characteristic of linear work is that each step can be specified in advance (i.e., Step A is composed of…and always precedes Step B, which is composed of…).

Knowledge work is non-routine and non-linear. Non-linear work is comprised of activities that can be done in parallel, separated from each other, or done in a variety of sequences. In non-linear work processes, future work cannot be decided until some of the results of the current work activities are completed. Non-linear knowledge work in schools is the pattern of thinking and behavior called classroom teaching.

To improve linear work, you look for errors that occur early in the sequence of activities that cause most of the problems down the line. To improve non-linear knowledge work, you look for ways to improve the quality, quantity, and timing of information that is exchanged among knowledge workers. High-quality information in sufficient quantity needs to be exchanged early in the work system to prevent critical errors.

One of the primary goals of any work system is to identify and correct variances (errors or disturbances in the work process) so that the organization can achieve its performance goals successfully. According to socio-technical systems design theory, the way to identify and correct variances is to conduct a comprehensive analysis of the work processes.

A comprehensive analysis of the work system helps organizational members identify the boundaries of work units (e.g., departments, teams, or grade levels) within the work process from the point where inputs (human, financial, and technological resources) enter the system, are converted by passing through a work process, and are delivered as outputs (e.g., quality learning for all students) to the customer. Second, this kind of analysis identifies key variances (errors) in the work process, assesses their impact, and evaluates the current ways in which teachers, administrators, and supervisors control the errors. Third, this analysis diagnoses the impact of other related organizational variables on the work system, especially the impact of suppliers, customers, and support systems (e.g., administrative and supervisory processes). Fourth, a comprehensive analysis clarifies the demands that are made on the social system to operate, coordinate, and maintain the entire work system. Finally this analysis identifies opportunities to improve control of the work system.

Diagnosing the Linear Work System in Schools

Schools are knowledge organizations, and the work of schools is knowledge work. Knowledge work is work of the mind. It is "…characterized primarily by the creative manipulation of symbols by the mind, whereas so-called routine work is characterized primarily by the creative manipulation of objects by the body" (p. 3).[2]

In schools, knowledge work is classroom teaching supported by a linear work process (the instructional program, K–12). Additionally, other supportive work processes have an effect on the instructional program and classroom teaching (e.g., the work of administrators, supervisors, education specialists, and secretaries).

The process for diagnosing the linear instructional program of the target school is essentially an audit of the instructional program. This audit is conducted by the Redesign Management Team (RMT) with assistance from the consultant. The amount of time needed to conduct the diagnosis varies depending on the availability of RMT members, the complexity of the instructional program within the target cluster, and the accessibility of diagnostic data.

The diagnosis of the linear instructional program has two desired outcomes:

- Key players in the target cluster develop an in-depth knowledge of their whole system, including information about what *goes on* and what *goes wrong* in the instructional program.

- Key players reach agreement on requirements for redesigning the target cluster that prevent, eliminate, or control variances in the linear instructional program.

The major tasks to be completed when diagnosing the linear instructional program of the target cluster are shown in Worksheet 5.1. Each task listed in the worksheet is described in detail below.

1. Identify major inputs (e.g., human, financial, and technological resources; the quality and quantity of information and knowledge) and outputs (the goals and outcomes of the instructional program). To perform this task, the RMT collects diagnostic data to answer questions about the target cluster. Because the target cluster consists of interconnected schools, the instructional program is examined backwards, starting from the high school and ending with the elementary schools. The RMT collects data to answer the following questions:

- What are the distinguishing characteristics of our instructional program?

- What are the current inputs to our instructional program? (Inputs are the human, financial, and technical resources that come into

1. Identify major inputs (e.g., human, financial, and technological resources; quality and quantity of information and knowledge) and outputs (the goals and outcomes of the instructional program).
2. Describe major components of the instructional program (e.g., policies, procedures, curriculum).
3. Describe what happens during each step in the linear instructional program.
4. Identify variances (i.e., errors) found in the functioning of the linear instructional program.
5. Identify *key* variances in the linear instructional program and describe how they are currently managed.
6. Design ways to prevent or control key variances.
7. Summarize what was learned from the analysis of the linear instructional program.
8. Design specifications and generate ideas for redesigning the linear instructional program to move it toward higher levels of performance.

WORKSHEET 5.1   **Major Tasks for Auditing a Linear Instructional Program**

the cluster so that the instructional program can function.) Then the following questions are answered:

a. What are the inputs?
b. What are our specifications (criteria) for the quantity and quality of the inputs?
c. Where do the inputs come from (i.e., who supplies them)?
d. Where in the instructional program do key players gain ownership of the inputs?
e. How stable is the flow of the inputs (high, medium, or low)?
f. What problems exist with the inputs (quantity/quality specifications, ownership issues, stability, or impact on the instructional program)?
g. What ideas do we have for improvements?

• What are the current outputs, goals, and feedback for our instructional program? (Outputs are the "fruit of the labor"—the results produced through the current functioning of the instructional program.) The RMT finds answers to the following questions about outputs, goals, and feedback:

a. What are the desired outputs (goals and outcomes)?
b. What are the actual outputs?

 c. How were outputs measured?

 d. Who measured the outputs?

 e. When were the outputs measured?

 f. Who receives feedback on the measurement of the outputs?

 g. When is the feedback received?

 h. How is the feedback received?

 i. How is the feedback used?

 j. What problems exist with outputs and feedback (e.g., inappropriate goals, inferior results, inadequate measures, incomplete feedback loop, non-use of feedback)?

 k. What ideas do we have for improvement?

An alternative set of diagnostic questions is offered by Stephens and Herman.[3] They describe a comprehensive model for conducting an instructional audit. Their model collects diagnostic data on the following variables:

- Board of education policies
- Job descriptions
- Budget allocations
- Negotiated contracts
- Communications
- Instruction
- Elections
- Students
- Employees
- Administration

Although these variables are a mix of work and social system factors (e.g., job descriptions and communications are part of the social system, whereas instruction is part of the work system), their model could be easily adapted for diagnosing the linear work system of the target cluster.

After collecting the data, RMT members discuss the results. They use large pieces of flip-chart paper and colored markers. At the top of a sheet of flip-chart paper, they write "Our Instructional Program." Then, they draw or write the distinguishing characteristics of the instructional program and list the current inputs and outputs. Using these data as points of discussion, the RMT discusses the following questions in as many meetings as necessary to reach consensus:

- Are the distinguishing features of our instructional program acceptable to us?

- What criteria (or specifications) should we use to improve our major inputs?

- What criteria (or specifications) should we use to measure the quality of our major outputs? Goal attainment? Adequacy of feedback?

- What are the most important things we learned from this assessment of the linear instructional program? (The answers to this question are used to develop specific proposals for redesigning the linear instructional program.)

- What opportunities or creative ideas present themselves for redesigning the instructional program? (The answers to this question are used to develop specific proposals for redesigning the linear instructional program.)

2. Describe major components of the instructional program. Next, the RMT charts the work flow in the instructional program. To do this analysis, the RMT identifies the major steps that children must currently follow to move through the instructional program within the target cluster. Because the target cluster is a set of interconnected schools, there are multiple instructional program streams leading into the school that is farthest downstream—the high school. An example of a cluster of schools and their multiple instructional program streams is shown in Figure 5.1. The work flow of the instructional program that flows through each of the feeder streams into the high school is analyzed.

In the example in Figure 5.1, the high school is the farthest downstream. Because it is downstream of several other schools that feed into it, all of those feeder schools must also be redesigned along with the high school. This creates a cluster of interconnected schools. In this cluster, there are four instructional program streams leading into the high school (e.g., Stream A is composed of Elementary[1], Middle[1], and High School[1]).

Listing the major steps in the work flow as grades that children must complete is not sufficient for this analysis (e.g., it is not helpful to record Step 1: Kindergarten; Step 2: first grade; and so forth. Instead, the RMT does a finer analysis to identify the key steps in the instructional process (for example, Step 1: Children are identified for placement in kindergarten; Step 2: Upon entering kindergarten, the ability levels of the children are diagnosed; and so forth).

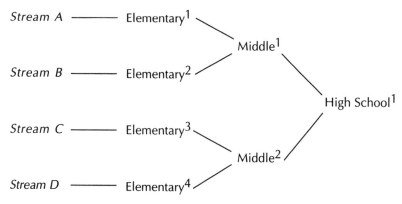

FIGURE 5.1 Multiple Program Streams Flowing into One Target High School

After charting the major steps in the linear instructional program of the cluster, the RMT members discuss the most important things they learned from their assessment and identify opportunities or creative ideas for redesigning the instructional program.

3. Describe what happens during each step in the linear instructional program. After identifying the major steps in the instructional program as described above, the RMT describes each step in detail. This description answers the following questions:

- What is the step?
- What number is the step in the full sequence of steps (i.e., Step 1, Step 2, Step 3, and so forth)?
- What is the goal of this step?
- What must the preceding step do, provide, or accomplish before this step can begin?
- What actually happens to or for the learning process in this step?
- What data do we need to know if this step is being performed at a high level of performance?
- What are the characteristics of the process that is used during this step?
- What equipment or technology is used in this step?
- How do we know when this step has accomplished its purpose?
- What are the major things we learned from this description?

- What opportunities or creative ideas presented themselves for improving performance in this step?

If the target cluster is a network of interrelated schools, the RMT identifies which schools in the network perform which steps in the linear instructional program. It is important to have a chart for each program stream (as illustrated in Figure 5.1) that "flows" into the high school. Charting the specific characteristics of the program streams is accomplished using a chart similar to Worksheet 5.2.

4. Identify variances (i.e., errors) found in the functioning of the instructional program. The RMT, at this point, has collected and analyzed a lot of data about the instructional program of the target cluster. It has also identified and described the major steps in the instructional program. Now, it begins hunting for errors (or potential errors) in the instructional program. This is done by using a worksheet similar to

(Fill-out one chart for each program stream (e.g., see Figure 5.1)		
Names of Schools Flowing into the High School	**What Are the Outcomes of the Instructional Program in Each School?**	**How Does the Work Performed by Each School Impact the High School?**
First School (the one farthest "upstream" of the target school):	What outcomes is this school responsible for?	
Second School:	What outcomes is this school responsible for?	
Third School:	What outcomes is this school responsible for?	
Fourth School:	What outcomes is this school responsible for?	
Fifth School:	What outcomes is this school responsible for?	

WORKSHEET 5.2   Identifying the Characteristics of the Program Streams Flowing into the High School

Worksheet 5.3. Use one worksheet for each step in the instructional program.

5. Identify key variances in the instructional program and describe how they are currently managed. Using the results posted on Worksheet 5.3, the RMT now charts the key variances. The charting can be done on large sheets of flip-chart paper. A sample of a variance matrix is shown in Worksheet 5.4. This matrix asks the RMT to chart the variance, where it occurs (i.e., which unit), why it occurs (i.e., probable causes), what its consequences are, and who currently controls it. Key variances can be marked by placing an asterisk (*) next to them.

Describe the step:	**Grade Level:**
Ideally, what should be happening during this step:	

Errors or potential errors occurring at this step:

1.

2.

3.

4.

5.

6.

7.

8.

9.

10.

Put an * next to those variances that have a *critical* impact on the functioning of the instructional program. These variances are called *key variances*.

** Remember, a work step is not synonymous with grade level. This distinction was made earlier in the chapter.

WORKSHEET 5.3 Errors Occurring in Each Step of the Instructional Program**

Error	Where It Occurs	Why It Occurs	Consequences	Who Should Control It?
Error #1:				
Error #2:				
Error #3:				
Error #4:				

WORKSHEET 5.4 Error Analysis Matrix

The variance chart is a useful visual display for identifying where in the instructional program key errors occur and for showing how those variances affect other steps in the instructional program. Use the following procedure to fill out the variance analysis worksheet shown in Worksheet 5.4:

- In the first column, list all of the errors (or potential errors) you have identified (make as many additional tables as you think you might need).
- In the second column, identify exactly where the error occurs.
- In the third column, list reasons why you think the error occurs.
- In the fourth column, identify or predict the impact of each error on downstream steps in the instructional program.
- Finally, in the fifth column, identify who ought to be controlling the error.

6. Design ways to prevent or control key variances (errors). After charting the errors on Worksheet 5.4 and marking those that are critical,

---

Key error:

Location: Where and when does the error occur?

Causes:
- Internal (inside the school)
- External (outside the school)

Impact: What are the consequences of this error?

Current error-control procedures:
- Where are the effects of the error?
- What corrective measures are currently taken to control the cause(s)?
- What current skills, level of responsibility, and resources are used to control the error? What is the current level of adequacy of these variables?
- Who currently has the authority to control this error?
- What problems do we have with the current control system?

Ideas for preventing the error and improving the error-control procedures:
- Technical improvements
- Changes in roles or jobs
- Changes in information sources and flow
- New skills required
- Changes in level of authority
- Changes in the overall organization

WORKSHEET 5.5   Key Error Control Chart

the RMT discusses how to prevent or control the critical (key) errors. Control measures are identified using a worksheet similar to Worksheet 5.5.

7. Summarize what was learned from the analysis. The RMT discusses and summarizes what it learned from the analysis of the instructional program. Major learning is used to develop redesign proposals later in the redesign process. Use Worksheet 5.6 to summarize the learning.

8. Design specifications and generate ideas for redesigning the instructional program for high performance. With the results of the above analyses still fresh in the minds of RMT members, they develop specifications for a new instructional program. These specifications become design criteria. The design criteria should not overspecify the desired characteristics of the new instructional program. Providing minimal

The most important things we learned about what really happens in our instructional program:	
The most important things we learned about what goes wrong in our instructional program:	
Given what we have learned, what opportunities or creative ideas do we have for correcting or minimizing the errors?	

WORKSHEET 5.6 **Summary of Major Learning from Assessing the Instructional Program**

specifications gives flexibility to the people who must implement the redesign proposal. Worksheet 5.7 is used to plan and organize the desired design specifications.

Remember, depending on the level of schooling being diagnosed (i.e., high school, middle or junior high school, or elementary school), the length and complexity of the instructional program and the number of program streams in the target cluster varies. For example, the instructional program stream for a high school has thirteen levels (kindergarten through 12th grade), but only four of those levels are within the high school. The remaining nine levels flow into the high school through several middle and elementary schools. For a K–5th grade elementary cluster, however, the instructional program is only six levels long and there are no other program streams feeding into it (again, refer back to Figure 5.1, which illustrates the concept of feeder streams). When examining the instructional program of a target cluster, it is critical to examine all the steps and grade levels within that cluster as well as *all* of the steps and levels of work flowing into the school farthest downstream in that cluster. This requirement helps you to view the systemic relationships within the district.

After collecting the diagnostic data, the RMT and consultant conduct a series of meetings to analyze and interpret the data. They also develop specifications for redesigning the instructional program for high performance. If there is a need for additional data, plans are made to collect them.

Variables Affecting the Instructional Program	Specifications for "Future" Instructional Program
What do our internal and external customers expect of our instructional program?	
Describe the quality, quantity, and timing of resources needed to operate a high-performing instructional program.	
Describe the quality, quantity, and timing of desired outputs of our instructional program.	
What do we need from people or organizations that act as suppliers to our instructional program?	
How will we know when we have a high-performing instructional program?	
How will we control for the actual or potential errors in our instructional program?	

WORKSHEET 5.7   Designing Specifications for Our New Instructional Program

These discussion meetings are scheduled to allow adequate time for examining data. The meetings are also designed as team-building opportunities for the RMT. Excellent communication skills are taught and practiced. Ways of managing conflict or differing opinions, perspectives, and values are developed. Decision making is consensual. (See Chapter 11 for information about effective interpersonal and group dynamics for running effective meetings.)

Diagnosing Non-Linear Knowledge Work in Schools[4]

Knowledge work is non-routine and non-linear. Non-linear work is a set of tasks where the sequence of work is optional or where several tasks occur in a parallel manner. The way to improve knowledge work is to assure an early, whole-system exchange of quality information among teachers, administrators, and supervisors in order to avoid critical errors and failures later on and to assure an ongoing exchange of information among the knowledge workers responsible for critical work activities.

In schools, the core knowledge work process is non-routine and non-linear. This process is classroom teaching. Thus, the way to improve classroom teaching is to assure that teachers and others have the opportunity to exchange high-quality information with each other and with administrators and supervisors on an ongoing basis and to assure that everyone has access to this information on a timely basis. By focusing on improving the quality, quantity, and timing of information exchanges, the focus on improvement shifts from the individual behavior of classroom teachers to an examination and improvement of the information base and information exchange process used by teachers, administrators, and supervisors (additional thoughts about this paradigm shift are provided in Chapter 12).

There are two desired outcomes of a diagnosis of knowledge work in schools:

- The RMT assesses the quality, quantity, and timing of the information exchange process that informs classroom teaching. This is done by developing an inventory of key information topics that teachers, administrators, and supervisors need to deliberate, identifying who needs to participate in these deliberations, describing where and how these deliberations take place, identifying the information participants need to bring to and take from the deliberations, and evaluating the adequacy of devices or procedures used to support classroom teaching.

- The RMT designs a set of specifications that are minimally defined to correct or avoid the errors caused by faulty or inadequate information exchanges (e.g., a lack of or badly timed information, inadequate involvement or commitment of the right participants, and inappropriate forums for deliberations). Some of the important concepts for diagnosis of non-linear knowledge work are explained below.

To analyze non-linear knowledge work, the RMT uses a technique different from that used for analyzing the linear instructional program. Because the work performed in classrooms by teachers is non-routine and non-linear knowledge work, the RMT cannot chart variances on a traditional matrix analysis table. Instead, it examines the information exchange process, identifies gaps and errors in the exchanges, and then redesigns the exchange process to eliminate or control the errors. The RMT also examines and corrects work procedures and technological devices that support classroom teaching (e.g., grade reporting procedures and computer networks). If the supportive work procedures are routine and linear (e.g., grading procedures, lesson planning procedures), then the RMT can use traditional analysis techniques to identify and chart errors in these supportive procedures.

The major tasks for diagnosing knowledge work are:

1. Identify by topic the critical information that teachers, administrators, and supervisors need to exchange so that teaching becomes more effective. Rank order the topics according to how critical they are to effective classroom teaching—from most important to least important. The RMT uses a worksheet similar to Worksheet 5.8 for this task.

2. Describe the characteristics of the *current* information exchange process (i.e., for each information topic, identify its forum, its participants, and the information that each participant is expected to bring to and take from the exchange). The RMT uses Worksheet 5.9 to chart this information.

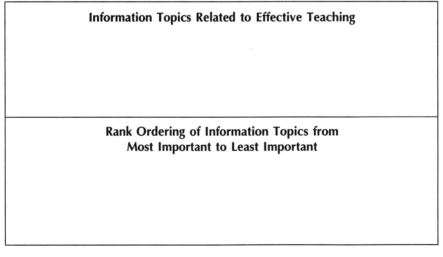

Information Topics Related to Effective Teaching

**Rank Ordering of Information Topics from
Most Important to Least Important**

WORKSHEET 5.8 Identify and Rank the Information Topics that Teachers, Administrators, and Supervisors Need to Deliberate to Increase the Effectiveness of Classroom Teaching

Critical Information Topics	Where Is Information Exchanged?	Who Participates in the Information Exchange Process?	What Information Do Participants Bring to the Exchanges?	What Information Do Participants Take from the Exchanges?
• What are they? • What topics are missing? • Is there any redundancy?	• Where are topics deliberated? • How are forums structured?	• Who participates? • Who makes decisions? How? • Is there any conflict among participants' values? What kind of conflict? How is conflict handled?	• What information are participants expected to bring to the exchange process? • What is missing or redundant?	• What information are participants expected to take from the exchange process? • What is missing or redundant?

WORKSHEET 5.9   Analysis of the Information Exchange Process

Description of the Information Exchange Process (from Worksheet 5.9)	Actual and Potential Problems/Gaps/Errors	Who Is Responsible for Controlling These Errors?

WORKSHEET 5.10   Identification of Errors in the Information Exchange Process

3. Describe errors in the information exchange process. Worksheet 5.10 is designed for this task.

4. Identify work procedures and technological devices that *currently* support classroom teaching. Worksheet 5.11 is useful for this task.

5. Summarize critical learning from the analyses. Worksheet 5.12 is designed for this task.

6. Design critical specifications to redesign the information exchange process for high performance. Worksheet 5.13 is useful for this task.

Supporting Work Procedures/Devices	Actual or Potential Problems/Gaps/Errors	Who Is Responsible for Controlling These Errors?

WORKSHEET 5.11   Identification of Work Procedures and Devices that Support Classroom Teaching

The most important things we learned about what really happens in our information exchange process.	
The most important things we learned about what goes wrong in our information exchange process.	
Given what we have learned, what opportunities or creative ideas do we have for correcting or minimizing the errors?	

WORKSHEET 5.12   Summary of Major Learning from the Diagnoses

Variables Affecting the Information Exchange Process	Specifications for "Future" Information Exchange Process
What are our internal and external customers' quality expectations for classroom teaching?	
How should our information exchange process function in support of effective classroom teaching?	
Describe the quality, quantity, and timing of information that we need to feed into our information exchange process so we can increase the effectiveness of classroom teaching.	
How will we know when we have a high-performing information exchange process that supports effective classroom teaching?	
How will we control for errors in our information exchange process?	

WORKSHEET 5.13   Designing Specifications to Improve the Information Exchange Process

CONCLUSION

This chapter described a process for diagnosing the linear instructional program and non-linear knowledge work process of the target cluster. This diagnosis is critical to the success of your redesign project because the results are used to develop critical specifications for proposals to redesign the target cluster.

Although diagnosing the work system of a target cluster is important, it is not the only diagnosis that occurs. In the next chapter, you will learn how to diagnose the social system of the target cluster. This diagnosis is equally important because we know from the literature on socio-technical systems design that the characteristics and elements of the social system have a significant impact on the functioning of the work system. In fact, one of the goals of the redesign project is to maximize both the work and social systems in relation to each other instead of maximizing one at the expense of the other.

REFERENCES

1. Lytle, W.O. (1991). *Socio-technical systems analysis and design guide for linear work.* Plainfield, N.J.: Block-Petrella-Weisbord, Inc.
2. Christensen, T. in Purser, R. (1991). "Redesigning knowledge work." *The FULCRUM Update: Newsletter of the Fulcrum Network for Human Systems Development.* Rohnert Park, Calif.: The Fulcrum Network, Department of Management, Sonoma State University.
3. Stephens, G.M. and J.J. Herman (May 1985). "Using the instructional audit for policy and program improvement," *Educational Leadership.* 42, pp. 70–75.
4. This section is significantly influenced by the writings of Calvin Pava. In particular, Pava, C.H.P. (1983). *Managing new office technology: An organizational strategy.* New York: The New Press.

CHAPTER 6

PHASE II: REDESIGNING FOR HIGH PERFORMANCE/ DIAGNOSING THE SOCIAL SYSTEM

STEP 2.1B: DIAGNOSE THE SOCIAL SYSTEM

Analysis Goals

The Redesign Management Team (RMT) analyzes the target cluster's social system by examining the interactions teachers, administrators, and supervisors have with the linear and non-linear work systems and with each other. The analysis also examines the quality of work life and identifies the essential skills workers need to function within the instructional program and within the classroom. The ultimate goal for improving the social system is to assure that teachers, administrators, and supervisors have *whole jobs*, that there is as high a *quality of work life* as possible for everyone, and that workers experience *effective working relationships* as they strive to perform their essential work activities together. These three principles are the basis of an error-free instructional program and classroom teaching and are essential to customer satisfaction.

There are two desired outcomes as the result of this analysis:

- The RMT describes the current quality of work life in the target cluster and the degree of satisfaction experienced by the teachers, administrators, and supervisors; analyzes how effectively workers interact individually and in groups; and assesses the degree to which various jobs satisfy basic psychological criteria that affect motivation.

- The RMT develops minimum critical specifications for new roles, relationships, ways of working together, and required job skills. These specifications empower people to take new responsibility in the redesigned target cluster for performing effectively within the instructional program and in classrooms and for managing errors in both work systems.

Analysis Tasks

The major tasks to be completed during this phase of the redesign project are shown in Worksheet 6.1.

Before providing specific guidance on how to accomplish each of the above steps, it is important to define several of the key terms used in this chapter:

1. **Motivators**—Those elements of work that induce teachers to learn and that compel them to achieve personal and organizational goals. Important motivators are autonomy, task variety, feedback, whole jobs, respect, and an opportunity to grow.

2. **Quality of work life**—The degree to which existing motivators and satisfiers in the organization meet teachers' needs.

3. **Satisfiers**—Elements of the workplace that respond to teachers' basic psychological needs (e.g., the needs for security, health, safety, equity and fairness, and due process).

4. **Skill**—A teacher's ability to use what he or she has learned to perform tasks essential to the functioning of an error-free knowledge work process.

1. Identify skills teachers, administrators, and supervisors need to work effectively in the instructional program and in classrooms and the skills needed to control errors in both work processes.

2. Identify skills needed to have effective working relationships.

3. Identify who needs to participate in exchanges of information about critical topics related to effective classroom teaching.
   a. What values do these participants have toward the critical topics?
   b. Which of these values are (or could be) in conflict?
   c. What trade-offs will participants need to make if their values are in conflict?
   d. Who should be participating in the information exchange process but is not?

4. Do a GAIL analysis.

5. Determine the degree to which various roles meet psychological criteria that contribute to motivation (*motivators*).

6. Determine the degree to which various roles offer job satisfaction (*satisfiers*) and quality working conditions.

7. Summarize important learning from the analyses.

8. Develop minimum specifications for redesigning the social system.

WORKSHEET 6.1   Major Tasks for Diagnosing the Social System

5. **Working conditions**—The culture, safety, and physical appearance of the workplace and the degree of physical and emotional effort required by the job (e.g., the number of hours of work, take-home work, number of breaks, planning time).

Tasks for Diagnosing the Social System

1. Identify the skills that teachers, administrators, and supervisors need in order to function effectively in the instructional program and in classrooms and the skills needed to control errors in both work processes. Teachers need to possess certain skills to perform effectively within the instructional program and for working in classrooms. The skills needed to perform in the instructional program are different from those needed for classroom teaching. For example, to function effectively in the instructional program, teachers need curriculum analysis

School Level (elementary, middle, or high):	Grade Level:
What skills do teachers, administrators, and supervisors need to meet the expectations of internal and external customers?	
What skills are needed by teachers, administrators, and supervisors to operate the instructional program at a high level of performance?	
What skills do teachers, administrators, and supervisors need to control key errors in the instructional program?	
What skills do teachers, administrators, and supervisors need for working with individuals, with groups, and within groups?	
What are the most important things we learned from the above analyses?	
What opportunities or ideas do we see to redesign the social system?	

WORKSHEET 6.2 Skill Requirements for Working in the Instructional Program

skills; however, to function effectively in the classroom, teachers need effective platform skills. The RMT assesses which skills are needed for each of the work processes.[1] Use Worksheets 6.2 and 6.3 to complete this task.

2. Identify the skills needed to have effective working relationships with co-workers, customers, and other stakeholders. The web of work relationships holds the entire school system together. Effective relationships between individuals, within and among groups, and with customers and stakeholders are critical for the effective functioning of the work system. Worksheets 6.2 and 6.3 can also be used to chart the skills needed for these relationships.

Required Skill Areas	Required Skills
What skills do teachers, administrators, and supervisors need to involve the right people in the information exchange process?	
What skills do teachers, administrators, and supervisors need to arrange the right place and time for the exchange of information?	
What skills do teachers, administrators, and supervisors need to facilitate the decision-making and problem-solving processes during the information exchange process?	
What skills do teachers, administrators, and supervisors need to surface and manage conflict during the information exchange process?	
What are the most important things we learned as a result of these analyses?	
What opportunities and ideas do we have for redesigning the social system to support the information exchange process?	

WORKSHEET 6.3 Skill Requirements for Exchanging Information About Effective Classroom Teaching

3. Identify and describe participants who collaborate on key exchanges of information about classroom teaching. Worksheet 6.4 is used for this purpose.

4. Do a GAIL analysis. Another level of analysis described by Cotter[2] relates four sets of organizational variables to vertical and horizontal relationships in an organization These variables are Goal setting, Adaptation, Integration, and Long-term development. The acronym for these variables is GAIL.

Critical Information Topic:				
Who Currently Participates in the Exchange of Information About This Topic?	What Are the Characteristic Values of the Participants Related to This Topic?	Which of Their Values May Be in Conflict?	What Trade-Offs Will They Need to Make to Resolve the Conflict?	Who Else Needs to Be Involved in This Exchange of Information?

WORKSHEET 6.4 Characteristics of Participants in the Information Exchange Process for Effective Classroom Teaching

Goal setting includes, for example, policies and practices for financial budgeting, allocating funds, degree of autonomy, clarity of goals, and coordination among units of the organization. Adaptation focuses on assessing the appropriateness of such current organizational practices as long-term planning, feedback from customers, managerial support for innovation, and measurement procedures. Integration refers to practices and structures such as disseminating information, communicating, coordinating, cooperating, and resolving conflict. Long-term development includes variables such as staffing plans, recruitment, selection criteria, and performance evaluations.

The analysis of the GAIL variables gathers data on who interacts with whom to perform goal setting, adaptation, integration, and long-term development functions. The interactions are evaluated in terms of who is involved, how often the interactions occur, how effective they are, and how people feel while participating in the interactions. This analysis is done using Worksheet 6.5.

5. Determine the degree to which various roles meet psychological criteria that contribute to motivation (called motivators[3]). Another important part of the analysis is the assessment of the degree to which

Roles	Goal Setting	Adaptation	Integration	Long-Term Development
Teachers				
Administrators				
Supervisors				
Level of involvement: 7 = too high, 6 = high, 5 = moderate-high, 4 = moderate, 3 = moderate-low, 2 = low, 1 = too low, 0 = non-existent.				

WORKSHEET 6.5   GAIL Analysis

organizational roles stimulate internal motivation in teachers, administrators, and supervisors. The psychological characteristics of a role that contribute to motivation are called *motivators*. Motivators, in conjunction with *satisfiers*, constitute what we call the *quality of work life* in an organization. Worksheet 6.6 is used to assess the degree to which these

	Criteria					
Roles	Autonomy and Discretion	Learning	Variety	Exchange Help & Respect	Meaningful Contribution	Meaningful Future
Teachers						
Administrators						
Supervisors						
Degree present: 7 = too high, 6 = high, 5 = moderate-high, 4 = moderate, 3 = moderate-low, 2 = low, 1 = too low, 0 = non-existent.						

WORKSHEET 6.6   Analysis of Degree to Which Knowledge Workers' Roles Meet Psychological Job Criteria (i.e., Motivators)

motivators exist. The psychological job criteria (motivators) on Worksheet 6.6 need to be defined.

- **Autonomy and discretion**—Psychologically attractive work provides a good mix of opportunities to be responsible and to exercise self-management in response to clear guidelines for behavior.

- **Opportunity to learn and continue learning on the job**—Psychologically attractive work provides many opportunities to learn new knowledge and skills, especially those that will improve on-the-job performance. However, these learning opportunities must offer reasonable challenges and timely feedback on the effects of one's learning.

- **Optimal variety**—Work that is psychologically attractive permits people to seek a reasonable amount of variety in their work activities. This opportunity helps reduce boredom and fatigue while simultaneously encouraging the development of a satisfying rhythm (i.e., an alternating cycle of variety) in one's activities.

- **Opportunity to exchange help and respect**—Work that is psychologically attractive generates conditions under which colleagues can and do exchange help and respect. Building in this feature requires making mutual help and assistance an intrinsic element of job expectations. It also requires encouraging recognition of individual capability and achievement.

- **Sense of meaningful contribution**—Psychologically attractive work provides workers with a sense that their contributions are important and valued.

- **Prospect of a meaningful future**—Work that is psychologically attractive promises advancement, which fosters personal growth and offers appropriately higher compensation.

6. Determine the degree to which various roles offer job satisfaction.

Describe what it is like to work in the target cluster in regard to factors that contribute to job satisfaction (satisfiers) and quality of work life. Herzberg, Mausner, and Snyderman[4] distinguish between motivators and satisfiers. Job satisfaction, they say, is affected by variables in the context of work. They call these hygienic factors. Motivators, on the other hand, are inherent characteristics of the work roles. Satisfiers that seem to be important to people in organizations are listed in Worksheet 6.7, which can be used to assess the degree to which the satisfiers exist

Role of Person Completing Survey:	
Satisfiers	**Degree to Which Each Is Present in the Work Environment**
Fair and adequate pay	(low) 1 2 3 4 5 (high)
Job security	(low) 1 2 3 4 5 (high)
Fringe benefits	(low) 1 2 3 4 5 (high)
Health	(low) 1 2 3 4 5 (high)
Due process	(low) 1 2 3 4 5 (high)
Other	(low) 1 2 3 4 5 (high)
Working Conditions	**Degree to Which Each Is Present in the Work Environment**
Safety	(low) 1 2 3 4 5 (high)
Climate	(low) 1 2 3 4 5 (high)
Appearance	(low) 1 2 3 4 5 (high)
Other	(low) 1 2 3 4 5 (high)

WORKSHEET 6.7   Identifying Satisfiers in the Work Environment and Assessing Quality of Working Conditions

in the work environment. One way to collect data on the degree to which these variables exist is to conduct a survey of teachers, administrators, and supervisors in the target cluster.

7. Summarize important learning from the analyses. After completing the analyses of the social system, the RMT summarizes important learning using a chart similar to Worksheet 6.8.

8. Develop minimum specifications for redesigning the social system. After summarizing and discussing the major learning from the analysis of the social system, the RMT develops minimum specifications for redesigning the social system. Worksheet 6.9 can be used for this task. Later in the redesign process, this information is used to develop specific proposals for redesigning the social system of the target cluster.

1. What were the most important things we learned about skills needed to work in the instructional program and in classrooms?
2. What were the most important things we learned about our information exchange process?
3. What were the most important things we learned from the GAIL analysis?
4. What were the most important things we learned from our assessment of work "motivators"?
5. What were the most important things we learned from our assessment of job satisfiers and quality of working conditions?
6. What opportunities and ideas do we have for redesigning the social system to better support the instructional program and classroom teaching, to increase motivation and job satisfaction, and to improve the quality of work life?

WORKSHEET 6.8   Summary of Important Learning from the Social System Analysis

1. What skills are needed to work effectively in the instructional program and in classrooms? (Use data from Worksheets 6.2 and 6.3.)
2. Which characteristics of the information exchange process do we need to achieve high-performance classroom teaching?
3. What is the ideal level of involvement in each element of the GAIL grid?
4. Which motivators should be present in our social system? How do we build them into the social system? To what degree should they be present for each role?
5. Which satisfiers should be present in our social system? How do we build them into the social system? To what degree should they be present?
6. Which working conditions should be present in our social system? How do we build them into the social system? To what degree should they be present?

WORKSHEET 6.9   Minimum Specifications for Redesigning the Social System

CONCLUSION

You have learned how to analyze the social system of a target cluster. This analysis, in conjunction with the environmental analysis conducted by the Steering Committee at the beginning of the redesign project and the analysis of the technical system, is used to develop specific proposals to redesign the target cluster.

The next chapter explains how to use the results of the three analyses (environmental analysis completed in Phase I by the Steering Committee and the analyses of the technical and social systems completed by the RMT) to develop and implement redesign proposals. Chapter 8 presents information on evaluating the process and outcomes of your redesign effort. Chapter 9 discusses making improvements permanent in the target school(s), diffusing the changes to other schools in your district, and moving the process to Phase IV, the continuous improvement of schooling.

REFERENCES

1. The field of performance technology offers practical guidance on how to identify critical work-related skills. For example, see Gordon, J. (1992). "Performance technology: Blueprint for the learning organization," *Training.* pp. 27–36.
2. Cotter, J.J. (1983). "Designing organizations that work: An open sociotechnical systems perspective." Paper distributed at a workshop on sociotechnical systems design. North Hollywood, Calif.: John J. Cotter & Associates.
3. Emery, F.E. and E. Thorsrud (1976). *Democracy at work: The report of the Norwegian democracy program.* Leiden: Nijhoff.
4. Herzberg, F., B. Mausner, and B. Snyderman (1959). *The motivation to work.* New York: Wiley.

CHAPTER 7

PHASE II: REDESIGNING FOR HIGH PERFORMANCE/ DEVELOPING AND IMPLEMENTING REDESIGN PROPOSALS

STEP 2.2: DEVELOP REDESIGN PROPOSALS

The Proposal Development Process

Preparation precedes action. The redesign process will not succeed without careful planning that is both systemic and systematic. The Redesign Management Team (RMT) is primarily responsible for planning the proposal development process. Worksheet 7.1 contains some planning guidelines you can use.

The proposal development process begins by compiling summaries of the major learning from the diagnoses. During Phase I: Preparing, the Steering Committee examined the various elements of the school district's environment. The major learning from this assessment is noted and summarized.

Planning Questions	Answers
1. Who needs to participate in the proposal development process?	
2. Who has final approval of design proposals?	
3. What sequence of steps must we follow to create and approve design criteria?	
4. Do the new designs need to be tested before implementation?	
5. How will the design decisions be communicated? • Who communicates? • What media do we use? • What audiences do we need to reach? • How will we solicit and use feedback and reactions?	

WORKSHEET 7.1   Planning the Proposal Development Process

Next, the RMT conducted in-depth analyses of the target cluster's technical system by examining both its linear instructional program and non-linear classroom teaching. Finally, the RMT examined the social system of the target cluster. The major learning from these analyses was also recorded for future use.

For this step of Phase II: Redesigning, the RMT begins developing specific proposals to redesign the target cluster by reviewing the summaries of major learning from each of three diagnoses mentioned above.

1. Learning From Open Systems Planning—The Open Systems Planning analysis of the environment identified needs and opportunities. The major learning provided information about:

• The school district's boundaries

• Major influences on the district

• The expectations of key stakeholders

- Information about how stakeholders' expectations are currently met

- An assessment of important environmental pressures on the district

2. Learning from the Technical System Analysis—Two primary work processes within the target cluster were identified and examined: the linear instructional program and non-linear classroom teaching. It was noted that these two processes were interconnected in a symbiotic relationship, with the linear instructional program playing a supportive role to non-linear classroom teaching. The diagnosis of the linear instructional program yielded the following learning:

- The major inputs and outputs for the instructional program
- A listing of the steps in the instructional program
- Identification of key variances in the instructional program
- A description of ways to control key variances
- Identification of internal and external customer requirements for quality and quantity

The analysis of non-linear classroom teaching produced the following learning:

- A list of the deliberations that teachers and others participate in to do their jobs
- Identification of key deliberations about classroom teaching
- For each deliberation, the identification of its topic, forum, participants, and the information that participants take to and from the deliberation
- Identification of the variances in the deliberation process
- An assessment of the work procedures and technological devices that support classroom teaching
- An ideal list of deliberations, participants, and forums for considering classroom teaching

3. Learning from the Social System Analysis—Following the completion of the technical system analyses, the RMT undertook an analysis of the target cluster's social system. The major learning from this analysis provided information about:

- The skills people need to function effectively in the instructional program and in the classroom

- The skills needed to have effective relationships with co-workers, customers, and other stakeholders

- For participants in key deliberations about classroom teaching, the identification of
  - Their characteristic values for each deliberation
  - Conflicts that exist between participants' values
  - A determination of who should be involved in the deliberation process

- An assessment of the degree to which various roles are meeting psychological criteria that contribute to motivation

- A description of what it is like to work in the target cluster with respect to job satisfaction variables

With all of this information in hand, the RMT now begins a series of comprehensive *design meetings* (advice on conducting effective meetings is provided in Chapter 11). These meetings are intended to produce a list of all the possible ways in which the target cluster's technical and social systems can be redesigned and ways in which the target cluster can improve its relationship with its environment. Each possibility must satisfy design criteria articulated in the school district's overall mission and vision and other criteria found in the results of the Open Systems Planning process.

Proposal Development Steps

Step 1: Decide Which Redesign Options to Pursue

It is easy to imagine the RMT having many more ideas for redesign than it can possibly use. Therefore, the RMT must have a set of criteria for deciding which ideas to pursue and which to set aside. Here are several sources of important design criteria.

Mission and Vision Statements—The prime criteria are found in the mission and vision statements of the school district. Whichever redesign ideas are accepted *must* be aligned with the mission and vision of the district. It is unwise to pursue redesign ideas that are in conflict with the broader mission and vision of the district or, for that matter, are innocuous but non-supportive. Like a fleet of ships all sailing in the same direction, even though each is under its own power, the schools in a district must move toward the mission and vision of the district while they are pursuing their particular redesign goals. In the lexicon of organization development this process is called *oneness*. "Oneness" means that all subsystems of a system respond to changes as if they were one system.

Expectations of Key Stakeholders—Remember that stakeholders are the people and groups that have a stake in the success of your school district. At several points in the diagnostic process, you collected information about their expectations. You must now review their expectations and decide:

1. If you want to accept their demands and try to meet or exceed them;

2. If you want to ignore their demands and risk losing their political support; or

3. If you want to disagree with their demands and try to convince them to change their minds.

The expectations you accept as valid are then used as criteria for selecting your redesign goals.

Organizational Design Criteria—As stated above, proposals for redesigning the technical and social systems of the target cluster must be created and measured against predetermined criteria. In addition to the sources of criteria listed above, the following other possible design criteria are adapted from Ackerman:[1]

- **Organizational constraints or "givens"**—The organizational factors that absolutely must be adhered to by the target cluster (e.g., money, equipment, people to be involved, and management processes)

- **Job requirements or tasks**—Any requirement for the work processes or content of specific jobs or functions

- **Political implications**—Any relationship or circumstance that involves political influence, turf, reputation, or power

- **Cultural implications**—Criteria related to supporting or nurturing organizational culture

- **Technological devices**—Criteria related to special technological devices needed to support the conversion processes

- **People requirements**—Criteria derived from an assessment of human needs

Another way to select redesign criteria is to construct a design options matrix. A redesign matrix, as shown in Worksheet 7.2, is constructed by listing specific design specifications in the left-hand column and redesign goals across the top of the matrix. Then, the RMT can make a prediction about whether or not a particular criterion satisfies a particular redesign goal. (If it does, mark it with an asterisk (*) or some other symbol.)

Planning Specifications for the Redesign—When considering criteria for redesigning the technical and social systems of the target cluster, keep in mind that your design specifications should have four levels of detail: Level 1: vision, Level 2: strategic design, Level 3: managerial design, and Level 4: operational design. The first level is very broad and far reaching. As you think through each succeeding level, your thinking becomes more specific and concrete—a kind of deductive reasoning process whereby you move from the general to the specific. The four levels of planning specifications are described in Worksheet 7.3

Step 2: Identify Important Improvement Targets

At this point in the process, you have analyzed the results of the diagnostic activities, reviewed the major learning from those analyses, and developed criteria for selecting your improvement goals. Now, you must actually develop the redesign goals. These goals focus on redesigning the target cluster's technical and social systems and its relationship with its environment. Do this carefully because you just might achieve the goals you set.

In selecting your goals, it is beneficial to target some improvements that could be done relatively soon and without great risk or cost. These early "successes" re-energize the RMT and the target cluster. "Quick" successes can do wonders for morale and can also reduce cynicism and resistance to change.

Design Options That Satisfy Design Criteria	Design Criteria					
	Commitment/ Energy	Joint Optimization	Environmental Agility	Human Resource Development	Innovation	Cooperation
Cooperation is recognized and rewarded						*
Managerial information is widely shared	*		*		*	*
Job rotation					*	*
Multi-skilling	*	*		*		*
Integration of quality control with work processes		*				
Involvement of people in improvement of work processes	*	*		*		
Technical problems solved at their source		*		*		

WORKSHEET 7.2 Sample Organizational Design Options Matrix

Design Levels	Description	Has Planning Been Completed at This Level? (Y/N) What Work Remains to Be Done?
Level 1: Vision	Thinking at this level focuses on how to relate the redesign project to the school district's vision.	
Level 2: Strategic Design	Thinking at this level identifies long-range alternatives for achieving the vision of the district through the redesign project.	
Level 3: Managerial Design	Thinking at this level considers management systems, controls, work flow, linkages between functions, and committees needed to carry out and maintain the redesign effort.	
Level 4: Operational Design	This level of thinking examines job descriptions, operational details, records needed, and work schedules to make the new designs work.	

WORKSHEET 7.3 Levels of Design

Step 3: Do an Impact Analysis

Impact analysis is an example of systemic thinking. It can take two forms: (1) a prediction of how proposed changes may impact other parts of the target cluster's (or school district's) social and technical systems and its environment and (2) a cost-effectiveness analysis to assess costs and benefits in monetary terms. Let's consider the first kind of impact analysis.

Predicting the Impact of Changes

Sometimes it is not possible to assess costs and benefits in financial terms. However, it is usually possible to predict the consequences of implementing the redesign goals in terms of the impact they might have on the socio-technical system of the target cluster (and the entire school district).

We know from socio-technical systems theory that when change occurs in one part of a system, it frequently ripples through the entire system and affects some parts more than others. The purpose of an impact analysis is to predict where the proposed improvements will hit the hardest or produce the most benefit. An impact analysis can also be used to help manage the redesign budget, reduce negative impact on people, and help with the overall evaluation of the redesign effort.

The impact analysis varies in its degree of formality depending on the specific redesign proposal that is being assessed. In some cases, it is a formal study; in others an intuitive "scan." Either way, its purpose is to predict and clarify the consequences of implementing the redesign proposal. Worksheet 7.4 lists the steps in the impact analysis process.

The redesign may impact other organizational structures (an organizational structure is any device, policy, or procedure that is used to guide human behavior in an organization) and processes. Some examples of questions you might ask to assess the impact of the redesign project on organizational structures are provided in Worksheet 7.5.

Not only must the RMT predict the impact of the proposed redesign on the technical system of the target cluster (and school district), but it must also anticipate the impact on the social system—on the people, their roles, and their relationships.

People's responses to change are predictable. They respond in one or more of the following ways (emotional and psychological responses are discussed in Chapter 11):

- They may react with resistance, anxiety, or sadness because they will need to give up the old ways of doing things.

- They may react with enthusiasm, celebration, and inspiration because the changes herald a new order that they have been awaiting.

- They may respond with the use of negative political behavior and negative use of power.

- They may behave by expressing a need to control the redesign process.

Another variable in the social system that might be impacted by the redesign is the target cluster's culture and the school district's culture.

Step 1:	Identify issues and concerns about the improvements required by the redesign project. Issues and concerns may be raised about the following organizational elements: • Mission/vision • Formal organizational structure • Management processes • Instructional program and classroom teaching work processes and supporting equipment/procedures • Job specifications • Products and services • People—how many, their needed skills, systems that impact them (e.g., human resource systems) • Policies and procedures • Needed resources • Space requirements or physical layout of school building • Leadership style and skills • Relationships inside and outside of the target cluster • Image (how others perceive us) and identity (how we perceive ourselves) • Logistics • Relationship with the teachers' union (if relevant) • Government regulations
Step 2:	Search for patterns or themes among the issues.
Step 3:	Group similar patterns or themes into categories. Give each category a name (e.g., "organizational structures" or "people variables").
Step 4:	Examine each of the issues or concerns within the categories and prioritize them.
Step 5:	Assign responsibility to someone from the RMT to manage the predicted impact.
Step 6:	Individuals responsible for managing impact identify who needs to be involved in the process. Special task forces can be instituted to help out.
Step 7:	Establish a time line and process (i.e., who will do what, when, where, and how).
Step 8:	Follow through on impact management tasks. Report progress back to the RMT and Steering Committee.

WORKSHEET 7.4   Steps in the Impact Analysis Process

- What changes need to occur in our decision-making procedures (by individuals, committees, teams) to support the required improvements?
- Will we need to change any financial controls?
- Will we need to establish or change our computer system and programs?
- How will we need to change the flow of information within the target cluster and between the target cluster and other units of the school district?
- What changes need to occur in the reward system?
- Will we need to change our planning systems?
- Will there be changes in our administrative approval processes (e.g., delegation of authority and signature authority)?
- What changes need to occur in our student tracking systems?
- Will we need to change our scheduling patterns?
- Will there be changes in the span of control or unity of command for the target cluster's managers?
- What improvements will need to be made in our faculty and staff development systems?

WORKSHEET 7.5 Impact on Organizational Structures

An organization's culture is composed of values, norms, beliefs, expectations, heroes (men and women), and myths. The redesign will probably affect that culture.

Assessing the impact of the redesign proposal on people continues with a human resource management assessment (i.e., the RMT answers questions about personnel administration issues and concerns). Twelve possible human resource management questions that serve as examples of the kind of thinking that the RMT does for this assessment are shown in Worksheet 7.6.

Impact analyses are comprehensive and complex. Therefore, it is not enough simply to answer the questions. You need to make the required redesign improvements. To assist with this, you identify someone to "drive" the effort to implement various segments (or subsections) of the redesign proposal, define the competencies the "driver" needs, and identify who else must work with the "driver." Next, the person who is the "driver" must develop a plan of action to address each improve-

---

- Will district-level personnel policies need to change to support the redesign proposal? If yes, which ones and in what ways?
- Will faculty and staff need to learn new skills? If yes, which jobs will require skill "retooling"? What types of skills will need to be taught?
- Will the redesign result in position reductions within the target cluster? If yes:
  - ○ Which positions will be lost?
  - ○ What policies do we have (or will we need) to handle the loss (e.g., do we need outplacement counseling, an early retirement package, interim assignments, transfer policies, or retraining opportunities)?
- Will some positions stay in the target cluster but become vacant because of the redesign? If yes, what process will be use to select a replacement for those positions?
- Do we need to rewrite job descriptions?
- What effect will the redesign project have on the performance appraisal policies and processes used in the target cluster?
- What are the implications for our relationship with the teachers' union?
- Will there be any administrative changes (e.g., transfer of files, employee records, reporting procedures, or payroll administration)?
- What training and management development support is needed?

WORKSHEET 7.6 Impact on Human Resource Management

ment goal under his or her purview. These action plans not only include goals and objectives, time lines, and needed resources but also incorporate tactics for monitoring progress.

Do Cost-Effectiveness Analyses

"Cost-effectiveness analysis refers to the evaluation of alternatives according to both their costs and their effects with regard to producing some outcome or set of outcomes."[2] This kind of analysis in an education organization is a complex and difficult calculation. Some general guidelines for doing cost-effectiveness analyses are listed below.

1. Assess Economic Benefits—Although school districts are not-for-profit organizations, they still have economic goals (e.g., "doing more with less"). Thus, the RMT must try to determine, and quantify, any economic benefits that might be derived from the proposed redesigns. The following steps are part of cost-effectiveness analysis:

- **Get the facts**—Do not make decisions without first considering all of the data you have collected about the current functioning of the target cluster. In particular, look for poor labor utilization, errors in the linear instructional program and non-linear classroom teaching, and the amount of time it takes to do the work.

- **Convert the costs to dollar amounts whenever possible**—Once you have identified problems and errors, try to describe them in financial costs.

- **Describe the potential benefits**—Predict the effects of the redesign improvements. Examine the impact of the improvements on all aspects of the target cluster.

- **Convert potential improvements to annual dollar amounts**—Wherever possible, attach a dollar amount to the effects potentially produced by each redesign goal.

- **Compare the actual costs to the projected benefits**—By making a comparison between what the current functioning of the target cluster costs and the benefits that you think will accrue, you can make informed decisions about which redesign improvements to pursue and which to set aside.

2. Assess Potential Human Benefits—Most of the benefits that directly affect people are realized by redesigning the target cluster's social system. Predict the impact of the redesign on those psychological factors that affect motivation, job satisfaction, and quality of work life.

3. Determine the Total Cost of the Redesign Project—This is basically an accounting procedure where you specifically identify the costs related to the total redesign project (e.g., the cost of the initial diagnostic work, releasing people to serve on the RMT, training, and making visits to other school districts or organizations that are being redesigned).

Another cost factor that is often ignored is the cost of "doing business as usual." Some of the cost items of doing business as usual might be:

- Direct labor costs
- Operation and maintenance costs
- Planning, supervision, and control costs

- Turnover costs
- Absenteeism costs
- Quality costs
- Operating costs of facilities

After completing the impact analysis, the RMT moves to the next step in the proposal development process: selecting the best redesign goals.

Step 4: Select the Best Redesign Goals

At this point in the process, the RMT has collected, analyzed, and interpreted the results of all its diagnostic work. Further, it has developed specific criteria for selecting redesign goals. The RMT has also applied the selection criteria to establish possible redesign goals and assessed the relative costs and benefits associated with economic concerns, linked to the quality of work life and the cost of doing business as usual. Now, the RMT is ready to select the most promising (as judged in comparison to the design criteria reflected in the district's mission and vision statements) redesign goals.

Step 5: Develop the Redesign Proposal

After the RMT selects the most promising redesign goals, it develops a redesign proposal. The redesign proposal is a richly descriptive document that contains the following information:

- A rationale for the proposal
- The mission and vision statements of the entire school district
- A statement relating the redesign proposal to the vision statement
- A general description of the redesign process that was used
- A summary of the diagnostic methods that were employed
- A summary of the diagnostic results
- An explicit scenario describing the desired future state of the target cluster

- A description of the redesign improvements that must occur in the technical and social systems of the target cluster and its relationship with its environment if the desired future scenario is to become reality

- A summary of the impact and cost–benefit analyses associated with achieving the desired future state

- A description of "next steps"

The redesign proposal should be clear, concise, and cogent. Edit the proposal several times before submitting it to the Steering Committee (SC). If necessary, use the services of a professional writer. Also, prepare the proposal using a desktop publishing word-processing program. In addition to being written well, the document must also look professional and have a "user-friendly" design.

Step 6: Get Approval of the Steering Committee

After printing the final draft of the proposal, submit it to the SC for review and approval. Because one member of the SC has been on the RMT, there should be no surprises in the proposal for the SC. Thus, the review should be rather routine (this is not to imply that the SC simply "rubber stamps" the proposal).

STEP 2.3: DEVELOP IMPLEMENTATION PLANS

At this point, you may be feeling overwhelmed by the complexity of the planning that goes into developing the redesign proposal, but this is an appropriate level of complexity given the multifarious characteristics of a school organization. Also, it is important to remember that the proposal must serve as a map to guide the transition of the target cluster from the "present state" to the desired "future state." If you are trying to navigate through new and difficult terrain, isn't it better to have a topographic map and a compass instead of a road map? Further, this level of complexity is in response to findings in the field of organization development that attest to the fact that most organizational improvement efforts fail because of inadequate transition planning and incompetent management of the transition process.

Although the planning process is complex, there is no need to despair. The way to manage this complexity is to develop effective transition structures. These structures are discussed next.

The SC and the RMT are faced with a set of difficult and complex questions when planning to implement the redesign proposal. These questions include:

- How do we ensure that the target cluster keeps running relatively smoothly while the changes are in progress?

- How do we create and maintain the momentum needed to set the changes in motion?

- How do we respond to the psychological and emotional responses of our people to the redesign effort (e.g., feelings of anxiety, depression, frustration, resistance, and disappointment)?

- What is the best way to lead the target cluster through this difficult transition from the present to the future?

The responses to the above questions vary depending on particular circumstances. There are, however, some general guidelines that can be followed when moving any target cluster toward its desired future state.

Beckhard and Harris[3] tell us that the basic change process for an organization has three stages: examining the present state, defining the desired future state, and making the transition from present to future. Each stage has different change management requirements. The current state has its existing procedures, structures, processes, and so forth. The future state is designed conceptually on paper, mostly in the form of a vision statement, and in the minds of the SC and the RMT members. But the transition stage must accommodate the existence of both states (the present and the future); thus, change requires two parallel management systems. The first management system directs the target cluster in the interstice between present and future. The second management system monitors and leads the target cluster toward its vision (i.e., its desired future state). Without question, these two management systems are essential to the success of your redesign project. Yet, they must be handled as parallel tasks, not as combined tasks. Five organizational structures to help manage these parallel tasks are discussed below: the interim management structure, the transition manager, the transition team, the transition plan, and specific action plans.

The Interim Management Structure

The principals of the schools in the target cluster are faced with a complex challenge at the beginning of the transition phase: how to stay in control of their schools' operations once the changes begin. Two things are certain: the principals cannot stop the schooling process while the changes are being introduced and they must minimize any temporarily negative consequences of the transition phase on students. So, how do the principals keep their schools running while moving toward the cluster's desired future state?

One of the first steps is for the RMT and the principals to explicitly define the key managerial and operational decisions that must be made to keep the schools running (e.g., class scheduling, testing, and reporting). The decisions needed to keep the schools running are then delegated to the assistant principal or to a senior-level teacher (or committee). This delegation of authority and responsibility frees the principals to focus attention on moving their schools toward the cluster's desired future. As the target cluster gets closer and closer to its envisioned state, the acting managers for the "old" schools return to their normal duties or assume new duties as required by the "new" cluster.

Second, the interim management structure allows old committees, policies, and procedures to stay in place until new ones are constituted or developed. However, in some situations, temporary new committees and policies might need to replace old ones. These structures could be designated ad hoc. Once the "new" cluster is fully in place, the "old" structures, processes, and systems are abandoned or disbanded as needed.

The Transition Manager

Successful organizational transitions are managed by line managers whose full-time responsibility is to direct the transition of the target cluster from the present state to the desired future state. This person is called the transition manager (TM). The TMs should be principals within the target cluster (remember that authority and responsibility to run the "old" school are delegated to an assistant principal or senior teacher). Because the redesign project is focusing on a cluster of schools, principals from each school within the cluster serve as the TMs of their respective schools.

The TM, in collaboration with the RMT, develops and monitors the transition plan. Some responsibilities of the TM include:

- Secures resources for the transition

- Orchestrates the contributions of key players for the transition

- Manages the budget for the transition

- Serves as a center of information and direction

- Balances the competing needs of their individual schools and the target cluster

- Manages the conflict resolution process

- Maintains communication with the manager(s) in charge of running the "old" school

The TM must also maintain communication with the RMT. Because the RMT is managing the redesign of the entire cluster, it has a vested interest in the success of the redesign effort for the target cluster.

To function effectively in this role, the TM must have adequate resources, a clear and in-depth understanding of where the target cluster is heading, an in-depth understanding of the overall transition plan, full authority to make key decisions, and the support of the RMT and the consultant.

The Transition Team

Up to this point, the RMT has been responsible for planning the redesign project, collecting diagnostic information about the functioning of the technical and social systems of the target cluster, and developing redesign proposals. Now, the RMT takes on the role of a transition team.

The RMT supports the TM by helping him or her develop a transition plan. The RMT is also a point of contact for information about redesign specifics in addition to serving as a resource to others in the target cluster. Finally, specific functional responsibilities can be assigned to individual team members (e.g., individual members could be placed in charge of overseeing changes in management systems, human resource management systems, the technical system, or the social system).

The Transition Plan

Remember that the redesign proposal describes many changes that must occur if the target cluster is to be aligned with the mission and vision of the district. Because so many changes need to occur, a logical sequence for making those changes needs to be developed; for example, one principle for sequencing changes is to start from the outside and work inward. This means making changes at the broadest level of the organization first (e.g., at the policy level), then making changes that need to occur between organizational units or groups and within groups, and finally making changes that impact individuals. By organizing the transition in this fashion, the likelihood of completing a successful transition is increased. This kind of tactical thinking is what goes into the overall transition plan.

An effective transition plan has four major elements: identifying *what* has to change, *how* to change, *who* will be responsible for the changes, and *when* to change. Much of the information that the RMT needs for the transition plan has already been collected and analyzed, e.g., an identification of what needs to be changed (from the assessments and the impact analyses). Some of the additional thinking that needs to occur regarding transition planning includes the following questions:

- What communication strategy should we develop?

- How do we build commitment and understanding of the redesign improvements?

- How do we respond to resistance?

- How do we gather information and feedback from others?

- How do we best coordinate with the SC and school district?

- How do we manage conflict?

Thinking about *who* participates in the change process focuses on questions like:

- Who has the attitudes, knowledge, and skills to handle a particular change?

- Can these people be released from their regular duties to assume responsibility for the redesign changes?

- What resources will we need to get these people involved?

Planning *when* to introduce the improvement goals considers questions such as:

- How ready are people to move ahead with this particular change?

- Do people have the skills and knowledge needed to act on this change?

- How critical is this change to the success of our effort?

- What resources do we need to have in place before we can begin working toward each improvement goal?

- What is the logical order of implementation for all of these improvements? What needs to change first before other changes occur?

- How do we bring in (or phase in) such elements as new people, new teams, new departments, and new management systems?

- How do we handle the logistics of moving people, offices, records, and so forth?

Once all planning questions are answered, the RMT and TM can transfer the information to a transition plan, which serves as kind of a strategic plan for the redesign effort. There are alternative ways to design a transition plan. One example of a design divides the transition plan into four phases:

Phase I: Planning and organizing the implementation

Phase II: Implementing

Phase III: Evaluating the redesign

Phase IV: Achieving permanence and diffusing the changes

Planning sheets such as Worksheet 7.7 can be developed for each phase of the transition plan.

Another example of a transition plan is provided by Ackerman.[4] She displays a transition planning matrix that identifies nine planning steps across the top of the matrix and four levels of organization along the left margin of the matrix. The nine planning steps are:

1. Awareness of need
2. Assessment if changes needed
3. Influence on design of new state
4. Understanding impact on self

Phase I: Planning and Organizing				Page	of
Goal:					
Activities	Who's Responsible	Needed Resources	Starting Date	Completion Date	Criteria for Success

WORKSHEET 7.7   Transition Planning Sheet

5. Planning for transition
6. Support during implementation
7. Achievement of desired goal: formalization
8. Evaluation
9. Closure

The four levels of organization are (starting at the deepest level and moving outward to the most general level):

1. Individual level
2. Functional group level
3. Organization level
4. Environmental interface level

The intersection of the 9 planning phases with the 4 levels of organization creates 36 cells in the matrix. Ackerman describes transition activities that must be accomplished within each cell. For example, in the cell created by the intersection of "awareness of need" with the "individual level" of organization, she lists the following activities:

1. Test for understanding of the need for change

2. Ensure understanding of rationale for change and its impact on individuals

3. Test for readiness to change

The transition plan is used by the TM and the RMT to monitor the redesign of the target cluster. However, the SC also uses the transition plan to monitor the overall progress of the redesign effort. The SC has a vested interest in the success of the target cluster in implementing its redesign proposal because the cluster will serve as a prototype for all of the other clusters in the district when it is time for them to be redesigned.

Specific Action Plans

The implementation of the various elements of your redesign proposal unfolds as the TM and the RMT follow the transition plan. However, the transition must be guided by specific action plans designed and carried out by those responsible for specific changes. The action plans are tactical in nature. Specific action plans have the following elements:

1. **Statement of the redesign goal(s)**—For each improvement that must occur, there must be a goal statement defining the desired outcome.

2. **Specific objectives (or action steps) for each goal**—It is not good enough to have a goal; you also have to list specific steps to reach that goal.

3. **Time lines for beginning and ending**—You need to create a time bracket for beginning and ending the activity related to each goal and its supporting objectives.

4. **Who else needs to be involved and how they should be involved**—The change requires the cooperation of other people. It also impacts others. Who are these others? How should they be involved?

5. **Needed resources (human, technical, and financial)**—You need resources to accomplish a particular goal and its objectives. What or who do you need?

6. **Reporting requirements**—You have to make someone responsible for "driving" each implementation plan and require him or her to report to the TM and RMT on a scheduled basis. You cannot give

this person authority and responsibility and then cut him or her entirely loose. He or she must be accountable for making the improvements happen according to the overall transition plan.

7. **Evaluation criteria**—How will you evaluate the process and outcomes of this particular change activity?

8. **Indicators of successful implementation**—How will you know when you have reached your goal and completed your objectives? What indicators will you use to let you know that you have achieved what you set out to achieve?

STEP 2.4: IMPLEMENT SELECTED PROPOSALS

This step occurs after all the above planning is completed and the redesign proposal is reviewed and approved by the SC. The SC provides strategic oversight of the implementation (i.e., it assures that the implementation is aligned with the mission and vision of the district). The RMT and the consultant assist other teachers and administrators in the target cluster with those aspects of the implementation that impact them. The implementation is evaluated periodically (formative evaluation) to assure that it is staying on course. Course corrections are made as needed.

CONCLUSION

Developing and implementing your redesign proposal is an arduous, complex task. Nevertheless, you must persevere because experience shows that most complex organizational changes fail because of inadequate transition planning and incompetent transition management. Take extra care to ensure success at this step in the redesign process.

Remember, you do not want to be like Christopher Columbus. When he started out on his fateful journey, he did not know where he was going. When he landed in the New World, he did not know where he was. And when he returned home, he did not know where he had been (source unknown).

REFERENCES

1. Ackerman, L.S. (1985). *Managing complex change.* McLean, Va.: Linda S. Ackerman, p. VI-6
2. Levin, H.M. (1983). "Cost-effectiveness: A primer." *New perspectives in evaluation,* Volume 4. Beverly Hills, Calif.: Sage Publications, p. 17.
3. Beckhard, R. and R.T. Harris (1977). *Organizational transitions: Managing complex change.* Reading, Mass.: Addison-Wesley.
4. Ackerman, L.S. (1983). "Structures for the management of organizational change," in *Managing complex change workbook.* McLean, Va.: Linda S. Ackerman, Section IX.

CHAPTER 8

PHASE II: REDESIGNING FOR HIGH PERFORMANCE/ EVALUATING THE REDESIGN PROJECT

STEP 2.5: EVALUATE THE PROCESS AND OUTCOMES OF THE REDESIGN EFFORT

Leadership for evaluation comes from the Steering Committee. It is very important for the Steering Committee to evaluate the process and outcomes of the redesign project. The importance is couched in the fact that your district is committing significant resources to the project. You have to be accountable for the use of those resources and for demonstrating that the redesign project paid off with measurable improvements in the technical and social systems of the target cluster, and eventually of the entire district.

EVALUATION

Evaluation is a process for providing key stakeholders with feedback about the process and outcomes of the redesign project. Such information may suggest the need for further diagnosis or a modification in the direction of the redesign project. Evaluation considers both the initial success of the redesign project and the long-term results it produces. Two key aspects of an effective evaluation are measurement and research design.

Evaluating the redesign project requires judgments about whether the redesign improvements have been implemented as planned and, if so, whether they are producing the desired results. Because of the level of accountability that is often placed on top school administrators to justify the expenditure of scarce resources, the Steering Committee must conduct a rigorous assessment of the process and outcomes of the redesign project.

Two distinct types of redesign evaluation are described in this chapter. The first is a formative process called *implementation feedback* which occurs during implementation. It is an assessment of whether redesign improvements are actually being implemented as planned. The second is a summative process called *evaluation feedback* which occurs after implementation and serves as an evaluation of whether the redesign improvements produced expected results.[1]

One of the major reasons it is important to employ implementation feedback is related to one of the core principles of socio-technical systems design: the principle of *minimal specifications*. The principle advises Redesign Management Teams to define needed improvements by minimally specifying the characteristics of the desired improvements. In applying this principle, then, those responsible for implementing the action plans have the freedom and authority to add specificity as needed. This freedom to add specificity, however, creates a problem for the implementers—they have to translate the general redesign goals into specific actions, behaviors, and procedures. This freedom to turn general goals into specific actions can result in unintentional and intentional deviations from the transition plan. Implementation feedback helps keep the transition plan on course by providing decision makers with the information they need to correct deviations.

There are two types of information that are used for implementation feedback: data about the specific characteristics of the redesign improvements and data about the immediate impact of the changes. These data are collected frequently during the implementation. They are like instant photographs of the redesign improvements that provide practitioners with a better understanding of what is happening and provide guidance on which steps to take next.

At some point during implementation, feedback informs practitioners that all of the desired redesign improvements are in place. Once in place, the Steering Committee initiates evaluation feedback. Evaluation feedback is summative in that it looks at the overall process and outcomes of the redesign project. The results of evaluation feedback are used to make judgments about whether scarce resources should continue to be allocated as planned. This kind of evaluation is difficult to conduct because it takes longer to gather and interpret the data and it includes outcome measures on many redesign variables. Negative evaluation feedback indicates that either the initial diagnoses of the technical or social systems were incorrect or inadequate or the redesign goal being evaluated was wrong. Positive results indicate that the redesign goals produced desired outcomes and, therefore, the improvements should become permanent features of the target cluster.

REASONS FOR CONDUCTING EVALUATION RESEARCH

Burke[2] summarizes the main reasons for doing an evaluation of an organization development intervention such as your redesign project:

1. An evaluation forces the definition of change objectives.

2. An evaluation forces the clarification of the change outcomes that are expected.

3. An evaluation forces specificity with respect to how certain procedures, events, and activities will be implemented.

4. An evaluation helps to signal many of the problems and obstacles to be anticipated in the organization development effort.

5. An evaluation facilitates planning for the next steps and stages of organizational improvement and development.

Also, as we know from systems theory, there may be no single explanation as to why certain outcomes were achieved by your redesign project (i.e., there may not be a single cause for a single outcome). However, systematic evaluation can assist you in trying to provide causal explanations for the outcomes you do achieve. And evaluation will help you to define what effectiveness means for your school district and the target cluster.

MEASUREMENT

Two important principles affect measurement. The first is that the measures must be *accurate*. The second is that measures must be *precise*. Sergiovanni[3] suggests that we focus on both accuracy and precision. Accuracy, he says, means that you have the right goals—you are heading in the right direction. Precision, on the other hand, means that your goals are analyzed carefully to provide evaluators with precise ways to measure results. An accurate goal, for example, might be:

> Our teachers will recognize that they are both suppliers and customers within the linear instructional program.

However, this goal is too broad and imprecise to be measured, even though it is accurate. For evaluation purposes, it would need to be made more precise. To do this, you could restate the goal using specific behavioral language such as:

> Our teachers will explicitly define the desired outcomes of our instructional program and informally assess the actual outcomes of that program. They will then explain their roles as both "suppliers" and "customers" within the linear instructional program.

For measurement purposes, precision has more value than accuracy, although both are needed.

What to Measure

The redesign variables that are measured should be derived from the theoretical or conceptual models underlying the goals of the redesign proposal. For example, if one of the redesign goals is to establish self-managing teams of teachers, then a theoretical model of self-managing teams should be used as the basis for measuring the success of this improvement.

When deciding what to measure, remember to select variables for implementation feedback as well as for evaluation feedback. Historically, interventions such as socio-technical systems redesign have only measured outcome variables while neglecting process (or implementation) variables.[4] Contemporary evaluation requires the measurement of both process and outcomes.

Another historical problem with evaluation of outcomes is that the measures tended to collect data on attitude changes such as motivation or job satisfaction. Your measurement variables should also include behavioral measures (e.g., Macy and Mirvis[5] developed a standardized set of behavioral outcomes for evaluating the results of organization development interventions).

How to Measure

Following Sergiovanni's advice about precision, before measuring the outcomes of the redesign project you have to operationalize the variables so that appropriate data can be collected. This means that operational (or behavioral) definitions for each of the variables must be developed. These definitions not only specify the empirical information needed for evaluation but also describe how data will be collected.

Frequently, evaluators of interventions such as socio-technical systems redesign use perceptual measures to assess the outcomes of an intervention (e.g., they measure job satisfaction, commitment to organizational goals, and level of motivation). Because of the complexity of measuring human perception, it is mandatory to use instruments that have known validity and reliability.

Standard instruments for measuring perceptions and other intervention outcomes are growing in number. Some examples of these instruments are:

- The Job Diagnostic Survey[6]
- Survey of Organizations[7]
- Comprehensive Quality-of-Work-Life Survey[8]

Not only are there measurement instruments for assessing perceptions, but there are also "hard" measures of specific intervention variables, especially outcome variables such as productivity, absenteeism, and employee turnover. These measures are important because they are used in support of accountability.

There are several different techniques you can use to collect evaluation data. In addition to the survey technique, you can also conduct individual or group interviews, make observations, or analyze documents or other artifacts of the implementation. These techniques are described more fully in the literature on organization development.

RESEARCH DESIGN

Conducting an effective evaluation also requires using a solid research design. The key problem to be solved when considering research design is how to design the evaluation to demonstrate whether the redesign project did, in fact, produce the observed results (or whether something else produced the results). This concern is called *internal validity*. You also need to determine whether the redesign process will work the same way in the other clusters that need to be redesigned. This concern is called *external validity*. External validity is meaningless unless you first have internal validity; therefore, assessing internal validity becomes a primary focus for your evaluation.

Testing for internal validity is basically a test of a hypothesis (i.e., "x" redesign goal will result in "y" outcomes). Ideally, to assure your hypothesis has internal validity, you must reject all other competing hypotheses. In the behavioral sciences, however, the process of rejecting rival hypotheses is not easy.

In the behavioral sciences, rejecting rival hypotheses to your main hypothesis is not the kind of precise, controlled, experimental process that you find in a science laboratory.[9] The reasons for this complexity are as follows:

- Organization development interventions, like your redesign project, are complex and involve many interrelated changes that conceal whether an individual redesign improvement produced the desired outcome or whether some combination of improvements did the job.

- The redesign project is a long-term process and it takes considerable time to produce results. The longer the time period, the greater the chances that intervening variables are at play.

- Interventions are almost always used with intact work groups rather than with randomized groups. Without random sampling and comparison groups, it is almost impossible to precisely rule out competing hypotheses.

Because of these research design problems, behavioral scientists use *quasi-experimental* research designs.[10] These designs are not as rigorous as traditional experimental research designs, but they still allow evaluators to reject rival explanations about the causes of observed outcomes. There are three powerful quasi-experimental designs for assessing organization development interventions:[11]

1. **Longitudinal measurement**—This approach measures results repeatedly over long periods of time. For example, data collection would start before the implementation of the redesign proposal and continue for a period thought to be reasonable for producing desired outcomes.

2. **Comparison unit**—This method compares redesign outcomes achieved in the target cluster to another cluster where the redesign proposals were not used. Matching units (or groups) are rare, but most schools within a district share enough similar characteristics to make the comparison useful.

3. **Statistical analysis**—This technique uses statistical methods whenever possible to rule out the possibility that the observed outcomes were the result of random error or luck. There are several statistical procedures (not described in this book) that are compatible with quasi-experimental research designs.[12]

Quasi-experimental research designs using any of the three approaches just described will give you a reasonable evaluation of your redesign project. If you have to conduct repeated measures, it is advisable to use unobtrusive measures, such as reading documents or analyzing files or records. Unobtrusive measures are an important complement to the other measures because they do not interact with the redesign process or affect its outcomes. Obtrusive measures, such as interviews and observations, are reactive and they sensitize people to the redesign interventions. When people react to the interventions or become overly sensitized to what is happening, it is difficult to know whether the observed outcomes of the redesign project are the result of the redesign proposal, the measuring methods used, or some combination of both.

Using multiple measures (i.e., more than one data collection technique) is an important part of your research design because the more different kinds of data collection techniques you use, the more likely it is your findings will be valid.

GENERAL GUIDELINES FOR CONDUCTING EVALUATION RESEARCH

There are four general guidelines for doing an evaluation of your redesign project. First, Alderfer[13] says that the evaluator collaborates with all of the key players in planning the evaluation (i.e., administrators and teachers). This collaboration begins early in the redesign process.

Second, the evaluator develops a clear research design and strategy that defines what should be evaluated. Beer[14] lists four possible research strategies:

1. **Evaluation of total system effectiveness, efficiency, and health—** Whether or not the organization as a whole has changed

2. **Evaluation of attitudes toward the change process itself—**How organization members feel about the way changes have been managed

3. **Evaluation of a specific intervention—**Such as team building or some structural change

4. **Evaluation of performance outcomes—**Goal achievement, sales, turnover, productivity, and so forth

These strategies are not mutually exclusive—one or more could be used simultaneously or sequentially.

Third, the evaluation design is connected to the diagnostic model that was used. That is, if the diagnostic model examined the linear instructional program and non-linear classroom teaching of the target school, then the research design should be related to that model.

Fourth, the evaluator uses adequate and varied methods for collecting evaluation data. These methods should:

1. Help distinguish among different kinds of changes[15]
2. Provide valid information
3. Be tied to a model or theory
4. Be useful to the target school and the school district

SPECIFIC STEPS IN THE EVALUATION PROCESS

A comprehensive set of standards and guidelines for evaluating educational programs, projects, and materials was developed by the Joint Committee on Standards for Educational Evaluation.[16] These standards and guidelines support a 12-step evaluation process.

Ten of these steps are relevant to your redesign project. The following description of these ten steps has been modified to fit the language and goals of a redesign project.

1. Decide Whether to Evaluate—The first step in the evaluation process is to decide if you really want to do an evaluation. This decision is based on the purposes of the evaluation and the potential use of the evaluation data.

2. Define the Evaluation Problem—For valid and reliable measures, you need to be concerned with both accuracy and precision, but precision is more important than accuracy. Thus, when defining your evaluation problem (or the object of your evaluation), first be sure that you are measuring the correct variable, outcome, or object (accuracy) and then define the evaluation problem in precise, measurable terms.

3. Write a Contract to Cover and Control the Evaluation—If you are using an external evaluation specialist, your contract must specify exactly what you expect, define the boundaries of the evaluation, and describe the rules. If you are using a professional from your school district's staff, then you must also provide a "contract" that essentially includes the same information that you would give to an outside evaluation specialist. This contract is used to control the evaluation.

4. Design the Evaluation—The earlier discussion about research design and measurement issues also applies here. Design the evaluation carefully so that you get valid and reliable results that can be used to make informed decisions about the value and impact of the redesign project. In addition, you have to decide whether you want *implementation feedback* (i.e., formative evaluation) or *evaluation feedback* (i.e., summative evaluation) or both.

5. Budget for the Evaluation—Evaluation costs money. Resources must be appropriated and allocated for the evaluation. Do not underfinance the evaluation operation if you want valid and reliable results.

6. Staff the Evaluation—Not only do you need money to do an evaluation, you also need people. You must involve professionals who know how to plan, organize, and conduct excellent evaluations. There is no room for amateurs here (except as assistants to the primary evaluators).

7. Administer and Monitor the Evaluation Operation—Once the evaluation is underway, it has to be managed. The management of the evaluation is provided by the Steering Committee.

8. Produce and Communicate Evaluation Reports—If the evaluation is to provide implementation feedback, then reports must be provided periodically and communicated to those people who can use the results to make course corrections in the redesign process. If the evaluation provides summative judgments about the redesign process and outcomes, the final report must be communicated and explained to several audiences (e.g., the Steering Committee, the Redesign Management Team, professionals in the target cluster, and professionals throughout the school district).

9. Decide What to Do with Evaluation Results—Once you have finished the evaluation, decide what to do with the results. If the evaluation was for implementation feedback, the results are used in a formative way to make course corrections in the implementation of various elements of the redesign proposal. If the results are summative, then use them to make final judgments about the overall effectiveness and efficiency of the redesign process and outcomes. You can also use summative results to ensure accountability.

10. Evaluate the Evaluation—In addition to evaluating the redesign project, you must also evaluate the evaluation process. (Sometimes it seems that evaluation never ends.) Although this might sound like overkill, the purpose is to assure that the evaluation results are valid and reliable.

THE POLITICS OF EVALUATION

When there is a lot at stake, people become political. Political behavior is not inherently negative or positive. It is the intention of the individual using political behavior that makes it negative or positive. Because there is a lot at stake with your redesign project, including your reputation and possibly your career, you need to be careful to use only positive political behavior.[17]

Here are some hints for using positive political behavior with evaluation results:

- Do not use complex statistical techniques just to impress people.

- Consider alternative interpretations of reality or consider differing value perspectives on what is being evaluated.

- Justify the conclusions reached through evaluation explicitly so that key players can assess them. To be sufficiently defensible, the evaluation results must be reported with an accounting of the evaluation procedures and underlying assumptions. There should also be a discussion of possible alternative explanations of the findings and why these alternatives were rejected. This principle is important because unverified conclusions may be faulty, leading the audience to inappropriate actions.

- Advise the key players to be cautious in interpreting perplexing findings in the evaluation report.

- Provide safeguards within the evaluation procedures to protect the evaluation results, and subsequent reports, against distortion by the personal feelings and biases of any stakeholder. Reports are objective to the extent that they are based on impartially assembled facts and are not slanted to promote biased positions.

- Seek out and report to the fullest extent possible conflicting points of view about which conclusions and recommendations are warranted.

- Seek out, examine, and report biases and prejudices which may have influenced the evaluation results.

- Do not assume that all players in the evaluation process are operating from a position of integrity.

- Consider the need to safeguard reports and establish mechanisms to protect the reports against deliberate or inadvertent distortions.

- Do not relinquish the authority to edit evaluation reports.

- Be part of the public oral presentations of the evaluation findings to assure they are communicated accurately to stakeholders.

CONCLUSION

Evaluation is not an easy process. You can evaluate inaccurate goals using imprecise measures. Your research design can be faulty, which leads to inadequate or irrelevant findings. Your process can be corrupted by the interplay of negative political behavior. Even so, you must constantly evaluate your redesign project.

You must evaluate the redesign project because you need to make decisions about how to keep the process on track (using implementation feedback, or formative evaluation) and you need to make decisions about the ultimate outcome of the entire project (using evaluation feedback, or summative evaluation). You are also accountable to the taxpayers for the use of their scarce financial resources for this grand, yet expensive, endeavor.

REFERENCES

1. Cummings, T.G. and C.G. Worley (1993). *Organization development and change,* 5th edition. Minneapolis/St. Paul, Minn.: West Publishing, p. 573.
2. Burke, W.W. (1982). *Organization development: Principles and practices.* Boston: Little, Brown, p. 330.
3. Sergiovanni, T.J. (1977). *Handbook for effective department leadership: Concepts and practices in today's secondary schools.* Boston, Mass.: Allyn & Bacon, p. 322.
4. Cummings, T.G. and E. Molloy (1977). *Strategies for improving productivity and the quality of work life.* New York: Praeger.
5. Macy, B. and P. Mirvis (1982). "Organizational change efforts: Methodologies for assessing organizational effectiveness and program costs versus benefits," *Evaluation Review.* 6, pp. 301–372.
6. Hackman, R. and G. Oldham (1980). *Work redesign.* Reading, Mass.: Addison-Wesley, pp. 275–306.
7. Taylor, J. and D. Bowers (1972). *Survey of organizations: A machine-scored standardized questionnaire instrument.* Ann Arbor, Mich.: Institute for Social Research, University of Michigan.
8. University of Southern California (1981). *Comprehensive quality-of-work-life survey.* Los Angeles: Center for Effective Organizations.
9. Bullock, R. and D. Svyantek (1987). "The impossibility of using random strategies to study the organizational development process," *Journal of Applied Behavioral Science.* 23, pp. 255–262.
10. Cook, T. and D. Campbell (1979). *Quasi-experimentation: Design and analysis issues for field settings.* Chicago: Rand McNally.
11. Lawler, E. III, D. Nadler, and P. Mirvis (1983). "Organizational change and the conduct of assessment research," In S.E. Seashore, E.E. Lawler III, P.H. Mirvis, and C.T. Cammann (Eds.). *Assessing organizational change: A guide to methods, measures, and practices.* New York: Wiley-Interscience, pp. 19–47.
12. Cook and Campbell (see reference 10).
13. Alderfer, C.P. (1977). "Group and intergroup relations," In J.R. Hackman and J.L. Suttle (Eds.). *Improving life at work: Behavioral science approaches to organizational change.* Santa Monica, Calif.: Goodyear, pp. 227–296.
14. Beer, M. (1980). *Organization change and development.* Santa Monica, Calif.: Goodyear, pp. 250–251.
15. Golembiewski, R.T., K. Billingsley, and S. Yeager (1976). "Measuring change

and persistence in human affairs: Types of change generated by OD de-signs," *Journal of Applied Behavioral Science.* 12, pp. 133–157.

16. Joint Committee on Standards for Educational Evaluation (1981). *Standards for evaluations of educational programs, projects, and materials.* New York: McGraw-Hill, pp. 10–11.

17. For example, see Block, P. (1991). *The empowered manager: Positive political skills at work.* San Francisco, Calif.: Jossey-Bass Publishers.

CHAPTER 9

PHASE III:
ACHIEVING PERMANENCE
AND DIFFUSION AND
PHASE IV:
CONTINUOUS IMPROVEMENT
OF SCHOOLING

PHASE III: ACHIEVING PERMANENCE AND DIFFUSION

Lewin called it "refreezing."[1] Today, organization development specialists often call it "institutionalization."[2] Others call it "achieving permanence." These terms all refer to desirable changes that become a permanent part of the organization's normal functioning. When made permanent, changes are not dependent on any one person or group of people but rather exist as part of the organization's culture. This implies that support for the changes is widespread throughout the entire organization.

A Model for Achieving Permanence

Although unsupported with empirical research, the work of Goodman and Dean[3] provides a potentially helpful framework for achieving permanence. The framework suggests that two important sets of preconditions affect efforts to achieve permanence: (1) the characteristics of the organization and (2) the characteristics of the intervention that produces the changes. These two sets of conditions affect the institutionalization process. Each element of this proposed framework is described below.

Organization Characteristics

According to Goodman and Dean, there are three key characteristics of an organization that can affect the interventions used and the institutionalization process.

Congruence—This variable refers to the degree that members of the organization perceive the intervention (e.g., socio-technical systems design) to be in consonance with the organization's norms, values, beliefs, its current environment, and other changes that are happening concurrently.[4] If congruence exists, achieving permanence is easier. The opposite is also true.

Stability of Environment and Technology—This condition refers to the degree to which the organization's environment and technology (which includes both work processes and equipment) is changing. If there are a lot of changes impacting an organization (e.g., changes in federal and state laws, new organizational performance criteria mandated by accrediting agencies, changes in employment patterns), then it is more difficult for the intervention to become a permanent part of the organization's normal functioning because the constancy and frequency of the other changes undermine permanence.

Unionization—Achieving permanence, and, later, diffusing changes, can be more difficult in unionized environments. This is especially true if the changes have an effect on the terms of the union contract (e.g., salary, fringe benefits, and job design). On the other hand, unions can also be powerful supporters of change, especially when there is a solid and positive relationship between union and management.

Intervention Characteristics

Goodman and Dean theorize that there are five major characteristics of change interventions which can have an effect on the process of achieving permanence.

Goal Specificity—When intervention goals are specific, rather than general, socialization (e.g., training and employee orientation) of people toward the changes is facilitated. Goal specificity also supports the process of allocating rewards because it is easier to recognize behavior that is linked to specific change indicators.

Programmability—This refers to the degree to which changes can be programmed. Programming means the various elements of the intervention are packaged as a change program. Having a specific change program spelled out in advance facilitates other processes that support the change program (e.g., socialization and reward allocation processes).

Level of Change Target—The change target is the organizational unit that is the focus of change. Level refers to where the change target is located in the organizational chart or if the change target is the entire organization. Changes at levels other than the entire organization are highly susceptible to countervailing pressure to revert to "pre-change" behaviors. This pressure can work against efforts to diffuse improvements to other parts of the organization.

On the other hand, targeting the entire organization as the change target can also hinder the process of achieving permanence. The intervention can become bogged down in political resistance, overrationality, or the weight of sheer complexity.

Internal Support—This characteristic refers to the degree to which there is internal support for the intervention. Internal support can help get organizational members to make a commitment to the intervention. Internal support usually comes from an internal consultant, department, or unit within the organization that will be assisting with the intervention.

Sponsor—This refers to the presence of a powerful person(s) who can appropriate and allocate scarce resources for the intervention. Sponsors must come from high levels in the organization so they can exercise control over resources. They must also have the political skill and power to nurture and protect the intervention.

Institutionalization Processes

The Goodman and Dean model describes the following five processes that facilitate institutionalization (or permanence).

Socialization—This concept refers to the process of transferring organizational beliefs, values, norms, and preferences as they relate to the intervention. Because your redesign project involves ongoing organizational learning, you must also institute ongoing socialization activities to make improvements permanent. These socialization activities include staff development, celebrations, and award ceremonies.

Commitment—Commitment links people to new behaviors required by the redesign project. Initial commitment is required to get the redesign process started; periodic recommitment is needed to keep the redesign effort moving in the right direction. Opportunities to express commitment should be based on valid information and free, informed choice.[5] Further, commitment must emanate from every level of the organization, especially from managers who support (or interfere with) the intervention.

Reward Allocation—The organization needs to retool its reward system to reinforce new, desirable behaviors. Rewards help make changes permanent because behavior that is rewarded is repeated and behavior that is repeated becomes permanent—a basic principle of learning theory first espoused by Thorndike.[6]

To be effective, the reward system must provide both extrinsic *and* intrinsic rewards. Extrinsic rewards are given to people by the organization. Intrinsic rewards are internal to the individual and are experienced by taking advantage of opportunities for challenge, professional development, and accomplishment in one's work. Intrinsic rewards tend to be relatively stable over time but need to be enhanced with the prudent and equitable use of extrinsic rewards. Because the potency of extrinsic rewards tends to diminish over time, the organization's reward system needs to be retooled periodically.

Diffusion—This is the process of transferring interventions from one organizational unit to another. This process is discussed in more detail later in the chapter.

Sensing and Recalibration—These processes are used to detect deviations from the planned intervention and then to make course corrections. Invariably, interventions are confronted with destabilizing forces such as changes in leadership, the environment, or technology. Destabilizing factors can cause deviations in organizational and individual performance. Undesirable deviations need to be identified and corrected.

Sensing and recalibration are also important after changes become a permanent part of the organization's functioning. In this capacity, these two processes serve as integral functions in a formal continuous improvement program (Phase IV of the redesign model described in this book), whereby the organization continuously strives to improve itself.

Indicators of Institutionalization

It is important to note that Goodman and Dean suggest that institutionalization is not an all-or-nothing concept but rather that it reflects degrees of persistence or permanence. There are five indicators of the existence of institutionalization.

Knowledge—This refers to what organizational members know about the planned intervention, especially knowledge about new, desired behaviors. It is important for people to have the knowledge they need to behave in new ways and to recognize the impact that the new behavior will have on the intervention. For example, in redesigning organizations, teamwork is often built into the system. Organizational members need to know what a team is, how it develops, how it functions, and what impact teamwork will have on organizational performance.

Performance—It is not enough to have a conceptual understanding of the behaviors required by the intervention. People have to exhibit those behaviors in the performance of their roles. Thus, performance measures need to be designed and used to determine the degree to which the new behaviors are being manifested.

Preferences—Sometimes called attitudes, these variables seek to understand private feelings about the changes derived from the intervention. Private acceptance of change is often different than compliance resulting from organizational sanctions or group pressure. Private acceptance is reflected overtly in behavior when people openly and freely express positive attitudes toward change. These attitudes can be measured using surveys designed to identify the direction and intensity of people's attitudes.

Normative Consensus—A norm is a formal or informal expectation about what is good or acceptable for an organization. Consensus means that although people do not like everything about a change, they feel that it has been achieved fairly and positively and, therefore, they can live with it. The criterion of normative consensus means, therefore, that people in an organization can live with the changes that have been made and, then, make the changes part of the normative structure of the organization.

Value Consensus—Values, in this context, are beliefs about how people should or should not behave. They are derived from organizational norms. The degree of social consensus about these values is an indicator of the level of permanence that a change has attained.

The five indicators of permanence described above can be used to assess the level of institutionalization for the improvements realized through your redesign project. The more of these indicators present in your situation, the more likely it is that the redesign improvements will endure. Further, according Goodman and Dean, these five indicators unfold in a developmental order: knowledge → performance → preferences → norms → values. If this developmental hypothesis is true, it should provide some useful direction for the socialization activities referred to earlier in this chapter to support and nurture your redesign improvements.

Psychological and Emotional Considerations

People responsible for planning and implementing change go through an emotional cycle that starts with initial euphoria, proceeds to feelings of being overwhelmed, moves to a realistic sense of what they can and cannot accomplish, and concludes (or should conclude) with celebration. During the redesign process, these emotional variables must be managed because they can affect the degree to which the redesign improvements are made permanent. (Chapter 11 has more information on people's emotional and psychological reactions to change.)

Of special importance to achieving permanence is the celebration phase at the conclusion of the first cycle of the redesign process. In our often overrationalized organizations, we tend to ignore or suppress celebration. Yet celebration and recognition of contributions to the redesign process can be significant stimuli to your efforts to make your

Celebration/Recognition Category	Planning Considerations
Written Communication • Personal letters • Newsletter articles • Newspaper articles • Journal articles • Formal memoranda • Public news release	• To whom • From whom • Content • Mood/tone • To which journals • To which newspapers
Special Events • Celebration luncheon/dinner • Special meetings • TV news coverage • Celebration party	• For whom • Where • When • Who provides leadership
Mementos • Buttons/T-shirts/jackets/pens • Photographs/posters • Artifacts of the "old" schooling processes	• Design • For whom • With whom • Sizes/preferences
Recognition • Plaques • Certificates • "MVP" awards	• For whom • When • Where • How

WORKSHEET 9.1   **Planning to Celebrate Completion of Redesign Project**

redesign improvements permanent. Worksheet 9.1 can be used to plan a celebration for completing your redesign project and for recognizing those who made significant contributions to the success of the process.

Step 3.1: Conduct Double-Loop Learning Seminars

Argyris and Schön[7] discuss double-loop learning. They argue that most organizations achieve no more than "single-loop learning" (i.e., they see a problem and fix it, or try to fix it). According to Argyris and Schön, for significant organizational improvement to occur, and to ensure long-term survival and renewal of the organization, change must occur in more fundamental ways. They suggest doing this by first solving problems (single-loop learning) and then concurrently learning *how* to solve problems by changing the organization's norms. Thus, a second loop is added to the organizational learning process (i.e., double-loop learning occurs). The second loop is also constructed by encouraging people in the organization to question the unstated assumptions and values underlying organizational performance.

Building on Argyris and Schön's concept, you conduct double-loop learning seminars for members of the target cluster and, ultimately, for the entire school district. These seminars contribute significantly to the process of making your redesign improvements permanent. This occurs because people not only experience the process of making the improvements but also learn a process for continuously improving the district.

As a personal note, in 1980, Chris Argyris sponsored an honorary faculty position for me in the Harvard Graduate School of Education. Part of this post-doctoral study brought me into a learning seminar with Professor Argyris. The structure and process of this seminar is a good model for the kind of double-loop learning seminars proposed here.

Argyris's seminar brought people together to explore group norms, values, and authority structures. We learned and practiced skills for confronting issues directly and openly, expressing feelings in a positive way, taking risks, collaborating, and exercising individual and group responsibility. Double-loop learning seminars to support your redesign improvements could include similar activities for members of the Steering Committee, the Redesign Management Team, and, in time, teams of teachers within the target cluster and then throughout the school district.

A Proposed Structure for Double-Loop Learning Seminars

Double-loop learning seminars can be scheduled periodically. The Steering Committee and the Redesign Management Team would be the first participants in double-loop learning seminars. The first seminar would be facilitated by the consultant. As the seminar participants gain experience in this process, they assume facilitation responsibilities, with the external consultant serving as a process observer. Eventually, as expertise is gained, the external consultant's presence is not required.

A Proposed Process for Double-Loop Learning Seminars

Double-loop learning seminars focus on the redesign project. Participants discuss not only what happened but why it happened. Theories
of action explaining the "whats" and the "whys" are devised and tested.
A theory of action, according to Argyris and Schön, is an explanation
about what happened and why it happened. Some theories of action are
espoused theories of action, which verbally describe a phenomenon, and
others are *theories of action-in-use,* which are behavioral descriptions of
phenomena. Theories of action-in-use are more valid. The double-loop
learning seminars would seek to uncover or construct the theories of
action-in-use that guided the redesign project.

During discussions, the participants continually seek valid information. This is done by challenging untested assumptions, examining the
validity of attributions, and confronting incongruities. Participants examine the "whats" and "whys," assuming that there is more than one
explanation.

Step 3.2: Renew Commitment to the Changes Made

Loucks-Horsley and Hergert[8] address the issue of renewing commitment to continue a school improvement project. This advice applies to
the redesign process as well. They say, "Beginning a new effort results
in a concentration of energy that raises morale and effort. Once the new
effort is transformed into 'the way we do things here,' that energy can
be lost. In addition to losing the burst of energy, old habits may reassert
themselves and the practice itself may be lost." To prevent a decrease in
energy and morale and to limit any organizational backsliding, you
need to renew people's commitment to the redesign project. This renewal helps to make the redesign improvements permanent and helps
the school district get ready for the next round of redesign work. Renewing commitment to the redesign process occurs when you begin
diffusing the redesign improvements throughout the school district.

Step 3.3: Allocate Rewards for Desired Behaviors

The school district's reward system needs to be redesigned to reward
desirable new behaviors. Desirable behaviors are those that support the
target cluster's redesign goals and that are congruent with the school

district's overall mission and vision. A variety of intrinsic and extrinsic rewards are used to increase the power of the reward system. Extrinsic rewards are those material things given to people in recognition of their achievement or behavior (e.g., money, plaques, and certificates). Intrinsic rewards are opportunities for people to meet their higher level psychological needs[9] (e.g., the need for recognition, the need for achievement, and the need for self-actualization).

Step 3.4: Diffuse Changes to Entire District

What Is Diffusion?

Diffusion is the process of transferring interventions from one cluster of schools to all clusters until the entire district is redesigned for high performance. Diffusion facilitates and supports your efforts to achieve permanent improvements in your district. Redesign improvements in the target cluster(s) can fail to persist if they are in opposition with the values and norms of the larger organization—the school district. Sometimes, rather than supporting the redesign improvements, other clusters in the district reject the improvements and often put pressure on the first cluster to revert to old behaviors. Timely diffusion of the redesign improvements to other clusters reduces this counter-implementation reaction. Moreover, spreading the redesign improvements to other clusters communicates clearly your commitment to the redesign process.

Why Is Diffusion Important?

Experience with socio-technical systems design tells us that if only one unit of an organization is redesigned, the rest of the organization eventually pressures the changed unit to revert to its old ways. Another way of saying this is that the dominant unchanged organizational culture forces the redesigned unit to reconform. The consequences of this kind of changing/reverting pattern are wasted resources (human, financial, and technical), demoralization of the people who committed a lot of time and effort to the redesign, and increased cynicism and resistance toward future change efforts. The changing/reverting pattern is also the basis of an old French saying: "The more things change, the more they stay the same."

Diffusing the improvements made in the target cluster is important because if your goal is to design a high-performance school district, then you must spread these changes to *every* school in the district. You need to demonstrate to taxpayers, parents, and other key external stakeholders that you are serious about redesigning the entire school system, and you need to assure your internal stakeholders (i.e., teachers, building administrators, staff, students) that the improvements made in the target cluster(s) will also be spread to all schools in the district.

How Do You Diffuse Redesign Improvements?

1. Plan for Diffusion—You need to plan the diffusion as carefully as you planned the first redesign. Identify the next target cluster, meet with the key players of those schools, educate them about the process, and so on. Follow the same planning steps as you followed for the initial redesign.

2. Identify New Target Cluster(s)—Selecting target clusters for the second round of redesign work is very important because you want to maintain the momentum of your initial successes. Therefore, select those clusters you feel are ready to participate in the next cycle of the redesign process.

For the second cycle of redesign work, more than one target cluster can participate in the process. This is possible because your Steering Committee (SC) and Redesign Management Team (RMT) will have the expertise needed to work as internal consultants to guide new RMTs as they begin the process. For example, if your original RMT had seven members, some of those seven members could be assigned to one new RMT for new clusters, where they would serve as internal consultants to the new RMTs.

The SC maintains its original membership and continues to function as originally designed—as an oversight committee. Members of the SC can be assigned to the new RMTs to serve as communication links between the RMTs and the SC. The external consultant would continue to provide guidance on the overall process but to a lesser degree because of the evolving in-house expertise of the original RMT and SC members. The consultant would then be able to divide his or her time among the various RMTs.

3. Form and Train New RMTs—Each new cluster needs an RMT. Because there are several RMTs functioning simultaneously, the work of the SC becomes very important. As the redesign process expands to include several RMTs working simultaneously, the SC begins to focus on coordinating the work of those teams. Although each team is encouraged to create redesign improvements that fit their particular schools, all improvements must be aligned with the overall goals and objectives of the redesign effort and with the mission and vision of the entire school district. It is the SC's responsibility to assure that the individual RMTs are working within these boundaries.

The new RMTs are trained in the principles of socio-technical systems design in the same way as the original RMT was. Members of the original RMT and the external consultant provide this training. The experiences of the first RMT are useful for making modifications in the redesign process to make it more effective and efficient.

4. Repeat the Redesign Process—After completing the second round of redesign work, you then repeat the redesign process until the entire school district is redesigned. For the third and fourth rounds of redesign work, you can have even more target clusters working simultaneously on redesign because you will have that many more experienced members of several RMTs to serve as internal consultants to the process.

The amount of time to diffuse improvements throughout an organization varies. The literature[10] suggests that the average amount of time is anywhere from 18 months to 3 years. The variability is related to the complexity of the organization and the problems it faces.

Finally, after all of the clusters are redesigned, you will once again need to pay attention to institutionalizing these improvements so that the entire district remains improved. This is done by repeating the "achieving permanence" activities described above and moving into Phase IV of the redesign model: the continuous improvement of schooling.

Step 3.5: Detect and Correct Deviations from Desired Outcomes

After making improvements permanent in clusters of schools and diffusing the changes throughout the entire school district, the various RMTs, with input from the SC, monitor the outcomes of the redesign project to detect and correct deviations from what is desired and expected. This is done by periodically reviewing the school district's progress and seeking ways to assure that the district stays on course toward becoming a high-performance organization.

PHASE IV: CONTINUOUS IMPROVEMENT OF SCHOOLING

Finally, a permanent formative evaluation process must be instituted. This process monitors the status of changes that were made, provides data for correcting unwanted deviations from desired outcomes, and helps surface new opportunities for future improvements. This formative evaluation becomes the basis for continuous improvement of the school system and is represented as Phase IV of the redesign model. Important activities during the continuous improvement phase are described below.

Step 4.1: Supervise System Boundaries

One thing known about systems is that they are composed of subsystems. There are boundaries between these subsystems. In schools, these boundaries represent functional differences (e.g., 5th grade teachers do not teach 6th grade subject matter, and instruction in elementary schools differs from instruction in high schools). There is a boundary between the linear instructional program and classroom teaching. There are also boundaries between levels of schooling (i.e., between elementary, middle, and high school levels). There is also a permeable and invisible boundary between the entire school system and its environment. All of these boundaries are represented by policies, procedures, rules, regulations, and norms that govern the exchange of information between and among systems. These boundaries must be managed to reduce variances (i.e., errors in the work processes), ensure quality, and reduce stress on the social system.

A new process proposed for redesigned school districts to help manage the redesign process and the system boundaries described above is Knowledge Work Supervision.[11] An overview of this new paradigm of supervision is found in Chapter 12. In addition to managing the redesign process, a Knowledge Work Supervisor supervises the boundaries described above. The supervision of boundaries includes, for example, developing information management procedures to control the quality and quantity of information passing through and coming into the system, assuring quality communication between and among grade levels (especially between elementary and middle schools and between middle schools and high schools), acting as a buffer to protect teachers from environmental stimuli that might hinder their efforts to teach, and assuring a good "fit" between the linear instructional program and the non-linear classroom teaching.

Step 4.2: Seek Opportunities for Continuous Improvement

After the knowledge work processes, the social system for the entire school district, and the district's relationship with its environment are redesigned for high performance, the redesign process shifts its focus to the continuous improvement of schooling. Continuous improvement is used to look for incremental ways to improve work processes on an ongoing basis. During this phase of the redesign effort, the RMT looks for opportunities to make ongoing incremental improvements in the technical and social systems of the district. The principles and tools of total quality management[12] are useful here.

CONCLUSION

This chapter described two very important phases in the redesign model: Phase III: Achieving Permanence and Diffusion and Phase IV: Continuous Improvement of Schooling. Achieving permanence is important because you do not want the redesigned clusters to backslide to old ways of doing things. Diffusion is important because you want desirable improvements to be spread to other schools in the district until the entire school district has been redesigned. Continuous improvement is important because the district needs to become a learning organization that continuously monitors its progress and seeks ways to fine-tune its organizational performance. Achieving permanence, diffusing improvements, and continuously improving schooling are too important to ignore; without them, the district will more than likely revert back to its pre-redesign characteristics.

The redesign process (preparing → redesigning for high performance → achieving permanence and diffusion → continuous improvement of schooling → preparing, and so on) continues for the life of the school district. By making the redesign process a formal part of the organization's design, a school district develops a permanent capacity to renew itself and, therefore, it moves toward higher and higher levels of organizational performance.

REFERENCES

1. Lewin, K. (1951). *Field theory in social science*. New York: Harper and Row.
2. For example, Cummings, T.G. and C.G. Worley (1993). *Organization development and change*, 5th edition. Minneapolis/St. Paul, Minn.: West Publishing.
3. Goodman, P. and J. Dean (1982). "Creating long-term organizational change," In P. Goodman (Ed.). *Change in organizations*. San Francisco, Calif.: Jossey-Bass Publishers, pp. 226–279.
4. Ledford, G. (1984). "The persistence of planned organizational change: A process theory." Ph.D. dissertation. University of Michigan.
5. These criteria are two of the three conditions for effective intervention as proposed by Argyris, C. (1972). *Intervention theory and method*. Reading, Mass.: Addison-Wesley. The third criterion for an effective intervention is internal commitment.
6. Thorndike, E.H. (1966). *Human learning*. Cambridge, Mass.: Massachusetts Institute of Technology Press.
7. Argyris, C. and D.A. Schön (1978). *Organizational learning: A theory of action perspective*. Reading, Mass.: Addison-Wesley.
8. Loucks-Horsley, S. and L.F. Hergert (1985). *An action guide to school improvement*. Alexandria, Va.: Association for Supervision and Curriculum Development, p. 68.
9. Maslow, A.H. (1954), *Motivation and personality*. New York: Harper & Row; Herzberg, F., B. Mausner, and B. Snyderman (1959). *The motivation to work*. New York: Wiley.
10. Pasmore, W.A. (1988). *Designing effective organizations: The sociotechnical systems perspective*. New York: Wiley & Sons.
11. Duffy, F.M. (1995). "Supervising knowledge work," *NASSP Bulletin*. 79, 573, pp. 56–66.
12. For example, Crosby, P.B. (1979). *Quality is free: The art of making quality certain*. New York: New American Library; Crosby, P.B. (1986). *Running things*. New York: McGraw-Hill; Deming, W.E. (1982). *Out of crisis*. Cambridge, Mass.: MIT Press; Ishikawa, K. (1985). *What is quality control? The Japanese way*. Englewood Cliffs, N.J.: Prentice-Hall; Juran, J.M. (1989). *Juran on leadership for quality*. New York: The Free Press; Taguchi, G. and D. Clausing (1990). "Robust quality," *Harvard Business Review*. 68, 1, pp. 65–72.

SECTION 3

IDEAS TO SUPPORT
A REDESIGN PROJECT

CHAPTER 10

INTRODUCTION TO CHANGE THEORY

OVERVIEW

As professional educators, you know that today, more than ever, school districts across the United States are being pressured to change. The agenda for change is driven by the current educational reform movement which had its beginning with the report *A Nation at Risk* (a more in-depth description of the mandate to improve schooling is found in Chapter 2). The kind of change required by this movement is now popularly referred to as restructuring. Some examples of the changes being recommended through restructuring are found in *Educational Leadership*.[1] For example, Ken Michaels says:

> The clear message of second-wave reform is that we need to examine our basic philosophical beliefs about teaching, learning, the nature of human beings, and the kinds of environments that maximize growth for teachers and students alike. We need to sort out our values, develop new belief systems, and ultimately create schools that educate as well as train (p. 3).

In the same magazine, Ann Lieberman says, "The recent shift in dialogue about reform calls for reshaping the role of teachers to give them greater autonomy, responsibility, and status" (p. 4). Finally, in that same edition of *Educational Leadership*, Arthur W. Combs says:

> The behavior we observe in ourselves or in the people around us at any moment is only the external expression of what is going on inside. Thus, to change behavior effectively, educational reform must concentrate not on external things like information, gadgets, and methods, but rather on altering the belief systems of the people who make the decisions and do the work (p. 39).

Reengineering a school district requires changes not only in the formal structures of the districts but, more importantly, in the informal, deep structures which involve attitudes, behaviors, values, and beliefs.[2] In other words, reengineering requires changes in the culture of an organization. Reshaping the formal and informal structures of a school district is best done through the kind of organization development described in this book. Because the model in this book is embedded in the field of organization development and because the model represents a change theory, this chapter describes not only many of the core concepts of organization development but also the management of change that underlie the model.

This chapter provides a map of the terrain called change management, so you can see the complex process that underlies all reengineering or redesign projects.

MANAGING COMPLEX CHANGE

Change is a process of becoming something different from what you are. Many times we say we intend to change, we begin changing, and before we know it we are back where we started. The French captured this phenomenon in one of their sayings: "The more things change, the more they stay the same." You know this phenomenon is at play when you hear comments like "Didn't we do this before?" or "We tried this three years ago; why are we doing it again?" or "I remember this. The last time we did this we called it something else, but it's still the same old thing," or "We can ride this out. It's like all the other fads that have come and gone."

If you truly want to redesign your school district into a high-performance organization, you need to understand the basic principles of change theory. A multitude of failed change efforts have come and gone in school organizations (e.g., new math, values clarification, open classrooms), and one of the major reasons why these and other changes failed to "stick" in school organizations is because basic principles of change theory were either ignored or misapplied. The purpose of this chapter, then, is to introduce these basic principles so you can understand how the process of change works and, more importantly, how it can be used to produce permanent change.

Long-lasting change can be developmental or revolutionary. Although revolutionary change can produce positive results, the process often leaves a lot of damage in its wake because of its nature. Revolutionary change takes people by surprise, it is violent and widespread, and it tends to eliminate old ways of doing things in a rather drastic manner. Developmental change, on the other hand, is a planned process of change that is kinder and gentler because it involves people in the change process, targets needed changes, produces changes over a period of time, gives people a chance to adapt to the changes, and gives the organization a chance to regain its equilibrium. The redesign process described in this book is a developmental change model.

Developmental change is couched in a time line: past → present → future. The past is used as a source of diagnostic information about the purpose of the organization, about the customers that are served, about the culture and history of the place. The present is used as the stimulus for change. It provides the context for motivating people to want to change. The future is where you want your organization to be and what you want it to look like 5, 10, or 15 years from now.

When thinking about how to redesign your school district, it is helpful to keep in mind four key assumptions about change:

- People must be "unfrozen" before they can begin to change. "Unfrozen" means that people must be released from the demands of existing patterns of behavior and organizational structures. Releasing people in this way creates a tremendous amount of energy for changing.

- Not only must you change the attitudes, concepts, and skills of your people, you must also change the organizational structures that shape behavior (e.g., policies, procedures, authority relationships, and the reward system).

- In general, people learn best from their personal experiences. Thus, your change process should include opportunities for people to experiment with new ways of doing things.

- People become internally committed to decisions and results they helped to produce.

These four assumptions are incorporated into the redesign model described in this book.

MODELS OF CHANGE

Beckhard and Harris's Model[3]

A basic model of change was developed by Beckhard and Harris. They depict three states of change as two circles with an arrow connecting them: The first circle represents State I, the existing state; the second circle represents State III, the new state; and the arrow moving from State I to State III represents State II, the transition state. Each state of existence presents particular problems that must be managed.

Essentially, the Beckhard and Harris model shows that change occurs by making a transition from the present to the future. You have your current organization with its old, comfortable roles and structures that are familiar and controllable. You have a vision of some future organization, with new roles, work arrangements, and so forth, that are unknown, unfamiliar, and therefore risky. To get from State I to State III, you must make a transition from the present to the future. To make the transition, your staff must let go of old work arrangements, take on new work arrangements, respond to changing tasks and demands, deal with uncontrollable and sometimes unpredictable events, and cope with a sense of loss and gain. Most organizational change efforts fail during State II, transition.

Lewin's Change Model

Kurt Lewin[4] provided practitioners with a basic model of change. He pictured change as a process that altered those forces keeping a system's behavior stable. He believed that the two forces were those striving to maintain the status quo and those pushing for change. When both forces are relatively balanced, current levels of behavior are maintained in what Lewin called a state of "quasi-stationary equilibrium." If you want to change that quasi-stationary condition, you can increase those forces pushing for change, abate those forces maintaining the current state, or apply some combination of both.

According to Lewin, the change process moves through three phases: unfreezing, moving, and refreezing. Each of these phases is described below.

Unfreezing—This step reduces forces maintaining an organization's current behavior (also known as the status quo). It sometimes is accomplished by introducing information that points to a discrepancy between desired conditions and existing conditions. Unfreezing also occurs by:

- Creatively exploring and experimenting with new behaviors that might reduce dissatisfaction

- Forming an action hypothesis (e.g., "If we try this new way of doing things, then we should expect these consequences.")

- Internalizing the values, attitudes, or behaviors that are selected (e.g., "We will try this new way of doing things because it will accomplish something of value to us.")

Moving—This step shifts the behavior of an organization to a new level. It focuses on developing new values, behaviors, and attitudes by changing organizational structures and processes. Organizations move toward their desired future by:

- Testing new ways of doing things that appear promising

- Seeking specific feedback about the relative effectiveness of the new arrangements from trusted, non-threatening sources

Refreezing—This step stabilizes the organization at a new state of equilibrium. It is often accomplished by using supportive mechanisms that reinforce the new organizational state, such as organizational culture, norms, policies, and structures. Specifically, the organization establishes new equilibrium by:

- Making generalizations about the new ways of doing things that are effective or ineffective based on valid feedback

- Organizing the new, effective ways of doing things into a coherent framework that facilitates understanding and action

- Tying the new ways of doing things into the organization's culture and relating these ways to the daily life of the organization

Lewin's change model suggests a developmental approach to change. An organization, or an individual, must pass through all the stages in order to accomplish true change instead of suffering from the illusion of change.

There are two implicit concepts embedded in Lewin's model: readiness for change and equilibrium. Each of these is covered below in more detail.

Readiness—One thing we know for sure about personal and organizational change is that if the individual or system does not recognize the need to change, he, she, or it will not change. Recognizing the need for change creates *readiness for change*. Readiness can be thought of using a mathematical metaphor developed by Beckhard and Harris.[5] According to those authors, change occurs if

$$(A + B + D) > Z$$

where A = dissatisfaction with the status quo, B = a shared vision of the future, D = knowledge of some first, practical steps, and Z = total cost (economic and psychological).

This metaphor suggests that organizational change will not occur unless A, B, and D are greater than Z. First, there must be dissatisfaction with the status quo. This is recognition of need. If your staff likes the way things are, there will not be a perceived need to change—no recognition of need. If the staff has tolerated a bad situation for a long time, they often accept it as inevitable (something they must live with) and there is, therefore, no active dissatisfaction—no readiness to change. In most circumstances, real pain is necessary to cause change. Dissatisfaction is an initial source of energy and power.

Second, for change to occur there must be a *shared vision*. Even though your staff members may not like the current situation in your school district, they will not want to move as a group toward change goals until they agree on where they want to go. Individual visions of the future are not enough—they must be widely shared and agreed upon.

Third, before your staff can begin moving toward some shared vision, they must have knowledge of some *first practical steps* that can be taken. The energy of many groups is immobilized by not knowing where or how to start changing. Dissatisfaction and a sense of where one wants to go are not enough. You must have some initial ways to move forward.

Fourth, the *cost of changing* must be known. Any change effort has both economic and psychological costs, and the latter are often more significant. Who is responsible for the status quo and what is the cost to these people of admitting that there is a much more effective, and different, way of doing business as a school district?

Of the four factors described above, two of them very often serve as significant obstacles to change (i.e., change agents assume a level of dissatisfaction with the current situation that does not actually exist and the cost of changing is often underestimated).

Finally, there are two kinds of readiness for change: conceptual and risk assessment. Conceptual readiness means that people understand the rationale for change, the logic behind it, and the structure of the process that will be used. Readiness as risk assessment is a process that reduces uncertainty for people by discussing and examining the relationships among people (trust), establishing compatibility among people, understanding the consequences of probable outcomes of the change effort, seeing how the changes and the change process relate to existing contractual arrangements, and defining what it means to work in a cooperative relationship instead of a competitive one.

Equilibrium—The field of organization development and change management borrows many terms and metaphors from other fields. For example, the terms critical mass (which in organization development refers to having an adequate number of people in support of a change), force field (which refers to those forces within an organization in support of or constraining a proposed change), inertia (which means that an organization is not moving), and momentum (which refers to the forward thrust that an organization gains as it starts to move) all come from physics. Another term borrowed from physics is equilibrium, which is a state of dynamic balance between opposing forces. In change management the forces are those for and against a particular change proposal. Usually, the opposing forces are relatively equal to the supporting forces and a state of balance, or equilibrium, is maintained. Three kinds of equilibrium—stable, neutral, and unstable—are depicted in Figure 10.1.

Stable equilibrium is that state of balance in an organization where a change is introduced into the system (represented by ↑), the organization temporarily changes, and then it returns to the same old ways of doing things. This condition happens when there was not enough initial support for the changes, the financial and psychological costs were underestimated, or the level of support needed to maintain the changes

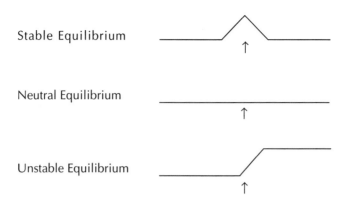

Stable Equilibrium

Neutral Equilibrium

Unstable Equilibrium

FIGURE 10.1   Three Equilibrium States

deteriorates or vanishes. For example, a school district experiments with a new way of organizing the daily schedule. This experiment continues for several months, but only a few people really wanted it in the first place even though many people did express an interest. Additionally, the amount of money needed to make this new arrangement work was not anticipated. The level of support for the change dries up and the innovation disappears like the setting sun on the horizon.

Neutral equilibrium is that state of balance in an organization where a change is introduced into the system (↑) and nothing happens—no changes. For example, a school district calls in a consultant to do staff development on a new teaching technique. All the teachers are forced to attend; they are physically, but not mentally, in attendance at the workshop, and then they return to their classrooms and continue doing what they have been doing all along. The reason for this condition is that basic requirements for change were not met (i.e., the people who were expected to change did not recognize the need to change and, therefore, did not change).

Unstable equilibrium occurs when a change is introduced into a system (↑) and the changes produce new attitudes, behaviors, and values that are "refrozen" to create a new level of equilibrium. This is the kind of equilibrium needed for your redesign effort.

The Planned Change Model

This model of change was first developed by Lippitt, Watson, and Westley[6] and later refined by Kolb and Frohman.[7] It takes the perspective of an organization development consultant working with a client. This model is significantly connected to three criteria developed by Chris Argyris[8] to judge the effectiveness of an intervention: (1) clients must be provided with valid information regarding their problems, (2) they must be given free and informed choice when making decisions about how to address the problems, and (3) they must be given the opportunity to develop internal commitment to the decisions that are made. This model of planned change has seven steps:

Step 1: Scouting	The consultant and the organization jointly explore the possibility of working together.
Step 2: Entry	A contract is developed between the consultant and the organization.
Step 3: Diagnosis	Data are collected, analyzed, and interpreted as part of a process to identify and examine organizational problems.
Step 4: Planning	Using the data from the diagnosis, action plans are developed to carry out desired changes.
Step 5: Action	The action plans are implemented and specific change interventions are started.
Step 6: Stabilization and evaluation	Actions are taken to stabilize the organization after the changes have been introduced. The process and outcomes of the change effort are evaluated.
Step 7: Termination	The consultant concludes work with the organization or completes one change project and plans to start a second.

Action Research

Action research is traditionally aimed at both helping specific organizations to implement planned change and developing more general knowledge that can be applied in other settings.[9] French[10] describes 14 steps in the action research model:

Step 1:	Problem identification
Step 2:	Consultation with a behavioral science expert

Step 3:	Data gathering and preliminary diagnosis
Step 4:	Feedback to key client or group
Step 5:	Joint diagnosis of problem
Step 6:	Joint action planning
Step 7:	Action
Step 8:	Data gathering after action
Step 9:	Feedback to client group by consultant
Step 10:	Rediagnosis and action planning with client and consultant
Step 11:	New action
Step 12:	New data gathering as a result of action
Step 13:	Rediagnosis of the situation
Step 14:	Repeat Steps 1 through 13

Integrative Model of Planned Change

"Recent conceptual developments in OD theory suggest that the concept of planned change implies that an organization exists in different states at different times and that planned movement can occur from one state to another."[11] If this observation is true, then practitioners need to look at the process of planned change as being developmental in nature. Bullock and Batten[12] conceptualized a developmental model of planned change that integrates the characteristics of more than 30 different models. This model describes planned change as having two major dimensions: change *phases* through which an organization moves as it begins planned change and change *processes* which are specific organization development methods used to help an organization move from one state, or phase, to another. Each phase is briefly described below.

Phase 1: Exploration—In this state of existence, the organization makes decisions about whether to begin a planned change effort. Decisions about the commitment of resources to the change effort are also made. The change processes used within this state focus on helping members of the organization recognize the need for change, searching for resources for the change effort, and establishing contracts for services and resources.

Phase 2: Planning—After committing resources to the change effort, the organization begins to plan. The change processes used here focus on trying to understand the nature of problems by conducting in-depth diagnoses, making decisions about change goals based on the results of the diagnoses, and designing appropriate action steps to improve the organization.

Phase 3: Action—After completing the work of Phase 2, the organization moves into the next state of existence, the action phase. In this state, the organization implements action plans designed in Phase 2. The implementation process and results are also evaluated so that corrections can be made to the course of the change effort.

Phase 4: Integration—It is not enough to produce changes in an organization. Those changes must become part of normal organizational functioning. In the language of organization development, the changes must become "refrozen," institutionalized, or made permanent. The change processes within this phase focus on stabilizing the changes, spreading the changes throughout the organization, and using the changes to renew the organization.

The above models of change—Lewin's model, the planned change model, and the integrative model—serve as examples of different approaches to planned change. The model described in this book is a fourth example; it views organizations as complete systems composed of interrelated parts, each of which must be improved.

CHANGE STRATEGIES

There are several strategies for introducing change in an organization, including top-down, or unilateral planning for change; bottom-up, or delegated planning; and shared planning. Beer's[13] criteria for evaluating the relative effectiveness of each strategy are concisely described below.

1. Multiple Constituencies Satisfied—This means the change strategy comes closer than any other choice to satisfying the needs of various interest groups in the organization. Top-down or unilateral approaches and bottom-up or delegated approaches result in low to medium satisfaction of this criterion. A shared approach results in a high level of satisfaction.

2. Speed—The change strategy is faster than any other competing option. Top-down or unilateral approaches respond at a high level of speed.

The remaining two approaches respond at a low to medium level of speed. This criterion does not imply quick results; it only refers to speed of response to a perceived need.

3. Immediate Results—The change strategy results in immediate, expected performance improvements. Bottom-up or delegated approaches, when used with a specific department or unit, realize a high level of immediate results. The top-down or unilateral approach potentially produces immediate results. The shared approach has a medium level of potential to produce immediate results.

4. Long-Term Results—The change strategy results in the expectation of long-term performance improvements. For long-term results, the most effective approach to change is the shared style. The two other approaches have a low to medium chance of producing long-term results.

5. Strain—The change approach results in the least possible psychological and organizational strain. Strain is anxiety caused by the change and/or the frustration that results when the change falls short of expectations. The top-down or unilateral approach and the bottom-up or delegated approach have the greatest chance of producing strain on the system. The shared approach has a low to medium chance of producing strain on the system.

6. "Take"—The change "takes" and is internalized by people throughout the organization, thus requiring no controls to sustain new behaviors. If you want to increase the likelihood that changes will "take," then use the shared approach. The remaining two approaches have a low to medium chance of producing changes that stick with the organization.

7. Dysfunctional Effects—The change strategy results in the fewest possible unanticipated and dysfunctional effects. The bottom-up or delegated approach produces the most dysfunctional side effects. The top-down or unilateral approach has a medium to high chance of producing dysfunction, while the shared approach has a low chance.

8. Renewal Potential—The change approach helps people feel more responsible for future organizational improvements after the change than they did before it. The organization has enhanced its potential for renewal in the future. If you want your organization to become a self-renewing entity, then the shared approach to change will help you more than the other two because it results in a high renewal potential.

Bennis, Benne, and Chin[14] described three additional strategies—empirical-rational, normative-re-educative, and power-coercive—for introducing change in an organization based on different assumptions than those described above.

Empirical–Rational—The fundamental assumption underlying this strategy is that people will respond to their rational self-interest once this is made clear to them. Using this strategy, changes are proposed that supposedly respond to the self-interests of the people in the situation. The change is characterized as desirable, effective, and responsive to self-interests. It is assumed that people will accept the change if they see and believe that it is rational and responsive to their interests. Behaviors of the sponsors of change include, for example, providing logical explanations, generating data to support the need for change, and looking for flaws in arguments that oppose the change.

Normative–Re-Educative—People using this approach do not put a lot of emphasis on rationality and logic. Instead, they focus on a variety of cognitive, affective, and social motives for encouraging people to accept changes. Thus, change planners must not only pay attention to people's thoughts about change but must also take their feelings and internal commitments into consideration. Additionally, the effects of group pressure and the cultural norms of the organization must also be factored into the planning activities.

Power–Coercive—This strategy involves the use of power. It is a strategy of influence aimed at forcing people with less power to comply with the directives and wishes of those with more power. Often, the kind of power that is applied is known as *legitimate power*, which is power derived from one's position in an organization. Other kinds of power played out while using this strategy are *reward power* (power derived from one's ability to dispense valued rewards) and *coercive power* (power derived from one's ability to dispense dreaded punishment).

MANAGING THE TRANSITION FROM THE PRESENT TO THE FUTURE

Every organization progresses through stages during a change effort.[15] First, the change agents seek to understand where the organization has been and assess its current state of existence. Second, they envision desired organizational conditions they would like to move toward. Third, and often overlooked or undermanaged, the change agents must plan and manage the transition of the organization from its current state to the future state of existence. During this transition, people must abandon old ways and structures, learn new ways of doing things, and, finally, adjust to all of the changes.

The transition phase is a challenge because there are often two kinds of management activities happening simultaneously. First, managers must run the "old" organization while the new organization is evolving. Second, managers are concurrently managing and guiding the transition activities. Structures for managing the transition of your district during the redesign process from the present state to the future state were described in Chapter 7.

For managing the transition phase, it is important to consider the pace and sequence of the transition events. Pacing refers to how quickly and how much change can take place in a given period of time. Several criteria are used to make pacing decisions:

- Are people willing to move ahead quickly?

- Are people capable of handling quick and substantive change?

- How urgent is the required change?

- How will the changes impact motivation and job satisfaction?

- To what degree will changes affect productivity?

When making decisions about sequencing a series of changes that need to occur, you have several options to consider:

- Figure out everything that needs changing and change everything at once.

- Implement changes gradually.

- Design the transition so that it happens in planned phases.

- Design a cyclical approach to change, where periods of quick and substantial change are followed by "downtime" for gaining stability and composure, which is followed by more fast-paced changing.

Each option has benefits and constraints. The option of choice for the redesign model described in this book is the fourth one—a cyclical approach.

CONCLUSION

To conclude this chapter, consider the following observations made by IMTEC–The International Learning Cooperative, located in Norway. In a 1988 newsletter,[16] IMTEC observed:

> Those who enter Teacher Training Colleges today, will, by their retirement, teach children who will be active in the work force in the 2090's. Reflecting on the major economic, technological, social, political and cultural changes that have taken place in this Century makes us realize that we are poorly prepared for the challenges ahead. There are good reasons to believe that changes will be even more fundamental in the next century.
>
> Our research on educational change shows how slowly educational systems respond to changes in society. Already we pay the price: Schools are increasingly difficult to manage, the teaching profession is less attractive than ever, achievement scores in many countries are declining. The total annual value of business and industrial in-service training is already as large as the entire annual college and university system budgets in the U.S. Moreover, of the 40 billion dollars spent yearly on industrial training in the U.S., some 8 billion was spent teaching basic skills!
>
> The reason for focussing on schools in Year 2020 is to provide room for a fundamental reconstruction of the educational enterprise. We believe that nobody will need today's schools in the year 2020—or will pay for them. Since it takes about a generation to fundamentally reconstruct schools, we need to start now. We need to build a capacity for change which enables us to create new opportunities for learning.

How can school districts respond to the challenges of the future as described by IMTEC and others? The answer is by redesigning themselves using a cyclical model like the one described in this book so they move continuously closer to higher levels of organizational performance. The need to redesign schools is recognized—the challenges are clear. What remains is for leadership to emerge within school systems to address these challenges in meaningful and substantive ways that go beyond superficial changes into the deep structures of the work and social systems of the school district and into the relationship of the district with its broader environment.

REFERENCES

1. Brandt, R., Ed. (February 1988). *Educational Leadership.* 45, p. 5.
2. Tye, B.B. (December 1987). "The deep structure of schooling," *Phi Delta Kappan.* 69, 4, pp. 281–284.
3. Beckhard, R. and R.T. Harris (1977). *Organizational transitions: Managing complex change.* Reading, Mass.: Addison-Wesley.
4. Lewin, K. (1951). *Field theory in social science.* New York: Harper and Row.
5. Beckhard and Harris (see reference 3).
6. Lippitt, R., J. Watson, and B. Westley (1958). *The dynamics of planned change.* New York: Harcourt, Brace and World.
7. Kolb, D. and A. Frohman (1970). "An organization development approach to consulting," *Sloan Management Review.* 12, pp. 51–65.
8. Argyris, C. (1970). *Intervention theory and method: A behavioral science view.* Reading, Mass: Addison-Wesley.
9. Shani, A. and G. Bushe (Spring 1987). "Visionary action research: A consultation process perspective," *Consultation.* 6, pp. 3–19.
10. French, W. (Winter, 1969). "Organization development: Objectives, assumptions and strategies," *California Management Review.* 12, p. 26.
11. Cummings, T.G. and E.F. Huse (1989). *Organization development and change,* 4th edition. St. Paul, Minn.: West Publishing, p. 51.
12. Bullock, R.J. and D. Batten (December 1985). "It's just a phase we're going through: Review and synthesis of OD phase analysis," *Group and Organization Studies,* 10, pp. 383–412.
13. Beer, M. (1980). *Organization change and development: A systems view.* Santa Monica, Calif.: Goodyear Publishing, pp. 58–59.
14. Bennis, W.G., D. Benne, and R. Chin, Eds. (1961). *The planning of change.* New York: Holt, Rinehart and Winston.
15. Beckhard and Harris (see reference 3).
16. IMTEC–The International Learning Cooperative (Spring 1988). *IMTEC Newsletter.* Oslo, Norway, p. 1.

CHAPTER 11

INTERPERSONAL AND GROUP DYNAMICS FOR CHANGE AGENTS

A BASIC PHILOSOPHY FOR INTERPERSONAL COMMUNICATION DURING CHANGE

Although the technical skills for redesigning a school district are difficult, communicating during times of complex change is even more challenging. Although miscommunication is common in human interactions, the potential for miscommunication during a redesign effort is significantly increased because of the inherent psychological stress for those directly involved in the effort. Developing or improving your interpersonal communication skills can reduce miscommunication, conflict, and stress during the redesign process.

If you want to increase your interpersonal effectiveness, you need a clear understanding of basic principles of communication. You also need to be aware of the implications of your role as a change agent and facilitator of human potential. Your communication tasks include helping people become more aware of their own resources, more sensitive to obstacles that prevent them from increasing their professional effectiveness, and more open to new ideas.

Your relationships with people in the district during the redesign project should be based on basic beliefs about people and about how one facilitates changes in attitudes, concepts, and skills. The relationship is based on a belief that the redesign effort is enhanced by shared problem-solving approaches and is *always* impeded by inappropriate superior–subordinate dynamics. During the redesign effort, teachers and other staff do not need to be told what to do; rather, you collaborate with them in a partnership to redesign the district in meaningful and lasting ways. Teachers' concerns can never be addressed effectively by any superficial approach that assumes administrators have all the answers and that the task of the teacher is to listen attentively and follow orders.

This chapter is not a primer on effective interpersonal communication skills. Instead, it highlights several critical communication issues that can have a serious impact on your school district reengineering project.

THE EMOTIONAL ASPECTS OF CHANGE

The Emotions of People Responding to Change

Many times we underestimate the emotional impact that change has on people. Yet, it is at the emotional level that people accept or resist change. Emotions affect the transition phase of a change effort in particular. During the transition from the present to the future, there are seven predictable emotional responses to changes:

1. **Paralysis**—When presented with massive change, people often react first by freezing in their tracks. This effect is often seen in the behaviors of people who become severe procrastinators when confronted with an enormous amount of change.

2. **Denial**—This emotional response is captured in comments such as "If we hold out long enough, this change will never happen," or "This, too, shall pass," or "There's no way they can make us do that."

3. **Despondency**—After people realize they have to change, they may experience feelings of depression or despondency. People begin to feel melancholy about the past—they begin to miss what they had, or what they think they had.

4. **Acceptance**—After working through their feelings of despondency, people begin to accept the reality of the situation. They see that changes have to be made and that they must participate in the process if they want to benefit. This is the point at which optimism begins to return.

5. **Experimenting**—The next phase of emotional reaction is to experiment with new behaviors, new structures, and new ways of doing things. People begin looking for ways of coping with the new situation that is evolving.

6. **Searching**—After experimenting with new arrangements and behaviors, people begin trying to understand what is happening and what has happened to them. They begin to search for meaning in the midst of change.

7. **Incorporating**—Finally, people accept and understand the changes. They have developed new attitudes, concepts, and skills. Now, with proper reinforcement, these changes are internalized and become part of their normal, daily behavior.

Although people do not move cleanly from one phase to the next, generally they experience each phase. Consequently, these feelings need to be anticipated by developing contingency plans for responding to these feelings when they are manifested.

The Emotions of People Planning and Managing Change

The people responding to change requirements are not the only ones who experience strong emotional reactions. The people planning and managing the redesign project will have emotional responses, too. They may experience the following emotions:

1. **Certainty**—At the beginning of a redesign effort, the Redesign Management Team (RMT) members will feel totally optimistic about what they can achieve and about the amount of time they have to accomplish the changes. This feeling of certainty results in an almost euphoric sense of optimism.

2. **Doubt**—After getting into the messiness of complex change, RMT members begin to have serious doubts about what they got themselves into. They begin to question their motivation, doubt their

abilities to carry out the redesign agenda, and feel that they have bitten off more than they can chew.

3. **Hope**—If RMT members persevere through the "doubt phase," they begin to see that although they may not be able to accomplish everything they had hoped for, they still can achieve some important goals and objectives. With this realization comes the return of hope.

4. **Confidence**—As the RMT continues with the redesign effort and as team members experience success, their level of confidence in themselves and in the redesign process increases. With confidence intact, the RMT moves steadfastly toward completion of the redesign effort.

5. **Satisfaction**—There is a great deal of psychological satisfaction in experiencing closure. Seeing a change effort to its successful completion provides an extraordinary "high." This feeling of satisfaction should be heightened by celebrating and rewarding completion of the redesign project. This act of psychological closure is often ignored to the detriment of the people involved and affects their future willingness to help solve problems for the organization. Members of the Steering Committee and RMT need to have this sense of closure and satisfaction after investing immense time and energy in the reengineering project. In addition, the faculty and staff who supported the redesign project also need to celebrate the successful completion of the redesign process.

RESISTANCE TO CHANGE

People resist change. Resistance is normal, healthy, and predictable. However, if you want your redesign effort to be successful, you must understand the sources of resistance and design ways to manage it.

Resistance is a symptom that tells you it is time to listen carefully to people to find out what is bothering them. Generally, people tend to resist change for three reasons:

- They are not convinced of the need to change.

- They fear damage to their relationships with friends and colleagues.

- They fear losing status, power, prestige, privileges, or their ability to use what they have worked so hard to learn about the organization. They may also fear damage to their careers.

Blockages to Change

Another way to understand resistance to change is to think of the resistance as blockages to change. There are two kinds of blockages you can experience during your effort to redesign your school district: personal and organizational.

Personal Blockages—Examples of these blockages are as follows:

- **Fear of failure**—People have a need to avoid the pain of failure. Consequently, they lay low, avoid risk taking, and often settle for less than what they might achieve.

- **Rigid perceptions**—Some people have rigid perceptions that cloud their insight, foresight, and hindsight. Often, these perceptions take the form of negative stereotypes that are used for making judgments about people and events. They make assumptions about people and attribute motivations to others without checking the accuracy or validity of their assumptions and attributions.

- **Fear of the unknown**—Some people have a strong need for clarity before they can proceed toward some hazy future. These people tend to resist or avoid change efforts that push them toward a fuzzy future. They need to know about the place you want them to go to before they start moving in that direction.

- **Need for structure and clarity**—Some people cannot tolerate ambiguity, disorder, or confusion. In the messy world of organizational change, these people become resistant to the redesign process because it lacks the order, symmetry, and clarity they need.

- **Pain avoidance**—Everyone has the need to avoid pain and seek pleasure. These are the two most basic human motivations. Change efforts are often painful or potentially painful. Thus, those who perceive the potential for a lot of pain will resist the change effort.

Organizational Blockages—There are four examples of blockages that are based in the culture of the organization:

- **Negative view of assertive behavior**—The culture of some organizations places a negative value on assertive or "pushy" behavior. When people responsible for planning change are perceived as being pushy, this perception results in resistance.

- **Lack of a shared vision**—If the organization does not have a clear vision of a desired future, or if the vision held by the decision makers is not shared by other members of the organization, then resistance emerges.

- **"Quick-fix" addiction**—Some organizations are addicted to the "quick fix." People in these organizations expect quick solutions to difficult problems. When the proposed changes do not promise quick solutions, resistance surfaces.

- **Excessive rationality**—The culture of some organizations is built on the cult of rationality. Every decision must be a rational one. Every action must be completely thought through so that there will be absolutely no surprises. There is no room for emotional or personal issues in the change planning process. When a change effort becomes messy, ambiguous, or charged with emotional electricity, an organization with this kind of culture becomes the wellspring of significant resistance to change.

Responding to Resistance

Resistance in organizations traditionally is seen as something to overcome. But it can be a positive force to strengthen people and meet goals. Karp[1] says managers can work with resistants—rather than against them—and achieve greater individual satisfaction and group effectiveness. Karp maintains, however, that resistance is not valued in organizations. Consequently, managers use three low-yield strategies for reducing or overcoming it. First, they may try to break down the resistance by making threats, coercing, selling, or reasoning. Second, managers sometimes try to avoid resistance by deflecting it using tactics such as ignoring it or inflicting guilt on the resistants. Third, managers might try to minimize the resistance by discounting the value or strength of it, by appealing to tradition, or by suggesting the need for unanimity. Although each of these strategies might produce temporary reductions in resistance, they rarely result in long-term solutions, are often costly, and may produce deeper resistance later.

Karp states two basic assumptions critical to forming an effective response to resistance. First, it must be assumed that people will always resist those efforts that are perceived as not being in their best interest. Second, it must be assumed that resistance should be honored and dealt with respectfully. Acting with these two assumptions as the basis of your response, resistance can become something that is positive and helpful to the change effort.

Karp's strategy for working with resistance has four steps, as follows.

1. Surface the Resistance—After beginning the planning phase of your redesign effort you must get the resistance out in the open. This is difficult because many people have been conditioned to believe that resistance is a negative thing and must be kept a secret. Others will fear retribution for expressing their resistance openly. Thus, you have to make it as safe as possible for people to express their resistance to the changes you are proposing. Be straightforward in expressing the direction of the redesign effort. State exactly what you expect to happen and ask people to tell you about any problems they see. Finally, keep asking people to express their resistance, and *avoid taking retribution* against anyone who takes the risk of publicly expressing their resistance in professionally acceptable ways.

2. Honor the Resistance—Resistance is honored in several ways. First, *listen—listen—listen.* You must develop active listening skills, one of which is to shut off your inner voice that keeps talking to you at the same time others are trying to talk to you. Also, resistance is honored by *not* trying to restate your original position in response to others' expressions of concern. Listen to what people have to say, demonstrate that you have heard and understood them, and accept their comments as valid expressions of their concerns.

Another aspect of honoring the resistance is to acknowledge it. Acknowledging the expressions of resistance is the only way you can show you have truly heard what has been said. Many aspects of acknowledgment use non-verbal cues (e.g., maintaining good eye contact, periodically expressing an "uh-hmm," or gently nodding your head). Verbally, you can acknowledge resistance by occasionally paraphrasing or restating what has been said to you or by asking relevant questions. Finally, one word of caution: Do not lead resistants to believe that you agree or support their views if you do not. You can acknowledge the validity of their perceptions without agreeing with them.

The final aspect of honoring resistance is to reinforce the "okayness" of the resistance. It is important to remember that resistance is normal, healthy, and predictable. People should not be made to feel inferior or disloyal because of their resistance to change. Therefore, it is good for your relationships to state periodically your belief that resistance is okay. Resistance is not okay, however, when the resistants become abusive, contemptuous, or destructive (suggestions on how to manage conflict situations are found in a later section of this chapter).

3. Explore the Resistance—Karp defines two kinds of resistance: pseudo-resistance and authentic resistance. To understand which of the two types you are up against, you must assess the nature of the resistance you are experiencing.

Pseudo-resistance has nothing to do with the redesign goals you are proposing. Usually, this kind of resistance is related to a resistant's past feelings toward some other event or person in the school district (e.g., a general mistrust of people, a learning style that demands concrete examples rather than abstract reports, a personality that requires lots of facts before making decisions, or resentment toward authority). Authentic resistance, on the other hand, is an expression of strength from the resistant, and it is directed specifically to the situation at hand. Once you figure out which type of resistance you are facing, then you can respond appropriately. You respond to pseudo-resistance by temporarily putting it aside as irrelevant to your change effort. You respond to authentic resistance by addressing it directly and authentically.

You continue your exploration of authentic resistance by engaging the resistant in the examination of his or her perceptions. Karp suggests two specific questions to probe authentic resistance: "What is your objection?" and "What would you prefer?"

The first question compels the resistant to respond specifically. If the response remains vague, continue to probe for clarity and specificity. The second question puts the resistant in a position of making a concrete recommendation that responds to specific concerns.

After surfacing, acknowledging, and exploring all of the authentic resistance, you must emphasize the positive nature of your change proposals. Inquire about what the resistant sees as positive about the change proposals or ask if there is any part of the proposals that might benefit the resistant's department or school. Avoid questions that start with "why" because these questions put resistants on the defensive. Instead, use questions that start with "how" or "what." Also, avoid leading questions, such as "Don't you think that...?"

4. Recheck—After completing the above steps in working with resistance, you and the resistant need to assess where you are in the process. Chances are that all parties have had some changes in their perceptions of the change effort. It is critical in this final step to ensure mutual understanding of what is to be done and what support is needed to make the change effort happen. If you do not accommodate any of the resistant's concerns, you should expect resistance to continue. Even if you do accommodate the resistant's concerns, you can expect some resistance to remain; however, it will not have the power it had before, and even if it does not diminish, it should, at least, not increase.

CONFLICT

Conflict is a natural consequence of any change process that produces emotional responses in people. Fear, anxiety, lack of communication, differing perceptions, differing values, differing personality styles, and differing expectations can all cause conflict.

Within every conflict situation there are opportunities for growth, change, and improvement. Managing conflict in a positive manner so people exit the conflict situation with their egos intact is an important leadership skill. When managed properly, conflict can motivate and energize people, provide a diversity of viewpoints that enriches the pool of possible solutions to a problem, set the stage for supporting opinions with facts, and help create mutual understanding among those who differ.

Ways to Manage Conflict

There are several different approaches to managing conflict. Two are described below. The first model, developed by Walton,[2] is called the *dialogue model*. The second is derived from the teachings of a Japanese martial art called *ki-aikido*,[3] as described by Thomas Crum.[4]

The Dialogue Model—Walton proposes that interpersonal conflict occurs in a repetitive cycle where issues confront a person. One or more of the issues serve as triggering events that lead to conflict behavior. The conflict behavior produces consequences, and the consequences raise new issues. The new issues become trigger points for more conflict, and so on.

Walton's model has four strategies for resolving conflict. The strategies are often employed by a neutral third party. The first three strategies attempt to control the conflict, whereas the last one attempts to change the underlying issues causing the conflict.

- **Strategy 1**—Prevent the conflict by seeking a clear understanding of the factors that trigger conflict; thereafter, modify the triggering stimuli to prevent the conflict from emerging.

- **Strategy 2**—Set limits on the form of conflict by, for example, setting rules of engagement or having informal meetings prior to the formal meeting during which conflict is expected to emerge.

- **Strategy 3**—Help the parties in conflict handle the consequences of conflict in a different manner.

- **Strategy 4**—Attempt to eliminate or resolve the underlying issues causing the conflict.

The Aiki Approach—Morihei Ueshiba[5] (the founder of *aikido*) and Koichi Tohei[6] (one of Ueshiba's top students and founder of *aikido* with *ki* or *ki-aikido*) teach us how to respond to conflict situations. Essentially, we are taught to avoid moving directly into an attack by blending with the attacker's energy so we can control the situation and bring it to a non-injurious, non-deadly conclusion. These principles have been interpreted and applied to common interpersonal conflicts by Thomas Crum.[7] Crum gives us several principles, derived from *ki-aikido*, for dealing with common, everyday conflicts:

- **Choose to be centered**—Centering occurs when the mind, body, and spirit become fully unified and connected to the world around us. Have you ever experienced reading a book and suddenly find your mind someplace else? This is *not* being centered. When you are fully focused on what you are doing, this *is* being centered. In conflict situations, you want to be fully focused and in the present moment—you do not want your mind to be someplace else.

- **Accept your connectedness**—Even in conflict, we are connected to the other person, no matter how diligently we work to separate ourselves. How often have you been in an argument where you are fighting to prove you are right and the other person is fighting just as hard to prove that he or she is? In situations like this, neither of you is listening because inner voices are racing ahead of you trying to formulate your next retort. You only see the differences between yourselves, and the more you struggle to be right, the farther you drive yourselves apart. Yet, according to Crum, the reality is that the two of you are connected by virtue of being in the conflict. Accepting and increasing the connectedness you have with the other person will always support the resolution of conflict.

- **Practice and cherish discovery**—Discovery means leaving yourself open to learning about others. It means allowing your belief system to be flexible and open minded. Rigid belief systems are the root of violence.[8] Belief systems create boundaries between you and others. Some people, ideas, values, and so forth fall inside those boundaries, while others are outside. In a rigid belief system, anything that threatens your boundaries is attacked or defended against. Discovery is a way of creating permeable boundaries that allows new ideas, beliefs, and so forth to enter into your world, a condition that is critical to the effective resolution of conflict.

- **Be willing to understand**—If you want to resolve conflict, you must be willing to understand the other person. One way to do this is to practice being appreciative of the other person's perspective. Move off your position to explore honestly and sincerely the feelings, interests, beliefs, and values of the other person. Once you move off the line of attack and try to explore the other's perspective, you begin to see commonalities. When you see commonalties, you are taking the first step toward conflict resolution.

- **Be willing to change**—Conflict is nature's prime motivator to change. If you are in a conflict situation, you have to be willing to change so that you can handle the situation. For example, have you ever tried to jump onto a moving merry-go-round while standing still? The way to get on a merry-go-round is to change your position in relation to the carousel by starting to run alongside of it. Then, when your speed is in proper relation to the speed of the carousel, you can hop on with ease. The same principle applies to a verbal attack in a meeting. To manage or reduce the conflict, you have to adjust the tempo of your response to match the tempo of the attack so that you can "join" with the attacker by blending his or her attack energy with your defense energy.

- **Choose to co-create**—According to Crum, choosing co-creation is an obvious step toward conflict resolution. Cooperating to resolve the conflict leads to significant benefits for both parties. It takes time, energy, and hard work to cooperate in a conflict situation because of the emotional context of that event. By joining with the other person's energy to co-create solutions, rather than remaining part of the problem, you move one step closer to positive conflict resolution.

MEETING MANAGEMENT

What Is a Meeting?

A meeting is any gathering of two or more people for the purpose of giving, receiving, or exchanging information; for solving problems; or for making decisions. Meetings can be formal or informal and can last for varying amounts of time. *Formal* meetings are announced in advance, have agendas prepared and distributed in advance of the meeting, and have minutes (or meeting summaries) distributed after the meeting concludes (usually within 24 hours). *Informal* meetings can be called at a moment's notice. Even though they are informal, the same general principles for conducting effective meetings still apply.

Whether formal or informal, meetings need to be effective. An effective meeting meets the following three criteria:

- The purpose and desired outcomes of the meeting are achieved.

- A minimum amount of time has been used to conduct the meeting.

- The participants and leader are satisfied with the meeting.

When Is a Meeting Necessary?

A meeting should be called only when you need people together at the same time and place to do the following:

- Exchange information (that cannot be exchanged in some other manner)
- Make a decision

- Solve a problem
- Resolve a conflict situation
- Conduct training
- Celebrate a "win"
- Build team effectiveness

Do not call a meeting when:

- The information to be shared can be distributed easily and clearly using other means (e.g., in letters, memoranda, face to face, over the telephone, in reports, or on bulletin boards)
- People who are key players for the meeting are not available
- There is not enough time to adequately prepare for the meeting
- People are too angry or upset to interact
- The purpose or need for the meeting is not clear

To determine whether or not to hold a meeting, ask yourself this question: What is the worst that would happen if there was no meeting? If you can live with the answer, do not hold a meeting.

Simple Solutions to Common Meeting Problems

Many of the problems associated with meetings are solved using simple solutions. These solutions are described below.

1. Prepare an Agenda—An agenda is essential. It should include the purpose, desired outcomes of the meeting, items to discuss with time allotments for each item, and a description of the process by which the desired outcomes will be achieved. The agenda serves as a road map for keeping the meeting focused. The agenda is prepared in advance and distributed before the meeting. If a meeting is called on the spur of the moment, one of the first activities for the group is to build an agenda for the emergency meeting.

Agendas are built in two ways. First, at the end of a meeting, a tentative agenda for the next meeting can be outlined. Second, after a meeting but before the next meeting, participants are surveyed for possible agenda items.

2. Review and Clarify the Purpose and Desired Outcomes of the Meeting—Always begin a meeting by reviewing the purpose and desired outcomes of the meeting. Then, move to a review of the agenda items. Modify the agenda if needed.

3. Limit the Number of Participants—Meeting participants should be limited to those people who are key players for the meeting. Limiting meeting participation to the key players ensures that people's time is not wasted. For information-sharing meetings, those who must attend include employees who need to know the information being discussed. For action meetings, those who need to attend include people who will be responsible for the decision or problem being discussed or who can make a significant contribution to the decision-making or problem-solving process.

4. Determine Roles for Participants to Play—It is important to consider the functions or tasks that need to be performed during a meeting. These functions or tasks need to be delegated or assumed by meeting participants. This is done by asking people to assume the following critical roles:

 a. **Leader/chairperson**—This person plays a critical role before, during, and after the meeting. Before the meeting, the leader determines the purpose and desired outcomes of the meeting, solicits input for the agenda from participants, plans and distributes the agenda, and determines process roles for the meeting. During the meeting, the leader:
 • Maintains authority to set limits and change the format of the meeting if it is not proceeding productively
 • Makes all final decisions about managing the meeting
 • Is an active participant in the meeting when seeking consensus on decisions or during collaborative problem-solving discussions
 • Urges participants to accept tasks and deadlines
 • Holds participants accountable by ensuring responsibilities and time lines are clearly understood
 • Leads the information-sharing portion of the meeting

 b. **Participant**—Participants play a key role in a meeting, too. Ultimately, the quality of their participation determines the quality of the meeting. The specific responsibilities of participants include:
 • Preparing adequately for meetings
 • Listening openly to the ideas of others

- Contributing ideas to the discussion
- Behaving in ways that are consistent with agreed upon ground rules
- Using effective group discussion skills

c. **Facilitator**—In some meetings, the same person holds the roles of the leader/chairperson and the facilitator. However, when the following conditions exist, it is advisable to use a neutral facilitator:
  - The meeting leader is highly invested in the content of the meeting and, therefore, has a need to participate actively and freely in the meeting
  - The meeting is totally devoted to problem solving or planning
  - A high degree of interpersonal conflict is expected

  The neutral facilitator can come from outside the group but inside the organization, from outside the organization, or from inside the group. The role of the facilitator is to:
  - Assist the chairperson in planning the meeting
  - Observe the group process and intervene when there is a breakdown in the process
  - Ensure that ground rules are observed
  - Protect participants from personal attack
  - Suggest methods and procedures for increasing the effectiveness of the meeting
  - Make sure that everyone has an opportunity to participate
  - Lead the problem-solving or decision-making portions of the meeting, thereby allowing the leader to act as a participant

  The facilitator's role is to assist the group and act more like a coach than a quarterback.

d. **Recorder**—During the meeting, the recorder transcribes important information for the group. Some examples of responsibilities often assumed by recorders are:
  - Summarizing agreements and commitments made during the meeting
  - At the close of a meeting, reviewing actions agreed upon by the team for the purpose of confirming responsibilities and time lines
  - Taking minutes

  This role is rotated among team members.

e. **Timekeeper**—The person filling this role does the following:
   - Monitors the amount of time the group spends on each agenda item
   - Periodically reminds the group about the amount of time used and about how much time is remaining (remember, always start and end meetings on time!)

5. Set Ground Rules for Interacting—It is very important for a new team to establish and review ground rules for interacting in meetings. The following are examples of ground rules for managing meetings:

a. Everyone arrives early and stays for the entire meeting.

b. No one can be called out of a meeting except for extreme emergencies.

c. Everyone shares in providing leadership to the team during the meeting.

d. Everyone can speak their mind about agenda items, but personal attacks are not permitted.

e. During the meeting, the ultimate goal is to ensure that the team conducts a highly effective meeting.

6. Manage Time Effectively—There is an old saying about meetings: "The amount of work tends to expand to fill the available time." This means that if you have a half hour's worth of agenda items and two hours of available meeting time, the meeting will last two hours—and then some. To prevent this phenomenon from occurring (and it does occur!), you need to manage the agenda and manage time.

Here are some ways to approach time management in a meeting:

a. *Always* start the meeting on time. Reward the people who made an effort to be there on time by starting on time instead of rewarding the late arrivals by postponing the starting time to accommodate their lateness.

b. Post the agenda in a conspicuous place and continually refer to it.

c. Repeatedly remind people of the agenda and the amount of time allotted for each agenda item. Keep the ending time clearly in your mind.

d. Allow people to digress from the agenda from time to time, but always bring them back to the agenda. Don't allow people to persevere on tangential discussions.

e. *Never* stop the meeting to summarize for late arrivals. Let them find out what they missed on their own time.

7. Keep Minutes—Someone must keep a record of the meeting's proceedings. Minutes should not be a verbatim, running description of everything that is discussed in the meeting. Instead, they should only highlight important discussions and decisions. Use the following sample list of categories to organize minutes:

a. Members present

b. Members absent

c. Purpose of meeting

d. Desired outcome(s)

e. Agenda

f. Discussion items (summaries of *significant* discussions related to the agenda)

g. Decision items (summaries of decisions made by the group—make sure you link relevant discussion items to decisions that resulted from the discussions)

h. Agreements and commitments (a list made by meeting participants)

The minutes should be typed and distributed within 24 hours of the conclusion of the meeting.

8. End the Meeting with a Summary—People have a psychological need for closure. Completing an agenda is important closure. People are very often frustrated by meetings that never accomplish their agenda. Work hard to ensure that the agenda is completed.

Another way to provide closure is to summarize what happened during the meeting by restating the meeting's purpose and desired outcomes and highlighting the group's progress toward meeting the purpose and outcomes. Include in the summary a reiteration of the agreements and commitments that were made.

Improving the Meetings You Conduct or Attend

Participants have a responsibility to help make their meetings more productive and satisfying. Here is some specific guidance on how to improve meetings that you attend as a participant:

- Prepare for the meeting.
- Use effective communication skills during the meeting.
- Contribute to the discussion.
- Listen actively.
- Consider others' opinions objectively.
- Provide feedback to the leader on the conduct of the meeting.
- Follow through on commitments.
- Comply with ground rules.
- Arrive on time and do not allow yourself to be called out of the meeting.
- Avoid side conversations that compete with other speakers.
- Keep your mind focused on the discussion.
- Be supportive of others' efforts to participate.
- Take notes.

GROUP PROBLEM SOLVING AND DECISION MAKING

Redesign Management Teams and Steering Committees will be confronted with problems to solve and decisions to make. Decisions (including decisions during problem-solving meetings) should be of the highest quality; they should meet the following criteria:

1. The problem is solved.

2. It is solved within existing human, technical, and financial constraints.

3. It is solved in such a way that people's feelings about the problem-solving process are not diminished and preferably are enhanced.[9]

A good decision that is not implemented is worthless. A decision that does not resolve the problem it is addressing is ineffective. A decision that solves a problem at extraordinary costs is inefficient and harmful. A decision-making process that solves a problem but leaves people feeling bitter and resentful about how the decision was reached is contrary to principles of effective group dynamics.

This section contains information about six different decision-making methods: lack of response, authority rule, minority rule, majority rule, unanimous decision, and consensus.[10]

Problem-Solving Methods

Methods for Generating Alternatives

To make a decision implies having alternative courses of action from which to choose. Developing multiple alternatives for the decision-making process is one of the challenges facing a RMT or a Steering Committee. Several structured approaches to generate alternatives for solving problems are nominal group technique, delphi technique, dialectical inquiry, and devil's advocacy. Let's look at each of these methods.

Nominal Group Technique[11]—This technique is structured to awaken creative decision making within a team. It is useful in situations where team members cannot agree or where individual team members have incomplete information about an issue or problem. There are five steps in the process:

- Team members write their ideas and potential solutions to a problem on a personal note pad.

- Each team member reads aloud his or her ideas and solutions. No criticism or discussion is permitted.

- The facilitator records all of the comments on a flip chart as each team member talks.

- After posting all of the input, the ideas and solutions are openly discussed for clarification only. No one is permitted to evaluate any of the ideas.

- Using a prescribed written voting procedure, team members prioritize each idea or potential solution. The facilitator then tabulates the votes to develop a prioritized list for the entire team. Occasionally, after discussing the prioritized list, a second vote is taken. This vote then represents the team's decision and provides the group with a sense of closure.

This technique has been shown to be effective with complex problems that have many elements. It seems to be less useful with simpler problems.[12]

Delphi Technique[13]—This approach was developed at the Rand Corporation. Its purpose is to allow groups to make decisions without face-to-face meetings. It even works in situations where people who need to be involved in a decision-making process are in different geographic locations. There are four major steps:

- The facilitator prepares and sends a questionnaire that states the problem and asks for alternative solutions.
- The facilitator summarizes all of the solutions that he or she receives.
- The facilitator sends the summary to all participants and requests additional input.
- The input from the second round of responses is then summarized and sent out a third time with another request for additional input. This process continues by repeating Steps 3 and 4 until consensus is achieved.

This is a wearisome process because of the many rounds of "input–summarize–more input" that are required. It also depends on written communication, which, of course, has its limitations.

Dialectical Inquiry[14]—This technique and devil's advocacy were both developed to handle complex, strategic decisions. They both rely on passionate debate among team members. Dialectical inquiry follows these steps:

- The facilitator divides the team in half.
- One of the subgroups writes out its recommended solution to a problem and includes its assumptions and supporting data.
- The other subgroup is directed to identify credible assumptions that negate the other group's ideas. This group of respondents also prepares its own recommendations that counter the first group's solutions.

- Both subgroups present their reasoning to each other, orally and in writing. Then they conduct a debate.

- The two subgroups then strive to reach agreement on the assumptions or ideas that survive the debate. Then, these assumptions or ideas become the basis for recommended decision alternatives.

- The recommendations that move forward are put in writing.

Devil's Advocacy[15]—This technique is similar to dialectical inquiry, but with some distinct differences. These differences are reflected in the steps in the process:

- The group is divided in half.

- One subgroup develops a set of recommendations for solving the problem and an argument to support its position.

- The first subgroup presents its recommendations to the second subgroup.

- The second subgroup critiques the recommendations by trying to expose everything that is wrong with them.

- The first subgroup reviews the critique and uses the input to revise its recommendations.

- The above steps are repeated until everyone is satisfied with the surviving recommendations.

- The facilitator records the surviving recommendations.

This technique, like dialectical inquiry, can really generate a lot of heated debate, but it can also result in some high-quality solutions to problems. One research study reported that both the dialectical inquiry and devil's advocacy approaches resulted in higher quality decision alternatives than the consensus method of decision making. However, the same study discovered that the consensus approach resulted in higher satisfaction among the participants and a greater desire to continue working together.[16] Since a solution to a problem is only effective if it is implemented and since consensus methods clearly affect team members' willingness to work together (thereby having an effect on implementation efforts), using consensus methods for generating decision alternatives may be better than using approaches like dialectical inquiry and devil's advocacy.

Brainstorming—This technique is useful for producing creative or imaginative solutions to organizational problems. A very strict set of rules for conducting brainstorming sessions promotes the generation of ideas and simultaneously reduces team members' inhibitions for sharing ideas. The basic rules are:

- Encourage freewheeling thinking—don't hold back on ideas. Get as many ideas as possible out on the table no matter how silly or farfetched they may seem.

- Write *all* ideas that are vocalized on a flip chart and post the chart where all members of the team can see them.

- Do not discuss the ideas that are generated while they are being posted.

- Do not evaluate any of the ideas that are posted.

- Let people build on others' ideas.

Here's the general sequence of events for a brainstorming session:

- Define and clarify the problem statement. This is often best done in the form of a question asking why, what, or how (for example, "What is the best way to increase the effectiveness of instructional supervision in our redesigned school?").

- Give the team a couple of minutes to reflect on the problem statement.

- Start the brainstorming by inviting people to contribute. Enforce the rules listed above.

- One team member acts as a recorder.

- After concluding the brainstorming, begin using one of the other decision-making techniques described in this chapter to narrow down the alternatives and, finally, to select a solution for which there is consensus.

Decision-Making Methods

Once a RMT has alternative courses of action to consider, it needs to decide which alternatives to implement. Several decision-making methods are described below.

Lack of Response—Silence, in the letter of the law, is agreement. This observation applies to decisions that are made by a lack of response. Another way of describing this method is to label it "decision by default." Basically, it means an idea is accepted if no one speaks either for or against it. With decisions made this way, it is difficult to assess the quality or level of acceptance of the idea. It might be a good idea that is ignored or it might be ignored because it is a bad idea. This kind of decision making usually occurs when the idea that is suggested is not very controversial. People internally feel "Yeah, okay. That's fine. Nothing needs to be said. Let's move on to more important issues."

Authority Rule—The leader makes the decision for the group. This kind of directive leadership often occurs when a group is stuck in its process and cannot figure a way out. This method works only if the leader has enough information to make an informed and effective decision. Otherwise, the leader's decision can be a poor one.

Another significant problem with this method is getting team members to accept ownership of the decision when it is time to implement it. Compliance with the decision depends on the leader's position of power, relationships with team members, and communication skills.

Minority Rule—This method is often called "railroading."[17] Minority rule permits a few team members to make the decision for the entire team. Again, as with the authority rule approach, if the minority group has all the information it needs and has a good relationship with the rest of the team members, then this decision method can work well. But this is a big "if." Often, with decisions made this way, people who did not make the decision feel coerced or intimidated. Examples of these feelings are especially prevalent in organizational environments where "political correctness" is the norm, whereby decisions are made that support the political agenda of minority groups. (Minority, in this context, does not mean racial, ethnic, or gender minorities. It refers to the number of people supporting a particular decision—minority versus majority.)

Minority rule decisions are also experienced in situations where there is a dominant coalition (or clique) within the organization. The word "dominant" does not mean majority; it refers to the amount of influence a group has. Most people can think of examples of powerful cliques in their organization that have significant influence on the decision-making process even though the membership in those groups is small.

Majority Rule—People can be just as upset with decisions made by majority rule as those made by minority rule. Whenever there is a vote of any kind to make a decision, thereby creating a "majority in favor" of a decision, winners and losers are created. If the losers feel their opinions were not listened to or considered carefully, or if they feel they were "bulldozed" by the majority, feelings of resentment or anger can result.

This method, if used properly, can work very well. It is, after all, the core decision-making method of our democratic society—the decision-making principle upon which our governmental processes are based. The key is to allow sufficient time for people to present and argue their points. Participants need to feel they had a chance to convince their colleagues of the merits of their ideas, values, beliefs, opinions, and so forth. If discussion and debate are cut short and an early vote is forced, feelings of anger, resentment, or lack of commitment to the decision may surface.

Unanimous Decision—With this approach, the entire team supports a particular alternative. With this high level of acceptance, a unanimous decision can be relatively easy to implement (in terms of getting the support needed for implementation). One problem with getting a unanimous decision, however, especially for complex issues, is that a great deal of discussion needs to occur before people feel comfortable throwing all of their support behind the decision.

Another problem with using this approach is that the team can often succumb to a group dynamic called "groupthink."[18] Groupthink occurs when the team's value for cohesion takes precedence over an honest appraisal of alternative courses of action. This phenomenon makes team members feel invulnerable. It also intimidates team members into complying with the team's wishes no matter how distorted or incorrect they may be.

Janis[19] describes the symptoms of groupthink and the potential hazards associated with each symptom:

- **The illusion of invulnerability that is shared by all or most of the members of the group**—This results in excessive optimism and extreme risk taking.

- **Collective efforts to rationalize the group's course of action**—This results in warnings being ignored.

- **Unwillingness to reconsider the assumptions underlying the course of action**—This results in group members recommitting themselves to past policy decisions without considering alternatives.

- **An unquestioned belief in the group's inherent morality**—This leads to members ignoring the ethical and moral consequences of their decisions.

- **Stereotyping of the "enemy" as evil, weak, or stupid**—This shuts off the possibility of negotiating with the "enemy" and results in an underestimation of the "enemy's" ability to pursue his or her goals or to resist attack.

- **Suppression of dissent within the group by applying direct pressure on "disloyal" members**—The consequence of this action is that group members hesitate to express any arguments against any of the group's stereotypes, illusions, or commitments.

- **Self-censorship of views that deviate from the group's apparent consensus**—When this happens, individuals censor their thoughts and feelings before expressing them. This results in other group members falsely assuming that the individual's silence means consent.

- **Shared illusion of unanimity and self-appointed "mind guards"**—These symptoms insulate group members from adverse information that might shatter their shared complacency about the effectiveness and morality of their decisions.

Consensus—One way to avoid groupthink is to use consensus decision-making techniques. William Ouchi[20] says that consensus is reached when team members accept (not necessarily fully agree with) a single solution or decision and each can say:

- I believe that you understand my point of view.

- I believe that I understand your point of view.

- Whether or not I prefer this decision, I will support it because it was reached openly and fairly.

- This decision or solution does not require me to compromise strong convictions or needs.

Reaching consensus does not mean unanimous agreement or majority rules. Instead, the team achieves consensus when a decision is made that everyone can live with and is willing to implement.

With complex problems or issues, consensus is probably the best that a team leader can hope for because seeking unanimity consumes too much time and resources. Furthermore, consensus decisions tend to be worth the effort because the process often results in high-quality decisions with a high level of commitment from team members.[21]

Consensus is gained by following these steps:

- Clarify the problem that is being discussed.

- Anticipate that discussion will take a lot of time. Allow time for people to state their opinions and beliefs openly and fully.

- Support differences of opinion as being valid and important to the team's decision-making process.

- Listen actively to others' viewpoints. Keep an open mind while seeking to understand another's perspective.

- Avoid arguments that are aimed at "getting your own way."

- Do not back down from conflicts of opinion; disagree without being disagreeable.

- Avoid conflict-reducing techniques like taking a "majority wins" vote, averaging everyone's priorities, using power plays, or flipping a coin.

- Be skeptical if the team reaches agreement too early on a complex problem.

- Test for consensus by asking participants where they stand. Do not misconstrue a nod of the head or silence as representing consensus—get a verbal response from everyone.

Consensus is best used:

- For making decisions about how the team should function

- Where effective implementation of a decision requires strong support from team members

- When you want team members to feel a sense of ownership for a decision

Multivoting and criteria rating forms are two tools for reaching consensus.

Multivoting[22]—This tool is used to reduce a long list of alternatives to a manageable number. It is useful after a technique like brainstorming, where many alternatives are available. Here are the steps in the process:

- Review each alternative and clarify those that are vague.

- Combine similar items (only if the team agrees that they are similar).

- Number all the alternatives.

- Ask each team member to select several alternatives from the numbered list. Each team member is given a limited number of alternatives to choose. The number of possible selections for each person should equal approximately one-third of the total number of alternatives (e.g., if there are 45 alternative solutions to a problem, each team member may select 15 of his or her personal favorites). The selections are kept private.

- After the team members have silently made their selections, the facilitator takes a tally of who is in support of which alternatives. Team members only raise their hands in support of their personal favorites.

- Reduce the list further by eliminating those items with few votes. If the team is small (five or less), then eliminate those items with only one vote. For 6 to 15 members, eliminate those items with fewer than three votes. For teams with more than 15 members, eliminate all items with fewer than four votes.

- Using the reduced list, repeat the above steps until the list cannot be reduced any further. Then ask the team members to discuss and prioritize the remaining items.

Criteria Rating Forms—These forms are constructed to prioritize a list of alternatives using an agreed upon set of criteria. These forms can be used during diagnosis to prioritize a list of possible changes that can be accomplished through the redesign process, or they can be used to prioritize a list of possible redesign alternatives. Here's how it's done:

	Alternative Solution #1	Alternative Solution #2	Alternative Solution #3	Alternative Solution #4
Redesign Criterion #1	1	5	3	2
Redesign Criterion #2	5	4	2	1
Redesign Criterion #3	2	5	3	1
Redesign Criterion #4	1	4	1	2
TOTALS	9	18	9	6

TABLE 11.1   Decision-Making Matrix

- As a team, create your decision criteria (e.g., use the design criteria described in Chapter 7).
- Decide if the criteria will all have equal weight or if they will have different weights.
- Construct a matrix with the alternatives across the horizontal axis and the decision criteria along the vertical axis (see Table 11.1).
- Discuss one alternative at a time, and ask team members to rate each alternative according to how well it meets the decision criteria. Rate the degree to which an alternative satisfies a decision criterion using a scale of 1 to 5 where:

  5 = definitely does satisfy the criterion

  4 = comes very close to satisfying the criterion

  3 = may satisfy the criterion—need additional information

  2 = comes very close to not satisfying the criterion

  1 = definitely does not satisfy the criterion

  In the example in Table 11.1, Alternative Solution #2 has the highest total value and is, therefore, the "best" choice.

- Enter the ratings in each cell of the matrix, as shown in Table 11.1.

• Total the ratings for each alternative, as shown in Table 11.1. The choices with the highest tallies receive top priority.

CONCLUSION

Your interpersonal communication skills explain 85% of your effectiveness at work; only 15% is explained by your technical skills. This startling fact was concluded after years of research by the Stanford Research Institute, Harvard University, and the Carnegie Foundation (which spent more than one million dollars on their research).[23] Think about the implications of this fact for a redesign effort. It seems that the success of your redesign effort is significantly linked to the quality and effectiveness of the interpersonal communication between and among the key players rather than to someone's technical redesign knowledge or skills.

This chapter highlighted critical interpersonal and group communication issues. During a redesign project, the RMT and Steering Committee will be confronted with the communication challenges described above, and their skill in handling the issues will be tested under fire. To succeed in explaining the vision, in communicating the redesign process, in dealing with resistance, in managing conflict, in running effective meetings, and so forth, the RMT and Steering Committee will both need superior interpersonal skills.

REFERENCES

1. Karp, H.B. (March 1984). "Working with resistance," *Training & Development Journal* (reprint). p. 1.
2. Walton, W. (1987). *Managing conflict*, 2nd edition. Reading, Mass.: Addison-Wesley.
3. Tohei, K. (1978). *Ki in daily life*. Tokyo: Ki No Kenkyukai H.Q.; Ueshiba, M. in Ueshiba, K. (1991). *Budo: Teachings of the founder of Aikido*. Tokyo: Kodansha International.
4. Crum, T.F. (1987). *The magic of conflict: Turning a life of work into a work of art*. New York: Simon & Schuster.
5. Ueshiba (see reference 3).
6. Tohei (see reference 3).
7. Crum (see reference 4).
8. Kramer, J. (1974). *The passionate mind*. In Crum (see reference 4), p. 114.

9. Duffy, F.M. (February 1990). "Soil conditions, cornerstones, and other thoughts: A treatise for school superintendents," *Wingspan.* 5, 2, pp. 3–7.

10. From Randolph, W.A. and R.S. Blackburn (1989). *Managing organizational behavior.* Homewood, Ill.: Irwin, pp. 524–528.

11. Delbecq, A.L., A.H. Van de Ven, and D.H. Gustafson (1975). *Group techniques for program planning: A guide to nominal and delphi processes.* Glenview, Ill.: Scott-Foresman.

12. Hegedus, D.M. and R.V. Rasmussen (1986). "Task effectiveness and interaction process of a modified nominal group technique in solving an evaluation problem," *Journal of Management.* 12, pp. 545–560.

13. Delbecq (see reference 11).

14. Cosier, R.A. (1982). "Methods for improving the strategic decision: Dialectic versus devil's advocate," *Strategic Management Journal.* 3, pp. 373–374.

15. Ibid.

16. Schweiger, D.M., W.R. Sandberg, and J.W. Ragan (1986). "Group approaches for improving strategic decision making: Analysis of dialectical inquiry, devil's advocacy, and consensus," *Academy of Management Journal.* 29, pp. 51–71.

17. Randolph and Blackburn (see reference 10), p. 526.

18. Janis, I.L. (1982). *Groupthink*, 2nd edition. Boston, Mass.: Houghton Mifflin.

19. Janis, I.L. (1972). *Victims of groupthink*. Boston, Mass.: Houghton Mifflin, pp. 197–198.

20. Ouchi, W.G. (1981). *Theory Z: How American business can meet the Japanese challenge.* Reading, Mass.: Addison-Wesley.

21. Wanous, J.P. and M.A. Youtz (1982). "Solution diversity and the quality of group decisions," *Academy of Management Journal.* 29, pp. 149–159.

22. Scholtes, P.R. et al. (1988). *The team handbook: How to use teams to improve quality.* Madison, Wisc.: Joiner Associates, pp. 2.39–2.41.

23. Ziglar, Z. (1987). *Top performance: How to develop excellence in yourself and others.* New York: Berkley Books, p. 9.

CHAPTER 12

SUPERVISING KNOWLEDGE WORK

INTRODUCTION

In ancient times there was a leader named King Gordius. He was the ruler of Phyrygia. According to legend, he tied a knot that could not be untied except by the future ruler of Asia. Faced with this problem, and knowing that others before him had failed, Alexander the Great cut the knot with his sword and went on to rule Asia and other parts of the world. Alexander succeeded because he approached the problem using a different paradigm.

In modern times, the term Gordian knot refers to an intricate problem, especially a problem that appears to be insoluble. In many ways, the problem of trying to improve instruction in schools through instructional supervision is a Gordian knot. Despite practitioners' best efforts and the field's best theoretical models, there is virtually no evidence that orthodox instructional supervision solves the problem of improving instruction throughout a school system. The problem seems insoluble unless it is approached from a different paradigm.

THE ORTHODOX PARADIGMS OF INSTRUCTIONAL SUPERVISION

A paradigm is a pattern, example, or model that guides thought or behavior. Barker[1] defines a paradigm as "...a set of rules and regulations (written and unwritten) that does two things: (1) it establishes or defines boundaries; and (2) it tells you how to behave inside the boundaries in order to be successful." Barker's use of this definition as a test to identify paradigms is enlightening. He says:

> Let us look at more important paradigms. Like your field of expertise. Almost everyone has one, either at work or at home. You may be an engineer, or a salesperson, or a chef or a carpenter or a nurse or an economist. Are these paradigms?
>
> Again, let us apply the test. What does the word "field" suggest? Boundaries. How do you feel when you are outside your field? Not competent, right? Not competent to do what? Solve problems. Why do people come to you? To receive help from you in solving problems in your field. That sounds like a paradigm, doesn't it? (p. 33)

There are two paradigms of supervision in the field of education. One is primarily espoused in the literature (clinical supervision and variations of it) and the other is primarily practiced in schools (supervision-as-inspection or performance evaluation).

The espoused paradigm of instructional supervision found in the literature (and occasionally in practice) focuses on helping individual teachers improve teaching and grow professionally. Although there are many approaches to these two important goals, the dominant theoretical paradigm for achieving these goals is the process of one supervisor working with one teacher at a time, collecting observational data about that teacher's classroom teaching, analyzing the observational data, reporting the analyses back to the teacher, making plans for that teacher's improvement of teaching and professional growth, and then moving on to work with another teacher. There are many variations of this approach, including clinical supervision,[2] differentiated supervision,[3] developmental supervision,[4] cognitive coaching,[5] and diagnostic supervision.[6] Some variations on this theme include teachers supervising teachers,[7] with the core supervisory process remaining focused on the classroom behavior of teachers.

Even though the research on the effectiveness of the clinical supervision paradigm is primarily anecdotal, many professionals have strong beliefs about the value of using this approach with individual teachers. However, an epistomological analysis of what is known about the effectiveness of clinical supervision indicates: (1) it is not commonly practiced in schools (supervision-as-inspection is the dominant paradigm in use) and (2) when it is used, there is no evidence that it is effective for improving teaching throughout an entire school system (although there is anecdotal evidence that it helps some individual teachers). Yet, professional educators are faced with the challenging task of trying to do just that—improve instruction throughout an entire school system. If the espoused paradigm of supervision cannot help educators improve instruction throughout an entire school system, then there is a need for one that can help them accomplish this goal.

There is also no research evidence that the supervision-as-inspection paradigm helps improve instruction. This paradigm probably prevails because it pretends to be scientific and objective and is relatively easy to use. Even so, it is very subjective in terms of how evaluation criteria are set, interpreted, and applied, and its subjectivity is increased because it relies on classroom observations as the primary source of data on a teacher's effectiveness (like its counterpart, clinical supervision). Its focus on individual behavior, as with clinical supervision, contributes to the inability of supervision-as-inspection to improve instruction throughout an entire school district. Beer, Eisenstat, and Spector[8] support this conclusion and note that change (e.g., improving instruction) does not happen by changing individual behavior. They say that attempts to change organizations are:

> ...guided by a theory of change that is fundamentally flawed. The common belief is that the place to begin is with the knowledge and attitudes of individuals. Changes in attitudes...lead to change in individual behavior...and changes in individual behavior, repeated by many people, will result in organizational change...This theory gets the change process exactly backward. In fact, individual behavior is powerfully shaped by the organizational roles that people play. The most effective way to change behavior, therefore, is to put people into a new organizational context, which imposes new roles, responsibilities, and relationships on them (p. 159).

Fundamental and enduring improvements in quality, therefore, come only with fundamental changes in the way an organization is structured, together with changes in the way people are viewed and managed and, therefore, with changes in the way work is thought of and performed—not by trying to change individuals.

SUPERVISING KNOWLEDGE WORK

In 1969, Peter Drucker[9] said, "To make knowledge work productive will be the great management task of this century." Twenty-four years later, in 1993, William Pasmore[10] said, "One of the most significant challenges for the 1990s and beyond lies in designing organizations to effectively manage and organize knowledge-based white collar and professional work." The proposed paradigm of Knowledge Work Supervision® described in this chapter responds to this challenge.

The paradigm of Knowledge Work Supervision[11] is an evolutionary step for the field of instructional supervision.[12] It is thought of as a new way to supervise knowledge work in schools. This new paradigm shifts the focus of supervision from the behavior of individual teachers to an assessment and redesign of the technical and social systems of a school district. This new approach is not an "add-on" responsibility for supervisors. Instead, it is conceived as a completely new way of doing supervision.

It is believed that practitioners working within the paradigm of Knowledge Work Supervision can solve the historically insoluble problem of trying to improve instruction throughout an entire school system. This belief is based on the fact that the proposed paradigm derives from *socio-technical systems (STS) design* theory,[13] which has guided the redesign of hundreds of organizations throughout the world. This belief is also linked to the premise that school systems are knowledge organizations and that teaching is knowledge work.

KNOWLEDGE WORK

I often consult and do research on organization development and change management; in particular, I specialize in systemic change (i.e., working to increase organizational effectiveness by viewing the organization as a system composed of interrelated parts). My consulting and research brought me in contact with the literature and practices of quality improvement,[14] knowledge work,[15] socio-technical systems design,[16] business process reengineering,[17] and organization development.[18] The concept of Knowledge Work Supervision is derived from the literature and practices of these areas and from my experience as an organization development consultant serving clients like State Farm Insurance Companies, the Association for Supervision and Curriculum Development, the U.S. Departments of Energy and Agriculture, and Fairfax County Public Schools (Virginia).

Knowledge work is any work that uses or produces knowledge to deliver products or services to customers or to produce new knowledge. Drucker[19] notes that in 1880, about nine out of ten workers made and moved things. Today that ratio is down to one out of five. The other four out of five workers, he says, are knowledge workers. These workers converse on the phone, write reports, and attend meetings.

Drucker[20] posits that the central social problem of our new, knowledge society is to make knowledge work productive and help knowledge workers achieve. Increasing productivity and achievement levels may best be changed by redesigning work processes and organizational structures. The paradigm of Knowledge Work Supervision offers a way to achieve these goals within school organizations by redesigning, reengineering, or restructuring work processes, the social system of the school district, and the district's relationship with its environment.

The importance of learning to manage knowledge work is also noted by Stewart[21] when he says: "What's at stake is nothing less than learning how to operate and evaluate a business when knowledge is its chief resource and result" (p. 68). Stewart also notes that there are many examples of organizations in the business world that are responding to this challenge. For example, the Canadian Imperial Bank of Commerce (CIBC), the Skandia Group (a financial services company), Dow Chemical, and Hughes Aircraft have made it clear that the knowledge assets of a company can be described, that processes can be developed to manage these assets, that it is possible to measure how knowledge adds value, and that managing intellectual resources improves organizational performance. In fact, some companies have even established specialized roles to manage knowledge assets (e.g., Dow Chemical has a director of intellectual asset management, and the Skandia Group has a director of intellectual capital).

Arian Ward,[22] a leader in the area of business engineering, talks about a problem faced by knowledge organizations. He calls it "losing the recipe." He says that knowledge hard won by a team two years ago, for example, may be unknown to a new team facing the same problem today, or a new team may know the solution to a problem but not know the research that underlies the solution. This lack of knowledge might result in the new team not seeing the applicability of the solution or not trusting it. This problem, he says, creates "islands of knowledge."

Ward believes that the best way to connect, or bridge, the "islands" is to realize that knowledge takes two forms: rules-based and context-based knowledge. Rules-based knowledge follows procedures that yield one correct answer to a specific problem. Context-based knowledge takes the form of wisdom, experience, and stories—not rules—and it varies with the context of the problem being addressed. Most knowledge, according to Ward, is context based. The knowledge that teachers work with is for the most part context based.

Leif Edvinsson,[23] a manager in the Skandia Group and the world's first director of intellectual capital, advises that to be an effective knowledge work manager, one must distinguish between two kinds of intellectual capital: human capital and structural capital. Human intellectual capital is the source of innovation and renewal for an organization. However, growth in this kind of capital through hiring, training, and education must be maximized. To capitalize on this kind of intellectual capital, managers must develop and manage structural intellectual assets. Structural intellectual assets include information systems, knowledge of how to access marketplaces, customer relations, and management processes. Structural intellectual capital counts the most, according to Edvinsson, because it is the means by which individual know-how is converted into organizational know-how. The proposed paradigm of Knowledge Work Supervision offers a mechanism to develop and manage structural intellectual assets in school systems.

Hubert Saint-Onge,[24] Vice President of Learning Organizations and Leadership Development for the CIBC, says that intellectual capital is created by the interplay of three elements: individual skills needed to meet customer needs (i.e., human intellectual capital), organizational capabilities as demanded by the marketplace (i.e., structural capital), and the strength of the individual division, unit, or franchise of the organization (i.e., customer capital).

To develop its human intellectual capital, CIBC, under the leadership of Saint-Onge, started by asking a simple question: What must our people know to serve customers? With this question as its guiding criterion, CIBC developed competency models that described the various talents needed for each category of employee. Each model contained about four dozen competencies. Next, CIBC abolished training. Instead, it made employees responsible for their own learning by asking them to use competency models to plan their own training and education to do their current jobs better—not to win a promotion. Then supervisors were expected to track how fast their teams learned and to identify gaps in required skill areas. The paradigm of Knowledge Work Supervision uses methods that involve teachers and "Knowledge Work Supervisors" in discussions about what teachers need to know to serve the educational needs of students and then guides them in the use of that knowledge to redesign their school system to serve these needs.

KNOWLEDGE WORK SUPERVISION: CONCEPTS AND PRINCIPLES

The paradigm of Knowledge Work Supervision is specially designed for school organizations. It is a special paradigm that shifts the focus of supervision from the behavior of the individual professional to the work processes and social system of an organization. Peter Drucker[25] seems to support the need for this shift:

> An old definition of "professionals" was people who could not be supervised in their work. That definition is now the rule rather than the exception. People on the assembly line have no choice but to perform their given task on that line. That is not true of service workers; their focus can wander from the task at hand. You cannot supervise them or, in many cases, give orders. The knowledge worker has to consider the job important and *want* to do it. You can train these workers, work on their specifications, retrain them, transfer them, and reward them, but in their job you *cannot* [emphasis added] supervise them.

THE STRUCTURE OF THE PARADIGM

The Knowledge Work Supervision paradigm is a modification of the redesign model described in this book. The modification exchanges a Knowledge Work Supervisor for the role of consultant. The paradigm is depicted in Figure 12.1. It has four phases and is cyclical in nature. Phase I is a set of preparation activities completed by a district-level

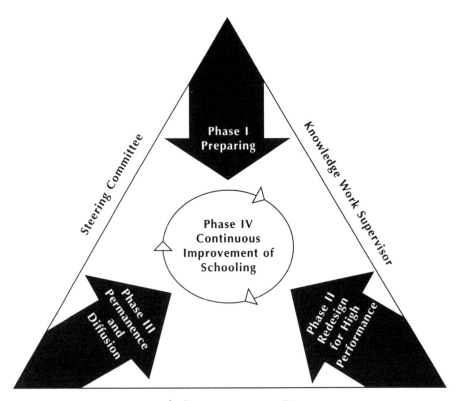

FIGURE 12.1   The Paradigm of Knowledge Work Supervision

Steering Committee that assesses the expectations and requirements of the district's environment. Phase II is a supervisory process to redesign the work and social systems of a school district and to improve its relationship with its environment for the purpose of moving that school district toward higher levels of organizational performance. Phase II begins with a cluster of interrelated schools (i.e., the *target cluster*). The process is managed by a Knowledge Work Supervisor (a role similar to those found in the Skandia Group and Dow Chemical Company cited earlier) in collaboration with Redesign Management Teams composed of teachers and building-level administrators.

After improvements are made in the target school(s), Knowledge Work Supervision strives to stabilize the changes and then diffuse the improvements throughout the school district until the entire organization is redesigned through Knowledge Work Supervision. Achieving permanence and diffusion are Phase III of the paradigm.

After the changes are stabilized and diffused, Knowledge Work Supervisors then begin a process of continuous improvement that identifies and acts upon opportunities for incremental improvements in both the work and social systems of the district and in the district's relationship with its environment. The continuous improvement of schooling is Phase IV of the paradigm.

After a predetermined period of time within Phase IV, the district returns to Phase I of the paradigm. Knowledge Work Supervision continues for the life of the organization. Because the supervision process is cyclical and because it is a permanent part of the organization's structure, the process of school renewal is ongoing and moves the district continuously closer to its vision of high performance.

The ultimate goals of Knowledge Work Supervision are to redesign the work system of the school district (which is composed of two work processes: the linear work process, known as the instructional program, and the non-linear work process, known as classroom teaching), redesign the web of roles, relationships, culture, and skill sets (called the social system), and redesign the relationships the district has with its environment. Achieving these goals helps a school district move toward higher levels of organizational performance. Once the redesign goals are achieved, Knowledge Work Supervision focuses on the continuous improvement of these three critical sets of variables.

A key element of the Knowledge Work Supervision paradigm is the process of diagnosing and improving the deliberations of teachers. A deliberation is an exchange of information between and among knowledge workers. The key to improving teaching-as-knowledge work is in improving the quality of the exchange of work-related information between and among teachers. Although there is no research to support this conclusion, the literature on school improvement indicates that efforts to improve teaching using traditional methods of clinical supervision and in-service training have not worked. Further, the literature on improving non-routine work[26] suggests that improving the process of exchanging information will improve knowledge work.

Diagnosing and improving the deliberations (or information exchanges) is the key to improving knowledge work.[27] The terms associated with the process of analyzing deliberations require further explanation.

The thinking process that occurs within the heads of knowledge workers is called a *deliberation*.[28] Teachers-as-knowledge-workers deliberate (or think) about many topics. Some of these topics are critical to their effectiveness on the job. These are called *key deliberations*. Other topics are not critical. Some even distract the knowledge worker from those topics which he or she should be deliberating. Some deliberations result in decisions; others do not. To identify the key deliberations, a list of key work-related topics that teachers need to think and talk about is compiled by the Redesign Management Team and Knowledge Work Supervisor.

Occasionally, the knowledge worker's deliberation process reaches out to solicit the input of others. Knowledge workers exchange information by discussing key work-related topics with people they think can be of help. The places where these exchanges of information occur are called *forums*. Forums can be structured (e.g., regularly scheduled team meetings), semi-structured (e.g., off-site training workshops), or unstructured (e.g., two colleagues conversing over coffee).

The people the knowledge worker includes in his or her deliberations are called *participants*. These people participate in the knowledge worker's deliberations by bringing advice, opinions, additional information, and insights to the deliberation. They also take information from the deliberation. Thus, there is a give-and-take exchange of information. Sometimes a knowledge worker involves the right people in his or her deliberations, and sometimes he or she does not. The quality of information exchanged and the effectiveness of the forums affect the quality and effectiveness of the deliberation process.

When people apply the information gained from the exchange, they often follow prescribed work procedures (e.g., evaluation procedures) and use technological devices to assist them (e.g., computer systems). These procedures and devices are intended to support the work procedures used by the knowledge workers.

These deliberations, forums, participants, supportive procedures, and technological devices comprise the non-linear, non-routine work system of a knowledge organization. To analyze this kind of work system, the Redesign Management Team and Knowledge Work Supervisor engage in a diagnostic process that focuses on variances (errors or potential errors) that exist in the information-exchange process (i.e., errors represented by missing or incorrect information, forums, participants, and supportive work procedures and devices). To improve this non-routine work system, all other professionals in the school learn how to manage the deliberation process more effectively by deliberating appropriate topics, reaching out to appropriate participants, engaging others within appropriate forums, applying appropriate work procedures, and using appropriate technological devices. Pasmore[29] refers to this kind of improvement process as "managing deliberations."

CONCLUSION

The argument for reconceptualizing instructional supervision as described in this chapter is based on the premise that school districts are *knowledge organizations* and the work they perform is *knowledge work*. Because knowledge work is non-linear, non-routine, and often chaotic, a different kind of supervision is required.

Socio-technical systems and change theory suggest that supervisors cannot analyze and improve teaching one teacher at a time. Instead, groups of teachers and building administrators examine the content of their deliberations, select or design appropriate forums within which they exchange work-related information, involve the right people in their deliberations, and use effective supportive work procedures and devices. These groups of teachers and building administrators are called Redesign Management Teams and there is one team for each cluster of schools in the district. The Redesign Management Teams collaborate with specially trained Knowledge Work Supervisors who provide tactical guidance for the supervisory process. A district-wide Steering Committee provides strategic guidance for the entire Knowledge Work Supervision process.

School systems also have a linear and sequential work process, the instructional program, which is delineated using a sequential grade structure. There is a system boundary between the linear instructional program and non-linear classroom teaching. This boundary is represented by policies, procedures, rules, regulations, and norms. Knowledge Work Supervision analyzes this linear work process to identify and correct errors and manages the boundary between the two work systems.

There are also system boundaries between grades and between levels of schooling (i.e., elementary, middle/junior high, and high schools). System boundaries also exist between individual schools. An additional boundary exists between the entire district and its environment. Knowledge Work Supervision manages all of these boundaries.

A school system also has a social system. This system is a complex web of roles, relationships, organizational culture, skill sets, motivators, satisfiers, and so on. The social system also has to be redesigned concurrently with the work system. The social system operates and maintains the work system to produce organizational outcomes. In high-performing organizations, both systems are maximized in relation to each other.

A school district also exists within a broader environment. The environment is composed of people and organizations that have a vested interest in the outcomes of schooling. These interested people and organizations are called stakeholders. The quality of the district's relationships with elements of its environment is critical to its success. Consequently, these environmental relationships must also be redesigned through Knowledge Work Supervision.

Given the systemic characteristics of a school district, the dominant orthodox paradigms of supervision (i.e., clinical supervision and supervision-as-performance-evaluation) are inappropriate because they focus almost exclusively on the behavior of individual teachers. Even those supervision models that espouse the value of managing other aspects of schooling in addition to classroom teaching[30] do not focus on the variables that are part of the Knowledge Work Supervision paradigm. If a high-performance school system is desired, it makes sense, then, to reconceptualize the supervision process to support this goal. Thus, it is appropriate to shift paradigms to Knowledge Work Supervision so supervisors can manage the exchange of information in the work system, the quality of the various elements within the social system, and the quality of the district's relationships with its broader environment. Further, Knowledge Work Supervision manages the various system boundaries described above.

If the proposed Knowledge Work Supervision paradigm replaces the dominant orthodox paradigms of supervision, then there may be a better fit between supervisory processes and the purpose, goals, and outcomes of a school system that desires to become increasingly effective. If supervision becomes a process to move school districts toward higher levels of organizational performance, it could finally become a process that makes a difference for an entire school system instead of for selected teachers. Perhaps supervision could also respond effectively and simultaneously to teachers' needs and the needs of the entire school system, thereby helping move groups of teachers and the whole organization toward higher levels of performance. Further, by anchoring the organizational renewal process described in this book to a district structure and process (i.e., supervision), it is possible for a district to become a learning organization that moves continuously toward higher levels of performance.

Because Knowledge Work Supervision is offered as a new paradigm that appears to compete with the dominant ideology of supervision, it is sure to meet with resistance. The potential for resistance was noted by Nagatomo:[31]

> When the rise of a new theory suggests a change of direction in scholarship, history attests to a common pattern of reaction among the established intellectual community. There is often flat dismissal or at best vehement attack in order to kill and bury the theory, especially if it signals an imminent as well as immanent possibility of shaking the secure and comfortable foundation upon which the existing paradigm of thinking rests (pp. ix–x).

Even though the proposed paradigm may be resisted, it offers a significant paradigm shift from the focus of traditional supervision. This paradigm responds to a significant need in the field of education for a process of instructional supervision that can improve the quality and effectiveness of knowledge work throughout an entire school district.

REFERENCES

1. Barker, J.A. (1992). *Future edge: Discovering new paradigms of success.* New York: William Morrow, p. 32.
2. Cogan, M.L. (1973). *Clinical supervision.* Boston: Houghton-Mifflin; Goldhammer, R. (1969), *Clinical supervision: Special methods for the supervision of teachers.* New York: Holt, Rinehart and Winston; Goldhammer, R., R.H. Anderson, and R. Krajewski (1980). *Clinical supervision,* 2nd edition. New York: Holt, Rinehart, and Winston.
3. Glatthorn, A.A. (1984). *Differentiated supervision.* Alexandria, Va.: Association for Supervision and Curriculum Development.
4. Glickman, C.D. (1985). *Supervision of instruction: A developmental approach.* Boston, Mass.: Allyn and Bacon.
5. Costa, A.L. and R.J. Garmston (February 1993). "Cognitive coaching: A strategy for reflective teaching," *Wingspan.* 9, 1, pp. 4–7; Costa, A.L., R.J. Garmston, and L. Lambert (1988). "Evaluation of teaching: The cognitive development view," In S.J. Stanley and W.J. Popham (Eds.). *Teacher evaluation: Six prescriptions for success.* Alexandria, Va.: Association for Supervision and Curriculum Development, pp. 145–173.

6. Seager, G.B. Jr. (1978). "An introduction to diagnostic supervision." Unpublished paper. University of Pittsburgh.
7. Alfonso, R.J. and L.F. Goldsberry (1982). "Colleagueship in supervision," In T.J. Sergiovanni (Ed.). *Supervision*. Alexandria, Va.: Association for Supervision and Curriculum Development.
8. Beer, M., R.A. Eisenstat, and B. Spector (November–December 1990). "Why change programs don't produce change," *Harvard Business Review*. 68, 6, pp. 158–166.
9. Drucker, P.F. (1969). *The age of discontinuity: Guidelines to our changing society*. New York: Harper & Row.
10. Pasmore, W.A. (1993). "Designing work systems for knowledge workers," *Journal of Quality and Participation*. 6, 4, pp. 78–84.
11. Duffy, F.M. (1995). "Supervising knowledge work." *NASSP Bulletin*. 79, 573, pp. 56–66.
12. Duffy, F.M. (1995). "The ideology of supervision," In G. Firth and E. Pajak (Eds.). *The handbook of research on school supervision*. New York: Scholastic, Inc.
13. For example, Pasmore, W.A. (1988). *Designing effective organizations: The sociotechnical systems perspective*. New York: Wiley & Sons; Trist, E.L., G.W. Higgin, H. Murray, and A.B. Pollack (1965). *Organizational choice*. London: Tavistock Publications.
14. For example, Deming, W.E. (1982). *Out of crisis*. Cambridge, Mass.: MIT Press; Crosby, P.B. (1979). *Quality is free: The art of making quality certain*. New York: New American Library; Crosby, P.B. (1986). *Running things*. New York: McGraw-Hill; Ishikawa, K. (1985). *What is quality control? The Japanese way*. Englewood Cliffs, N.J.: Prentice-Hall; Juran, J.M. (1989). *Juran on leadership for quality*. New York: The Free Press; and Taguchi, G. and D. Clausing (1990). "Robust quality," *Harvard Business Review*. 68, 1, pp. 65–72.
15. For example, Drucker, P.F. (1985). *Management tasks, responsibilities, practices*. New York: Harper & Row; Drucker, P.F. (1993). "Professionals' productivity," *Across the Board*. 30, 9, p. 50; Pava, C.H.P. (1983). *Managing new office technology: An organizational strategy*. New York: The New Press; and Knights, D., F. Murray, and H. Willmott (1993). "Networking as knowledge work: A study of strategic interorganizational development in the financial services industry," *Journal of Management Studies* (Oxford, England). 30, 6, pp. 975–995.
16. For example, Pasmore, W.A. (1992). *Sociotechnical systems design for total quality*. San Francisco, Calif.: Organizational Consultants; and Lytle, W.O. (1991). *Socio-technical systems analysis and design guide for linear work*. Plainfield, N.J.: Block-Petrella-Weisbord.
17. Hammer, M. and J. Champy (1993). *Reengineering the corporation: A manifesto for business revolution*. New York: HarperCollins.
18. For example, Argyris, C. and D. Schön (1974). *Theory in practice: Increasing professional effectiveness*. San Francisco, Calif.: Jossey-Bass Publishers; Argyris,

C. and D. Schön (1978). *Organizational learning*. Reading, Mass.: Addison-Wesley; and Burke, W.W. (1982). *Organization development: Principles and practices*. Boston, Mass.: Little, Brown.

19. Drucker, P.F. (1993). "Professionals productivity," *Across the Board*. 30, 9, p. 50.
20. Drucker, P.F. (1985). *Management tasks, responsibilities, practices*. New York: Harper & Row.
21. Stewart, T.A. (October 3, 1994). "Your company's most valuable asset: Intellectual capital," *Fortune*. 30, 7, pp. 68–74.
22. Ward, A. (1994). In Stewart (see reference 21), p. 70.
23. Edvinsson, L. (1994). In Stewart (see reference 21), p. 71.
24. Saint-Onge, H. (1994). In Stewart (see reference 21), p. 74.
25. Drucker (see reference 19).
26. Pava (see reference 15).
27. Pava (see reference 15) and Pasmore (see reference 10).
28. Pava (see reference 15)
29. Pasmore (see reference 16).
30. Harris, B.M. (1975). *Supervisory behavior in education*, 2nd edition. Englewood Cliffs, N.J.: Prentice-Hall.
31. Nagatomo, S. (1993). "Translator's introduction," In Yuasa, Y. (1993). *The body, self-cultivation, and ki-energy*. Albany, N.Y.: State University of New York.

CHAPTER 13

WORKING WITH
A CONSULTANT

OVERVIEW

Because organizational redesign requires specialized consulting knowledge and skills, you must learn to identify the competencies of potential consultants. This chapter provides you with the practical guidance you need to make a very critical decision: selecting a consultant to guide your redesign project. The kind of consultant you will be looking for will be a generalist in the field of organization development (OD) and a specialist in organizational design or large-system change.

A consultant is a person who provides technical assistance, counsel, advice, training and support. Although the term *consultant* usually conjures up the image of a helper, there are many different types of consultants. The purposes of this chapter are to (1) describe the context for the role and function of an organizational redesign consultant, (2) examine the different types of consultants in the field of OD, (3) highlight the characteristics that are needed for effective consultation, and (4) share some insights about how to interview and select a consultant to help with your redesign project.

THE CONTEXT FOR ORGANIZATION DEVELOPMENT CONSULTANTS

There are so many different kinds of OD consultants that it becomes confusing to try to find someone to help you. OD consultants either work inside an organization or work independently. Those who work independently can do so on a full-time or part-time basis. OD consultants also have a multiplicity of specialty areas and skill sets that set them apart from other kinds of management consultants. These characteristics are examined below.

Where OD Consultants Are Located—OD consultants can be found either working inside an organization as full- or part-time employees in human resource or training departments or outside organizations as full- or part-time independent contractors. Internal consultants are usually placed in a staff function, and they serve line managers throughout an organization. External consultants may be working for themselves or for a consulting company, or they may have academic appointments and consult only part-time.

Multiplicity of Specialty Areas and Skill Sets—OD consultants come in a veritable rainbow of specialty areas and skill sets. A recent survey conducted by the Chesapeake Bay Organization Development Network (CBODN, p. 12)[1] identified 12 sets of OD skills among members, including career development, communication, conflict management, meeting/group facilitation, organizational design, and team building.

OD Consultants Are Different than Other Consultants—Edgar Schein[2] describes two kinds of consulting roles (the purchase model and the doctor–patient model) and then compares them to his model of a process consultant. According to Schein, the purchase model is the most prevalent form of consultation. Basically, this model is used when a client purchases expert services from a consultant. The doctor–patient model is used when (1) the client tells the consultant what is wrong with the organization and (2) then waits for the consultant to prescribe a remedy to the problem.

Schein's process consultation model, in contrast to the two other models, helps the client organization to (1) diagnose its own strengths and weaknesses more effectively, (2) learn how to see organizational problems more clearly, and (3) share with the consultant the process of diagnosis and the generation of a remedy. Schein also states: "It is of prime importance that the process consultant be expert in how to *diagnose* and how to *establish effective helping relationships* with clients. Effective [process consultation] involves the passing on of both these skills [to the client]" (p. 8).

Thus, the primary, though not exclusive, function of an OD consultant is process consultation to help clients learn to help themselves more effectively. Although consultants occasionally provide expert information and may sometimes prescribe a remedy, their more typical mode of operating is *facilitation*.[3]

Schein's process consultant is the kind of consultant you need to help manage your redesign project. You do not want a training consultant with a training package to sell. You do not want a consultant who offers solutions to your problems before performing a thorough diagnosis of your organization (e.g., be wary of an educational consultant who is trying to sell you outcome-based education). You want someone who will come into your school district, establish relationships with your Steering Committee and Redesign Management Team, and facilitate the entire redesign process from beginning to end.

CHARACTERISTICS OF EFFECTIVE OD CONSULTANTS

Beer[4] lists five characteristics that he considers important for the OD consultant:

1. **Generalist and specialist**—The OD consultant is a generalist in terms of knowledge of organizational design and structure and a specialist in conducting diagnoses and recommending interventions.

2. **Integrator**—The OD consultant builds relationships and networks among people and units of the organization and also brings resources and people together.

3. **Neutrality**—The OD consultant should be neutral with respect to the client organization's internal politics and should not have an ax to grind with respect to the organization's problems. The OD consultant should not have any influence over any employee's career growth and should not be trying to get hired for a permanent job in the organization.

4. **Credibility**—OD consultants need to be knowledgeable about the organization they are helping, and they need to be associated with previous consulting successes. As Franklin[5] noted, credibility is a critical variable linked to OD success.

5. **Marginality**—Beer accepts Margulies'[6] definition of marginality. According to Margulies, marginality implies that the consultant is in between or on the edge—at the periphery or boundary of the organization. He argues that effective OD consultants maintain this position throughout their relationship with a client organization.

Burke[7] lists the personal characteristics he believes are essential for effective consultation. He says the effective consultant is able to:

- Tolerate ambiguity
- Influence others
- Confront difficult issues
- Support and nurture others
- Listen well and empathize
- Recognize his or her feelings and intuitions quickly
- Conceptualize
- Discover and mobilize human energy, including personal energy
- Teach or create learning opportunities
- Maintain a sense of humor, both on the client's behalf and to help sustain perspective

Finally, an effective OD consultant should have skills and knowledge in the following areas:[8]

1. **Intrapersonal skills**—The consultant is the primary instrument of diagnosis and change. Therefore, consultants must possess considerable conceptual and analytical ability. They must also have personal understanding of their own values, feelings, and purposes. They must practice integrity from a clearly defined ethical base, and they need to know how to manage their own stress.

2. **Interpersonal skills**—Effective consultants create and maintain effective relationships. Critical interpersonal skills include listening, establishing trust and rapport, giving and receiving feedback, and coaching.

3. **General consultation skills**—Effective consultants have advanced graduate work in or plenty of direct experience practicing consultation skills. These skills include organizational diagnosis, designing and implementing interventions, process consultation, and interviewing.

4. **OD theory**—An effective consultant can describe his or her personal theory of OD and has a good basic understanding of other theories of OD, such as organizational design, group dynamics, power, motivation, learning theory, socio-technical systems analysis, and personality theory.

PREPARING TO HIRE A CONSULTANT

Before you begin looking for a consultant to work with you, you need to prepare by clearly defining your needs. What exactly do you expect of the consultant? If you want to plan and carry out a school reengineering project using a process like the one described in this book, you want a consultant specializing in organizational redesign who will:

1. Provide training to a Steering Committee on principles of organizational redesign

2. Assist in conducting Open Systems Planning for the district

3. Assist in the process of developing or refining the district's mission and vision statements

4. Assist in the selection and training of a Redesign Management Team

5. Assist in diagnosing the work processes and social system

6. Facilitate the development of redesign proposals

7. Assist in the implementation effort

8. Provide guidance on evaluating the process and outcomes of the redesign effort

9. Provide advice on how to make the improvements permanent and how to spread the improvements to all schools in the district

10. Stay with you until the job is done

Your preparation should also focus on testing the level of political support you have within the district to launch a redesign effort. One aspect of this support is to determine the adequacy of your resources for supporting a reengineering project to its completion.

To facilitate preparation efforts, sometimes it is helpful to develop a Request for Proposals. An RFP is a document that organizes your thinking about what you need from a consultant and lists the essential services you require from the consultant.

APPRAISING A CONSULTANT'S EXPERTISE AND CREDIBILITY

After you clarify your needs and expectations, perhaps using an RFP, you then identify potential consultants (either internal or external). Finding a competent consultant to assist you with your redesign project is very, very important. There are so many consultants marketing themselves as "Jacks-" and "Jills-of-all-trades" that it is a challenge to find a consultant who "fits" your needs. Here are a few tips to help you make the right choice in selecting a consultant.

1. Call your friends in other school districts and ask for the names of any consultants that have been successful working with them. Your professional network might be able to identify a couple of consultants who fit the bill.

2. Attend a seminar or workshop presented on a topic related to school restructuring. Size up the consultant to get a sense of whether he or she might be appropriate for your situation.

3. Contact a local university and ask for the names of faculty who do OD consultation. Often OD consultants are full-time faculty members in schools of business and education. OD consultants are also sometimes found in psychology (i.e., industrial psychology) and counseling departments. Some universities have departments of organization development (sometimes called applied behavioral science).

4. Read current books on OD or socio-technical systems. Contact the authors and ask for recommendations.

5. Take a graduate course on OD. Establish friendships with the other students. Ask them if they know of consultants who might be helpful. Perhaps the professor might be your candidate.

6. Contact a professional association of OD consultants, for example, the Organization Development Institute (Chesterland, Ohio, 216-461-4333) or the Organization Development Network (ODN) (Portland, Oregon, 503-246-0148). ODN is a national-level association of OD consultants. The Chesapeake Bay Organization Development Network (CBODN) is one of many regional networks of OD consultants (Washington, D.C., 202-686-1314). Ask them to announce your search for a consultant to their members.

Because there are no licensing or certification requirements for becoming a consultant, anyone can claim to be one. Here are some suggestions for finding a consultant who is skilled, knowledgeable, and who has superior interpersonal communication skills:

1. Narrow your long list of consultants to a short list of two or three. (You might do this by picking the best proposals submitted in response to your RFP or by picking the consultants who received the highest recommendations from your network.)

2. Schedule interviews with each one. Include at least two other people from your staff in the interview process. Seek the following information:
   a. A description of relevant experiences
   b. A description of their "sweet" successes
   c. A description of dismal failures with an explanation about why he or she failed (An effective consultant does not succeed all the time. Be wary of consultants who say they have never failed.)
   d. Their personal model of an organization—Effective redesign consultants have a mental model of an organization that organizes their thinking about organizational performance. Beware of the consultant who does not have one.
   e. A summary of their academic preparation for consulting—In today's marketplace, the more effective consultants have advanced graduate degrees in fields related to OD (e.g., education, training, applied behavioral science, management,

psychology, counseling, and human resource development).
An older, more experienced consultant may not have an
advanced degree, but professional experience may compen-
sate for this lack of theoretical education.

f. An assessment of their interpersonal skills (e.g., are they good
listeners, do they display a keen ability to relate to people,
and do they have a good sense of humor?)

g. An assessment of their intrapersonal skills (e.g., do they have
a value system they rely on, do they seem comfortable with
themselves, do they display keen conceptual ability, and do
they express their values?)

To derive this kind of information from an interview, you must plan the
interview carefully. Design interview questions that will produce the
information you are seeking.

After the interviews are completed, you might escort the consultants around your district to meet other people in the district. For example, you might have a group of building principals meet with pro-
spective consultants so they can provide you with their insights and
input. Remember, the consultant you select is going to be working with
a lot of people in your district. It is a good idea to ask some of those
people for their perceptions of the consultant's "degree of fit" with your
needs and expectations.

If you decide to have other people in the district meet and talk with
the prospects, be sure to share with them a list of the characteristics you
are looking for in a consultant. Explain the process and the desired
outcomes to them, and do not surprise people with an unexpected
visitor.

After the consultants leave, collect everyone's perceptions and judgments about the consultants. Consider all of this information carefully.
Weigh the pros and cons with due consideration and then make your
choice based on consensus among those who met the consultants. Be
sure that you build consensus for the choice you make because if you
choose a consultant that no one else supports, your redesign project will
probably get off to a bad start and might even fail. After making your
choice, inform all of those who participated in the selection process,
give them an explanation of why you selected a particular consultant,
and address any concerns they raise.

Within five days, contact each of the consultants that you inter-
viewed. Thank the runners-up for their participation and invite the

selected consultant back to the district for a more detailed "contracting" interview.

THE CONTRACTING PROCESS

Even if the selected consultant submitted a proposal in response to your RFP, you still need to engage in a contracting interview. Because you have made a decision to work with this consultant, you should be prepared to pay the consultant for participating in this interview—it is part of the redesign process (more about consulting fees appears later in the chapter).

Peter Block[9] advises consultants about what to seek during contracting interviews. He says that a consultant should be able to:

- Ask direct questions about who the client is and who the less visible parties to the contract are

- Elicit the client's expectations of him or her

- Clearly and simply state what he or she wants from the client

- Say no to or postpone a project that in his or her judgment has less than a 50/50 chance of success

- Probe directly for the client's underlying concerns about losing control

- Probe directly for the client's underlying concerns about exposure and vulnerability

- Give direct verbal support to the client

- When the contracting meeting is not going well, discuss directly with the client why the meeting is not going well

With this advice in mind, then, you can structure your contracting interview to facilitate the consultant's quest for the above opportunities.

The desired outcome of the contracting interview is a performance contract that represents a sharing of responsibilities for planning and carrying out your redesign project. These responsibilities are set forth in nine subsections of a contract. These subsections are also derived from Block's[10] work. A tenth subsection has been added to Block's list. The contract subsections are:

1. **The boundaries of the consultant's work**—This is a statement describing the consulting project. The statement limits the scope of the consultant's assistance.

2. **The specific objectives of the project**—This section defines desired outcomes of the redesign project in observable, measurable terms.

3. **The kind of information that will be sought**—The consultant must have access to people and information. This section of the contract specifies who, when, and how this will occur. General descriptions of diagnostic methods are provided.

4. **The consultant's role in the project**—In this section, the consultant defines, in general terms, the intent and spirit of the working relationship he or she wants with the client.

5. **The product (if any) that will be delivered**—This section specifies exactly what the consultant is offering. For example, will diagnostic feedback be oral or written? How will the feedback be organized? Will actual solutions to problems be presented or will the consultant simply point out the direction that should be followed? Will a final report be submitted?

6. **The level of support and participation needed from the client**—This section specifies what the consultant expects of the client to make the project successful.

7. **The projected time schedule**—This is a "best guess" of the time line for the project: starting date, intermediate mileposts, and anticipated completion date. Interim progress reports should be scheduled at this time and deadlines for submitting information set.

8. **Measures that will be taken to protect confidentiality**—The consultant must be concerned with organizational politics. This is the subsection where those concerns are addressed through decisions like "who gets the report first." Experience suggests that the consultant should allow the client to decide on the distribution list for feedback reports, progress evaluation reports, and final outcome reports.

9. **Assurances that feedback on the outcomes of the project will be provided to the consultant at a later time**—Because consult-

ants have a psychological need to know if their work made a difference, assurances are made to the consultant that he or she will receive a progress report on the redesign project six months after the consulting contract is terminated.

10. **Projected costs**—The client needs an estimate of how much the consultant's services will cost. Thus, the contract should include an estimate of the consultant's fees and related expenses (consultants' fees and expenses are discussed in the next section of this chapter).

The level of formality for the contract varies. It may be a complex legal document or a simple letter of agreements and commitments drafted by the consultant and client and signed by both parties. In rare cases, it is an oral agreement sealed with a handshake. Because most contracts are broken through neglect rather than intent, it is best to at least have a letter of agreements and commitments on file. This letter can then be referred to periodically to determine whether everything is going as planned.

PREPARING FOR "STICKER SHOCK": CONSULTANTS' FEES AND EXPENSES

If you have not worked with OD consultants before, you are going to experience what automobile customers call "sticker shock." Consultants are expensive (and the more famous they are, the more expensive they are). As a case in point, in 1989 I was helping develop a proposal seeking funding for a training project. We wanted to invite an internationally known consultant specializing in change management to speak to the training class. I called her office and spoke with her secretary about our needs. The secretary said, quite routinely, "Yes, she would be willing to do that. She charges $16,000." And that was just to make a speech!

The average daily rate in 1995–1996 for OD consultants specializing in socio-technical systems redesign is about $1,250 per day (this estimate is based on informal interviews with several well-informed OD consultants). Good consultants are not inexpensive, but be careful applying the old principle "you get what you pay for." When working with consultants, this is not always true. There are many examples of consultants who charge exorbitant fees but are less than effective and consultants who charge lower fees and are highly effective. Do not equate the size of the consulting fee with consulting competence. Be sure to check the consultant's references and assess his or her competence during the screening interview.

You probably cannot afford to have a consultant working with you every day for several years (remember that a redesign project requires anywhere from 18 to 36 months to complete) unless the consultant is hired on a yearly retainer that is significantly lower than the daily rate. A good contract, as described earlier, helps you manage these costs in an effective manner by defining when and to what degree the consultant will be working with you for a fee.

When thinking about consultants' fees, also consider how much you will pay them. Sometimes you can work out a creative agreement where, for example, the consultant might accept a significantly lower daily rate in return for a long-term contract or provide an added value, such as free telephone consultation for one year following the completion of a consulting project. Bellman[11] described six other payment options:

- **Per diem**—For each day a consultant works, he or she gets a day's pay. The amount of the fee is set during the contracting phase.

- **Fixed amount**—A consultant agrees to do the work for a fixed fee. The fee is based on an educated guess. If the project takes more or less time to complete, the consultant still gets the agreed upon amount.

- **Variable amount**—The consultant quotes the client an estimated cost for the project. The consultant keeps track of his or her time on the project and submits time records to the client. The consultant keeps track of actual costs in relation to estimated costs and adjustments are made as needed. (Note: this method is also known as actual cost.)

- **Retainer**—The client pays the consultant a given amount per month or per year to have his or her services available to the organization. For example, suppose a consultant's daily rate is $1,000, and you expect you will need 50 days of consulting help. The consultant might be willing to accept the security of a $40,000 guaranteed retainer fee in return for the 50 consulting days even though that would mean being paid less than his or her full daily rate for the 50 days. With this arrangement, the consultant is paid whether or not the client uses his or her services. If the client wants to use these services more than the agreed upon amount, then the consultant is paid more.

- **Product**—The consultant develops a product that stays with the client after the consultant leaves (e.g., a training curriculum for administrators). The client pays the consultant a proprietary fee for use of the product.

- **Goodwill (sometimes known as *pro bono* work)**—The consultant agrees to work for nothing because he or she recognizes that the work serves a higher purpose. However, the praise and recognition that accompany this kind of service can pay off by generating a lot of goodwill, which the consultant can convert into future paying consulting assignments and future references.

Another important point to remember is that most consultants also charge for work done in preparing to work with you. For example, a consultant may need a minimum of two days to prepare a one-day training workshop for your Steering Committee. Thus, the cost of one day of training is really $1,250 + $2,500 = $3,750. Charging for preparation time is a reasonable and common practice, because if the consultant is preparing your workshop, he or she is not earning money on some other project. It is only right to remunerate consultants for their preparation time.

Some consultants will bill you for the time they spend talking with you on the telephone. (Most often, if your phone call is only for a few minutes there is no charge.) The standard practice is to bill in quarter-hour increments. Whether you use one minute or fifteen minutes, you are billed for a full fifteen minutes.

Often, consultants will bill you for travel related to their contract with you. Their rationale is that if they were not traveling to work with you, they could be earning fees from other clients or generating new business.

Consultants will also charge you for expenses directly related to the project. The specific expenses charged vary according to the consultant. Here are some common billable expenses:

- Round-trip travel expenses
- Meals while working with you
- Cost of a hotel room while working with you
- Cost of preparing overheads and other visuals for presentations
- Cost of preparing reports (typing, copying, binding)
- Postage related to the project
- Telephone calls related to the project

Because of the potential for abuse when charging for expenses, you should follow standard accounting procedures for documenting these expenses (e.g., require original receipts).

Because of the various ways in which you can pay a consultant, it is advisable to negotiate the daily rate and the method of payment. Most consultants are flexible as long as you bargain in good faith and do not try to overly devalue the worth and significance of their services.

Because consultants are expensive, you want to design their contracts so they gradually work themselves out of a job. Very good consultants will initiate a discussion of ways to do so. If your consultant does not raise this point, then you should. You must gradually reduce the consultant's involvement from a high level of involvement at the beginning to very little involvement near the end.

CONCLUSION

Selecting a knowledgeable and skilled consultant to assist you with your redesign project is very important. Screen potential consultants very carefully. Involve many people from your district in the selection process. Build consensus for the consultant that is to be chosen.

Work with the consultant to develop performance requirements for him or her and you and your staff. Reduce the requirements to a letter of agreements and commitments. Be sure that the content of the letter is mutually agreeable and that both parties sign the letter.

Remember that consultants' fees are high. Their contract-related expenses will also add to the cost of working with them. Plan to use their time very carefully. Require the consultant to teach others in the district how to do the work so the consultant can gradually work himself or herself out of a job.

Negotiate with the consultant about fees and expenses. Make sure you are very clear about the consultant's definition of a "day," what his or her hourly and daily rates are, what he or she will or will not bill you for, and what expenses will be billed. You want to avoid billing surprises.

OD consultants who specialize in organizational redesign have the technical knowledge and skills to assist you with a redesign project. They also have the objectivity of an outsider who can make observations without fear of retribution. Consultants are expensive, but necessary, resources for your redesign effort. Like any resource, they need to be managed carefully and prudently.

REFERENCES

1. Davidson-Randall, J. and K. Quam, Eds. (1995). *The CBODN OD career guide.* Washington, D.C.: Chesapeake Bay Organization Development Network.
2. Schein, E.H. (1969). *Process consultation.* Reading, Mass.: Addison-Wesley.
3. Burke, W.W. (1982). *Organization development: Principles and practices.* Boston, Mass.: Little, Brown, p. 345.
4. Beer, M. (1980). *Organization change and development.* Santa Monica, Calif.: Goodyear, p. 222.
5. Franklin, J.L. (1976). "Characteristics of successful and unsuccessful organization development," *Journal of Applied Behavioral Science.* 12, pp. 471–492.
6. Margulies, N. (1978). "Perspectives on the marginality of the consultant's role," In W.W. Burke (Ed.). *The cutting edge: Current theory and practice in organization development.* La Jolla, Calif.: University Associates, pp. 60–69.
7. Burke (see reference 3), pp. 353–354.
8. Cummings, T.G. and C.G. Worley (1993). *Organization development and change,* 5th edition. Minneapolis/St. Paul, Minn.: West Publishing, pp. 29–30.
9. Block, P. (1981). *Flawless consulting.* San Diego, Calif.: Pfeiffer & Co., p. 45.
10. Ibid., pp. 46–52.
11. Bellman, G.M. (1990). *The consultant's calling: Bringing who you are to what you do.* San Francisco: Jossey-Bass Publishers, pp. 206–207.

INDEX

Acceptance, 209
Accountability, 9, 27, 160
Action plans, 156–167
Action research, 199–200
Administrative progressives, 17–18
Administrators, in effective schools, 12
Agenda, 219, 222
Aiki approach to managing conflict, 216–218
"All-hands" meeting, 39, 72, 77
Alternative schools, 18
American Federation of Teachers, 26
Analysis goals, 123–124
Analysis tasks, 124–125
Argyris, C., 55, 179, 180, 181
Arnn, J.W., 10
Assertive behavior, 212
ATLAS Communities, 30
Attitudes, 166
Auditing a linear instructional program, 106
Audrey Cohen College, 30
Authority, 26
Authority rule, 229
Autonomy, 50, 130

"Back to Basics" movement, 19
Barker, J.A., 238
Batten, D., 200
Beckhard, R., 150, 194
Beckhard and Harris model of change, 194
Beer, M., 65, 74, 201, 239, 256
Belasco, James, 87

Benne, D., 203
Bennis, W.G., 203
Bensenville New American School, 29
Bias toward action, 7
Bilingual education, 18
Borger, J., 12
Brainstorming, 228
Brown versus Board of Education, 18
Bullock, R.J., 200
Burke, W.W., 161, 256
Business focus, 6
Business process reengineering, 240–241

Career development, 22
Career planning, 20
Carnegie Foundation for the Advancement of Teaching, 19
Carnegie Schools, 29
Carnegie Task Force on Teaching as a Profession, 21
Celebration, 179
Chairperson, 220
Change
    cost of, 197
    emotional aspects of, 208–210
    readiness for, 38–39, 64–74, 196–197
    resistance to, 210–215
Change agents, interpersonal and group dynamics for, 207–235
    conflict, 215–218
    emotional aspects of change, 208–210
    group problem solving and decision making, 224–235

meeting management, 218–224
philosophy for, 207–208
resistance to change, 210–215
Change management structure, 42–43,
  95–99
Change strategies, 201–203
Change target, 175
Change theory, 191–205
  change strategies, 201–203
  managing complex change, 192–194
  managing transition, 203–204
  models of change, 194–201
Chesapeake Bay Organization
  Development Network, 254, 259
Chicago's Corporate/Community
  School, 28
Chin, R., 203
Chiron Middle School in Minneapolis,
  Minnesota, 28
Chubb, John, 25
Classroom teaching, 105, 116, 137
  skills needed for, 125–126
Clinical supervision, 238
Close to the customer, 6
Coalition of Essential Schools, 27
Coercive power, 203
Combs, Arthur W., 192
Commitment, 4, 5, 11, 55, 176, 181
Community Learning Centers of
  Minnesota, 30
Comparison unit, 165
Comprehensive Quality-of-Work-Life
  Survey, 163
Conceptual readiness, 197
Co-Nect School, 30
Conflict, 215–218
Congruence, 174
Consensus, 178, 231–232
Consultant, 253–266
  appraising, 258–261
  characteristics of effective, 255–257
  context for OD, 253–255
  contracting, 261–263
  external, 76
  fees and expenses, 67, 263–266
  internal, 76
  knowledge and skills needed, 43

preparing to hire, 257–258
role of, 98
Context-based knowledge, 242
Contextual environment, 41
Continuous improvement, 56–58,
  185–186
  opportunities for, seeking, 57–58, 186
  system boundaries, supervising,
    56–57, 185–186
Contracting phase, 40, 76–78
Contribution, 51, 130
Corcoran, T.B., 12
Cost, 147–148
Cost-effectiveness analyses, 146–148
Credibility, 256
Criteria rating form, 233–235
Critical mass, 38–39
Critical success factors, 93
Crum, Thomas, 215, 216
Cultural implications, 139
Culture, 4, 143, 145, see also Social
  system
Curriculum, 18, 20, 26
Customer requirements, 5, 6
Customers, 80–82, 126

Dade County, Florida, 29
Dannemiller, K.D., 39
Dean, J., 174, 175, 176, 177, 178
Decision making, 8, 24–25, 26, 224–225,
  228–235
  matrix for, 234
Deliberation, 46, 47, 137, 246
Delphi technique, 226
Denial, 208
Depth, 38
Desegregation, 18
Despondency, 208
Developmental change, 193
Deviations, detecting and correcting,
  56, 184–185
Devil's advocacy, 227
Dialectical inquiry, 226–227
Dialogue model for managing conflict,
  215–216
Diffusion, 53, 54–56, 176, 182–184
  resources for, 68

Discretion, 50, 130
Double-loop learning, 54–55, 179–181
Doubt, 209
Doud, J.L., 10
Drucker, Peter, 240, 241
"Duffy's Laws of Human Behavior,"
    77–78

Economic benefits, 146–147
Edmonds, Ronald, 12
Educational reform movement, history
    of, 17–27
    schools of choice, 25–27
    site-based management, 24–25
Educational Research Service, 12
Edvinsson, Leif, 242
Effective schools, 9–11
Effective working relationships, 123
Eisenstat, R.A., 239
Ellett, C.D., 12
Emotional aspects of change, 208–210
Emotional considerations, 178–179
Empirical–rational strategy, 203
Environment
    analysis of, 79, see also Open
        Systems Planning
    Open Systems Planning and, 41–42,
        see also Open Systems Planning
    organization's relationship with,
        5–6
    stability of, 174
Equilibrium, 197–198
Equipment, 68
Error analysis matrix, 112
Ethnic curricula, 18
Evaluation, 53–54, 159–170
    criteria, 157
    feedback, 160
    guidelines for, 165–166
    measurement, 162–163
    politics of, 168–169
    research, 161–162, 165–166
    research design, 164–165
    steps for, 166–168
Evans, H. Dean, 23
Expeditionary Learning, 30
Experimentation, 7

Experimenting, 209
External customers, 81
External validity, 164

Facilitator, 221
Failure, 7
Fear of failure, 211
Fear of the unknown, 211
Feedback, 46, 106–107, 159–161, see
    also Evaluation
Feeder schools, 75
Feeder streams, 108, 109, 110
Fees, consultants', 263–266
Fixed fee, 264
Flexibility, 4, 20
Focus, 6
Force-field analysis, 69, 70
Ford Motor Company, 39
Formative evaluation, 53
Forums, 47, 137, 246
Fragmented centralization, 19
Frank, G., 74
French, W., 199
Frohman, A., 198
Funding, 9, 38

GAIL analysis, 49, 127–128, 129
Gainey, Donald, 13
Gleicher, D., 39
Goal specificity, 175
Goals, 5, 7, 45, 105–108, 140, 148, 156
    analysis, 123–124
Goals 2000: Educate America Act,
    31–32
Goodlad, John, 20, 22, 27
Goodman, P., 174, 175, 176, 177, 178
Goodwill, 264
Groupthink, 230

Hall, G., 38, 53
Harris, R.T., 150, 194
Hergert, F., 181
Herman, J.J., 107
Herzberg, F., 130
Hewlett-Packard, 7
High performance, redesigning for, see
    Redesigning for high performance

High-performance organization, 3–14
  change in, see Change theory
  characteristics of, 3–5
  environment, 5–6
  management of, 6–8
  schools, 8–13
High-performance schools
  characteristics of, 11–13
  designing, see Redesign process
  leadership in, 8–11
High-performing system
  measurement variables, 3, 4–5
  organizational-level variables, 3, 4
  social system variables, 3, 4
High schools, ideas for improving, 21
Holmes Group, The, 21, 22
Hope, 210
Hugh Russell, 7
Human benefits, 147
Human capital, 242
Human resources, 4

Impact analysis, 142–146
Implementation feedback, 160
Implementation plans, developing, 52,
  149–157
Improvement targets, 140
Incorporating, 209
Incremental reform, 23
Information exchange process, 46–47,
  117–120
Inputs, 105–108, 137
Institutionalization, see Permanence
Institutionalization process, 176
Institutionalizing, 65
Instructional program, 105–115
Instructional supervision, 238–240
Integrative model of planned change,
  200–201
Integrator, 255
Intellectual capital, 242
Interim management structure, 151
Internal customers, 80
Internal environment, 41
Internal support, 175
Internal validity, 164
Interpersonal effectiveness, 207

Interpersonal skills, 257
Intervention characteristics, 175
Interviews
  group, 71–74
  one-on-one, 70–71
Intrapersonal skills, 256
IQ testing, 19
Islands of knowledge, 242

Jacobs, R.W., 39
Janis, I.L., 230
Jefferson County, Kentucky, 29
Job Diagnostic Survey, 163
Job requirements, 139
Job satisfaction, 50, 130–131
Joint Committee on Standards for
  Educational Evaluation, 166

Karp, H.B., 212
Kelley, E.A., 12
Key deliberation, 46, 246
Key player, 82, 105
Key stakeholders, 41, 51, 81, 159
  expectations of, 139
Key variances, 104, 111–113, 137
Knowledge work, 44, 46–47, 104,
  115–120
Knowledge Work Supervision®, 57,
  237–249
Kolb, D., 198
Kotter, J.P., 37, 38, 42, 52, 53, 54

Leader, 220
Leadership, in high-performance
  schools, 8–11
Leadership vision, 6–7
Learning, 130
Legitimate power, 203
Lewin, Kurt, 71, 72, 173, 194
Lewin's change model, 194–198
Licensing, 21
Lieberman, Ann, 192
Linear work, 44, 45–46, 103–115
Lippitt, Ronald, 42, 198
Longitudinal measurement, 165
Los Angeles Learning Centers, 29
Loucks-Horsley, S., 181

Macy, B., 163
"Mafia Contract," 75
Majority rule, 230
Management, 6–8
Manager, 6–8, 65–66
Mangieri, J.N., 10
Marginality, 256
Marguilies, N., 256
Maslow's hierarchy of human needs,
    77
"Mastery in Learning" project, 29
Mausner, B., 130
Meaningful future, 51, 130
Measurement, 162–163
Measurement variables, 3, 4–5
Meeting management, 218–224
Meeting room, 67–68
Meyer, John, 19
Michaels, Ken, 191
Miles, R.E., 75
Miller, S.K., 12
Minimal rationality, 7–8
Minimal specifications, 160
Minority rule, 229
Mirvis, P., 163
Mission, redefining, 42, 86–95
Mission statement, 86, 88, 138–139, 148
Modern Red Schoolhouse, 30
Moe, Terry, 25
Mosley, Elaine, 28
Motivation, 4, 50
Motivators, 124, 128–130
Moving, 195
Multivoting, 233

National Alliance for Restructuring
    Education, 30
National Association of Secondary
    School Principals, 85
National Commission on Excellence in
    Education, 19
National Governors Association, 26
National Network for Educational
    Renewal, 27
Needs, recognizing, 37–38, 63–64
Neutral equilibrium, 198
Neutrality, 255

New American Schools Development
    Corporation, 29
Newman, F.M., 22
Nominal group technique, 225–226
Normative consensus, 178
Normative–re-educative strategy, 203

Odyssey Project, 29
Office space, 67
O'Neil, John, 13
Open Systems Planning, 41–42, 79–86
    learning from, 136–137
Opportunity, 93
    for continuous improvement, 57, 186
    recognizing, 37–38, 63–64
Opportunity analysis, 85
Organization characteristics, 174
Organization development, 241
Organization development consultant,
    see Consultant
Organization Development Institute,
    259
Organization Development Network,
    259
Organizational blockages to change,
    211–212
Organizational constraints, 139
Organizational design, criteria for,
    139–140
Organizational-level variables, 3, 4
Organizations, purpose of, 3
Ouchi, William, 231
Outcomes, 8
Outputs, 105–108, 137

Pain avoidance, 211
Pajak, E., 11
Paralysis, 208
Parental involvement, 18
Parents, 41
Participant, 47, 137, 220, 246
Partnerships, 9, 20
Pasmore, W., 47, 69, 74
People planning, 209
People requirements, 140
Per diem, 264
Performance, 177

Performance evaluation, 238
Performance measures, 45
Performance outcomes, 166
Performance technology, 50
Permanence, 54–56, 163–185
  commitment, renewal, 55, 181
  deviations from desired outcomes,
    56, 184–185
  double-loop learning seminars,
    54–55, 179–181
  model for, 174–178
  psychological and emotional
    considerations, 178–179
  rewards for desired behaviors, 55,
    181–182
Personal blockages to change, 211
Peters, Thomas, 5
Planned change model, 198–199
Political implications, 139
Political support, 69–74
Politics of evaluation, 168–169
Power–coercive strategy, 203
Preferences, 177
Preparing, 37–43, 63–100, 243, see also
  specific topics
  change management structure, 42–43,
    95–99
  contracting phase, 40, 76–78
  mission and vision, redefining, 42,
    86–95
  Open Systems Planning, 41–42,
    79–86
  starting point, identifying, 39–40,
    74–76
  steering committee, formation of,
    40–41, 78
  support, building, 37–39, 63–74
Principal, 41, 66, 78
  behavior in effective schools, 10
Proactive response, 6
Problem solving, 224–228
Pro bono work, 264
Programmability, 175
Proposals
  developing, 51–52, 135–149
  implementing, 52–53, 157
Pseudo-reform, 22–23

Psychological considerations, 178–179
Purkey, S.C., 12, 22

Quality, 5
Quality improvement, 240
Quality of work life, 123, 124, 129
Quasi-experimental research design,
  164–165
Quasi-stationary equilibrium, 195
Quick fix, 13, 212

Rand Corporation, 226
Rationality, 212
Raywid, Mary Anne, 22, 23, 24, 25, 78
Readiness for change, 38–39, 64–74,
  196–197
Recalibration, 176–177
Recognition, 179
Recorder, 221
Redesigning for high performance,
  44–54, see also specific topics
  evaluation of process and outcomes,
    53–54, 159–170
  implementation plans, developing,
    52, 149–157
  proposals, developing, 51–52, 135–149
  proposals, implementing, 52–53, 157
  social system, diagnosing, 48–51,
    123–133
  technical system, diagnosing, 44–47,
    103–121
Redesign Management Team, 43
  charter for, 96–97
  establishing, 95–98
  formation of, 183–184
  membership, 96–97
  purpose of, 96
  resources, 98
  responsibilities of, 97–98
  time frame for, 98
  training, 98, 183–184
Redesign process, 35–58, see also
  specific phases
  continuous improvement, 36, 56–58,
    185–186
  permanence and diffusion, achieving,
    35–36, 54–56, 173–185

preparing, 35, 37–43, 63–100
redesigning for high performance,
    35, 44-54
  developing and implementing
    redesign proposals, 51–53, 135–157
  diagnosing the social system, 48–51,
    123–133
  diagnosing the technical system,
    44–47, 103–121
  evaluating the redesign project,
    53–54, 159–170
Redesign proposals, see Proposals
Reengineering, 192
  errors, 52–53, 54
Refreezing, 195–198, see also
  Permanence
Rehm, R., 74
Relearn Network, 29
Reorganization movement, 17
Reporting requirements, 156
Research design, 164–165
Resistance to change, 210–215
Resources, 9, 68, 105–108, 156
Respect, 50, 130
Restructuring of schools, 23
  examples of, 27–31
  history of, 22–24
Retainer, 264
Revolutionary change, 193
Reward, 4
  allocating, 55, 176, 181–182
Reward power, 203
Rigid perceptions, 211
Risk, 93
Risk assessment, 197
Roots and Wings project, 30
Rosenthal, J., 38, 53
Rules-based knowledge, 242
Rutter, R.A., 22

Saint-Onge, Hubert, 49, 242
Santa Fe, New Mexico, 29
Satisfaction, 210
Satisfiers, 124, 129
Schein, Edgar, 254
Schön, D.A., 55., 179, 180, 181
Schools for the 21st Century, 29

Schools of choice, 25–27
Schools within schools, 18
Schools without walls, 18
Searching, 209
Sensing, 176–177
Sergiovanni, T.J., 162
Shanker, Albert, 26, 42
Sirotnik, K.A., 39, 40
Site-based management, 24–25
Sizer, Theodore, 13, 21, 23, 27
Skandia Group, 242
Skill, 124, 125–127
Smith, D.C., 10
Smith, M.S., 12
Snyderman, B., 130
Social system, 143, 145
  analysis, learning from, 137–138
  defined, 48
  diagnosis of, 48–51, 123–133
    analysis goals, 123–124
    analysis tasks, 124–125
    tasks for, 125–132
Socialization, 176
  variables, 3, 4
Socio-technical system, 79, 104, 143,
    240
Spector, B., 239
Speicher, D., 8
Sponsor, 175
Stable equilibrium, 197–198
Staff development, 9
Staff roles, 26
Stakeholders, 38, 41, 81, 126, 159
Starting point, identifying, 39–40,
    74–76
Statistical analysis, 165
Steering Committee
  approval of, 149
  change management structure and,
    95–99
  formation of, 40–41, 78
  in Open Systems Planning, 41–42,
    79–86
  purpose of, 40–41
  redefining mission and vision of the
    district, 42, 86–95
  role of, 98

Stephens, G.M., 107
Stewart, T.A., 241
Strategic advantages, 87
Structural capital, 242
Student progress, 9
Students
  in effective schools, 12
  with disabilities, 18
Substitute teachers, 66–67
Success factors, 38
Superintendent, 41, 66, 78
Supervisory excellence, 11
Suppliers, 80, 81, 82
Support
  building, 37–39, 63–74
    recognizing need and opportunity,
      37–38, 63–64
  internal, 175
  political, 69–74
Survey, 70
Survey of Organizations, 163
SWOT analysis, 82, 83
Symbolic politics, 22
System
  defined, 3
  defining, 79–82
  high-performing, see High-
    performance system
System boundaries, supervising, 56–57,
  185–186

Target, 140
  diagnosing the technical system,
    44–47, 103–121
  level of, 175
  selection of, 74–76
Target cluster, 43, 183
Task force, 23
Teachers, 78, 246
  in effective schools, 12
  in schools of choice, 25
  preparation of, 21
  substitute, 66–67
"Teachers-as-Leaders" project, 29
Technical system
  analysis, learning from, 137

defined, 44
  diagnosis of, 44–47, 103–121
Technological devices, 140, 246
Technology, stability of, 174
Threat analysis, 84
Timekeeper, 222
Time lines, 156
Tohei, Koichi, 216
Total quality management, 57
Transactional environment, 41, 79
Transition manager, 151–152
Transition plan, 155–156
Transition team, 152
Travel expenses, 68

Unanimous decision, 230–231
Unfreezing, 195
Unionization, 174
Union representative, 41
University of Georgia at Athens, 29
Unstable equilibrium, 198

Vaill, Peter, 3
Validity, 164
Value consensus, 178
Variable fee, 264
Variances, 104, 110, 111–113, 137
Variety, 50, 130
Vision, 4, 196, 212
  leadership, 6–7
  redefining, 42, 86–95
Vision-building workshop, 90–95
Vision statement, 86–90, 138–139, 148

Wade, J., 38, 53
Walberg, H.J., 12
Walton, W., 215, 216
Ward, Arian, 241–242
Waterman, Robert, 5
Watson, J., 198
Welch, Jack, 6
Westley, B., 198
Whole jobs, 123
Wilson, B.L., 12
Working conditions, 125
Work procedures, 246
Work system, see Technical system